YOUTH GANGS AND STREET CHILDREN

Social Identities

General Editors: Shirley Ardener, Tamara Dragadze and Jonathan Webber

Based on a prominent Oxford University seminar founded over two decades ago by the social anthropologist Edwin Ardener, this series focuses on the ethnic, historical, religious and other elements of culture that give rise to a social sense of belonging, enabling individuals and groups to find meaning both in their own social identities and in what differentiates them from others. Each volume is based on one specific theme that brings together contemporary material from a variety of cultures.

YOUTH GANGS AND STREET CHILDREN

CULTURE, NURTURE AND MASCULINITY IN ETHIOPIA

Paula Heinonen

berghahn
NEW YORK · OXFORD
www.berghahnbooks.com

First published in 2011 by
Berghahn Books
www.berghahnbooks.com

Library of Congress Cataloging-in-Publication Data

Heinonen, Paula.
  Youth gangs and street children : culture, nurture and masculinity in Ethiopia /
Paula Heinonen. — 1st ed.
    p. cm. — (Social identities ; 7)
  Includes bibliographical references and index.
  ISBN 978-0-85745-098-2 (hardback : alk. paper) — ISBN 978-0-85745-099-9
(institutional ebook) — ISBN 978-1-78238-132-7 (paperback : alk. paper) —
ISBN 978-1-78238-133-4 (retail ebook)
  1. Gangs—Ethiopia. 2. Street children—Ethiopia. 3. Ethiopia—Social
conditions—21st century. 4. Ethiopia—Social life and customs. I. Title.
  HV6439.E78H45 2011
  362.740963—dc22

                                                                        2010050321

British Library Cataloguing in Publication Data

A catalogue record for this book is available from the British Library

Printed in the United States on acid-free paper.

ISBN: 978-1-78238-132-7 paperback   ISBN: 978-1-78238-133-4 retail ebook

For Diego and Mika

CONTENTS

ACKNOWLEDGEMENTS

I owe an immense debt to the children, parents and others who welcomed me into their families and communities. The narrated facts are theirs. Any mistake in contextualising and interpretation are mine. I have written this book as if the street children were my principal critics. I have changed their names to respect their privacy. Love and gratitude to Diego Hidalgo, who makes the impossible in my life always possible. To Shirley Ardener, my teacher and friend, who read the original manuscript and told me to publish it and kept on prodding me to get on with it; her encouragement and her faith in my possibilities meant an enormous amount to my ability to write this book. To Sian, Lady Crisp, a very good friend, who read the subsequent text at an early stage and saved me from my own mistakes. After reading several draft chapters, she told me: 'All this is very interesting, but I think that the book you want to write is still in your head'. I threw everything out and began all over again. A special thank you to Dr. Tamara Dragadze, my editor, for her very helpful comments and criticisms without which this would not be the book it is now. I would like to thank the Abner Cohen memorial fund for the financial assistance they gave me to complete the manuscript. My deepest thanks to my sisters Theresa, Carla and Luisa, and brother-in-law Dimitri Geralis, each of whom fed my spirit during difficult times; our mother Atsede Demisse and grandmother Mintewab, long departed but never forgotten; our brother and childhood playmate Yonas Haile-Yesus, murdered by the *Derg*'s henchmen in his early twenties and whose memory I took with me to every backstreet of Addis Ababa. Last but not least, Chris Cochran, who also read the original manuscript and successive revisions with the same enthusiasm and constant encouragements.

INTRODUCTION

This book is based on six years of ethnographic research among homeless youth gangs and home-living street children in Addis Ababa. It has evolved over subsequent years of follow-up research and further reflection on the cumulative causes and consequences of persistent poverty and gross inequalities in Ethiopia. It attempts to combine theme, places and the voices of individual children and parents to elucidate the problem surrounding gang life and streetism,[1] without resorting to stereotyping and simplifications. It also deals with socio-economic factors that commonly affect their everyday well-being.

The rapidly expanding population of youth gangs and street children is one of the most disturbing phenomena in the urban centres of the developed and developing world. Such children are found in Bucharest, Rio de Janeiro, Cairo, Accra, Rome and London. Globally, youth gangs and street children are considered as children whose lives involve a constant state of destitution, violence and criminality. They are seen as a serious threat to society and in need of heavy-handed intervention, stabilization and control by a concerned adult world. As part of the 'vulnerable' categories of young lives, whose apparent plight require international attention, they have become a focal point for social and material development concerns. This has contributed to their institutional segregation within development agencies such as UNICEF, Save the Children and other NGOs.

The attribution of a negative signifier to a social group creates that social group. For example, in the UK, politicians, the media, academics and NGOs, through their constant advertising of the plight of children in order to raise funds, play a role in influencing our attitudes towards destitute children, street children and youth gangs. It is easy to spot the same rhetorical themes re-emerging. This is because the messages they promote can be conflicting and project a plethora of injustices. They range from poverty, to child neglect and abuse, to domestic violence, lack of good parenting by single mothers, poor health care, lack of clean water and sanitation, low education provision and more recently lack of leisure

---

[1] The word *streetism* was first used in relation to the street children of Ethiopia in a report written by MOLSA/Rada Barnen (1988: 4). It was defined as follows: '*streetism* to mean children who for various reasons work and/or live in the street. This is also intended to indicate the way of life of the children who consider the street in its widest sense, with its own esoteric rules, customs and vocabulary as their work place.'

facilities and absentee fathers. The suggested solution has been a combination of more social welfare provision, 'tough love' and/or the long arm of the law. The recent alarming media coverage of youth gangs and knife murders in the UK attests to this. The British government has recently unveiled a £100 million 'Youth Crime Action Plan', which is meant to address antisocial behaviour, victim support and sentencing. The plan is also expected to tackle inadequate parenting and the problem of absentee fathers under its Family Intervention Projects (FIPS) 'which work intensively with the most problematic families, and an incumbency on parents to ensure that their children serve community sentences or risk jail themselves' (*Guardian*, 19 July 2008).

Familiar sights of Addis Ababa during my childhood years in the 1960s and 70s included donkeys carrying unendurably heavy loads on their backs while dodging cars in heavy traffic and peddlers and beggars swarming around pedestrians and cars. Child beggars then were few and far between among the street-living fraternity. The very young ones were there to guide their blind or severely handicapped parents to lucrative begging spots or potential clients. There were hardly any girls or women amongst them. Homeless youth gangs were non-existent. Begging was not confined to the asphalted main roads; not a day passed without several beggars asking for leftover food alms at my Ethiopian mother's gate.

When I began my research in 1995, some things were the same and many had changed beyond recognition. Donkeys were still being used as beasts of burden and peddlers and beggars were a ubiquitous part of the scenery. However, nothing I had read or seen during my fleeting visits home during the 80s and early 90s had prepared me to cope with the explosion in the street children population, homeless beggars and youth gangs or the indescribable chaos caused by uncontrolled traffic jams once I was in the field as a researcher. In July 2001, I was obliged to stop my field work and leave Ethiopia. This was due to ill health and the emotional stress of doing field work among destitute children and their families without a pause or time to analyze my empirical data.

The long-term field study was not intentional. Every time I thought that I had captured the essence of who they were, further revelations and their actions shattered the certainty of my deductions. This was partly due to the inconsistency of their life circumstances and their passage from infancy to childhood and then adulthood. The vulnerable pre-teen street boys I knew entered puberty as sexually active teenagers, right before my eyes. As soon as I established the type of violence meted out to them by members of the public and the police, I was confronted by the violence amongst them, which was more frequent and lethal as well as being emotionally damaging to the children. Membership in a gang did not provide the homeless children with a long-lasting affective and economic support group as depicted in the literature on street and homeless children (see Sharf et al. 1986; Swart 1988; Aptekar 1988). The ones I worked with were not only at odds with one another most of the time, but frequently went in and out of groups. Chapters 4 and 5 include detailed analysis of the type of crime and violence the youth gang members I worked with were involved in as well as the retribution they suffered at the hands of their own comrades, members of the public and the police. Furthermore, seemingly dependent children were not only socializing their parents but had taken over adults' role in the public as well as the domestic sphere. They were active entrepreneurs themselves teaching their parents, siblings and even adult street workers the tricks of trading in the informal sector as well as parenting their parents and siblings. This book is about how the above-mentioned phenomena occurred in their homes and in the street.

In Ethiopia, the public assumes that street children are more or less outside the direct guidance, moral inculcation and economic dependence of their parents. This is in spite of the fact that most of them, if not all, live with their biological families. Worse still, they perceive homeless youth gang members who do not live with their families as being juvenile delinquents, prostitutes, drug abusers, petty thieves, vagrants, dropouts or deviants. During the six years I was in the field, members of my family, friends, the police and even the street-trading fraternity advised me to disassociate myself from their company because I risked being robbed or physically attacked. I suffered occasional acts of violence from adult beggars, unemployed youths or neighbours who felt that I was not paying equal attention to their plights. At the beginning of my field work, most of the gang members I met regularly lied to me. I have provided examples in chapters 3, 4 and 5. However, the street children and their families, including the female and male gang members I worked with, treated me with overwhelming kindness. None of the parents and children I worked with physically or verbally attacked or robbed me.

There were more than three hundred international and local NGOs based in Addis Ababa in 1995, many of which were purporting to help street children. Numerous foreign NGOs were operating without having registered themselves as non-governmental voluntary organizations. Many of their internationally recruited staff were working without the required work permit. They would enter the country on a tourist visa and every six months would fly to Eritrea and re-enter the country with a new tourist visa. The government was aware of this anomaly. Throughout 1996 and 1997, they closed down NGOs operating illegally in the country. During the same period, several NGOs working with street children were duplicating each other's projects and undercutting each other by producing hard-hitting pamphlets with the most heartfelt pleas in order to attract funding from Western donors. As Naila Kabeer (1994: 72) put it: 'There is an intimate relationship between the world-view of powerful developmental agencies and the kinds of knowledge that they are likely to promote, fund and act upon.' There is also a growing alarm and distaste about the 'iconography of African children's misery', which is used by NGOs and others to solicit donations and promote their campaign. Africans, including those living in Diaspora, agree that this is unacceptable because this masks the underlining political and economic factors causing this misery and thus prevents effectively addressing it. It also mutes the voices of the Africans impeding them from speaking for themselves or choosing the way they wish to represent themselves globally. I knew several children who had simultaneously registered themselves with different NGOs helping street children in the same area. Although the sums raised by the NGOs based in Ethiopia must have been considerable, in terms of the practical steps to eliminate poverty and streetism, they barely scratched the surface of the problem. In chapter 3, I have indicated how NGOs' agendas were partly influenced by the action of the children and their parents who at times went to any length in order to create an image of themselves, which they perceived NGOs' agents wanted to hear, in order to benefit from development projects. I have provided additional commentary on the role of international humanitarian agencies' efforts to help children and families living in difficult circumstances in the concluding 'Discussion and Conclusion' chapter.

Poverty and Streetism in Ethiopia

The origin of street children in Ethiopia has been rightly attributed to the onset of urbanization after the birth of Addis Ababa as the capital city of Ethiopia in 1887 (see Andarkatchew 1976, 1992; Zenebe 1996; Tedla 1999). Streetism has also been correlated with civil strife, famines and social change (see MOLSA et al. 1993; Central Statistical Commission 2002; UNICEF 2003). Whether these are the underlying causes for the unprecedented levels of childhood poverty, prevailing violence against children or the proliferation of street children in modern Ethiopia is a moot point. Poverty and begging preceded urbanization. Furthermore, there has never been a time in recorded history when Ethiopia and Ethiopians were not either at odds with each other, with their geographical neighbours or repulsing European or Muslim invaders. As indicated in chapter 1, famines, wars, insurrections, social change and social conflict are part of Ethiopia's ancient and modern history (see Bahru 1986, 1991; Turton 2006; W. James et al. 2002; Marsden 2007). Even though they have contributed to underdevelopment, they are not the sole cause for poverty and streetism in Ethiopia.

Very few of my contemporaries in Ethiopia had any doubt that the country was imploding in the late 1960s and early 70s. It was not whether the Imperial Regime of Emperor Haile Sellassie would be overthrown but when. In 1974, when the revolution happened, it took the form of a USSR-backed brutal Marxist military dictatorship that lasted seventeen years (see W. G. Dawit 1989 for a detailed analysis of this period in Ethiopian history). As put by one of my school friends who now lives in Diaspora: 'The Soviets hijacked our revolution and the revolution ate its children.' There was still a sense of doom and the feeling that the country was going to implode while I was carrying out field work from 1995 to 2001. In March 2001, a peaceful students' demonstration at the University of Addis Ababa complaining about the closure of their student magazine was met by brutal repression. This triggered street riots all over Addis Ababa by disaffected citizens and the hundreds of unemployed youths, which resulted in the death of many and a new wave of educated Ethiopians joining the earlier 1974–1980 exodus to the West in search of a better life.

The first decade of the new millennium saw the continuation of the 1998 Ethiopian/Eritrean cross-border war; Ethiopian soldiers were embroiled in the Somali civil war; and there was an uneasy truce with Sudan and civil unrest in the north and south of the country. The nationalist/separatist movements I was familiar with during my early childhood in the late 1960s, namely the Afar Liberation Movement, the Oromo Liberation Front and the Ogaden Liberation Front, had now been joined by the Gambella Peoples' Liberation Front and many others. Political instability continues to afflict Ethiopia, thus impeding any international aid efforts and the government in power to focus on economic and social development.

Rural poverty due to droughts and famine spurring rural to urban migration is often cited as contributing to the proliferation of street children in Addis Ababa (see Andarkatchew 1976; Ottaway 1976; Solomon and Aklilu 1993; Fitsum 1994; Tedla 1999; MOLSA 1993; Central Statistical Commission 2002). As I shall demonstrate in chapter 1, there are written records of droughts and famines dating back to the first half of the ninth century (see R. Pankhurst 1961, 1968). In June 2008, once again the world media zoomed their lenses on starving Ethiopian children and women, this time around the agriculturally fertile southern states. The crisis warranted a cover story in *Time Magazine* (18 August 2008), with the ubiquitous iconographic picture of a distraught Ethiopian mother with a starving child in her arms. Over a year later, the UK based *Independent on Sunday*'s front page news 'Millions facing famine in Ethiopia' dated 30 August 2009, had a poignant picture of a starving Ethiopian child with leading articles inside entitled: 'Twenty Five Years after Band Aid' and 'Our Ship is Sinking: We must act now'. It attributed the present tragedy and looming famine primarily to climate change. The caption under the picture of the Ethiopian ambassador to the UK quotes him as saying: 'the international community isn't living up to its promises'. In the words of one of my former students at the University of Addis Ababa who wishes to remain anonymous:

> The Ethiopian political leadership is busy disputing the number of people without food, which they claim is exaggerated and they suspect the NGOs are behind it. The vice prime minister was heard arguing that it is 5.4 million that are food insecure and not 6 million! I would say that one hundred starving Ethiopians are too many! What were they doing at the so-called 'Disaster Prevention and Preparedness Agency'? The government keeps telling us that our economy is growing. I cannot help wondering

what they mean when they say it is growing. The more we are told our economy is growing, the tougher life is getting for my folks and the streets are still full of child and adult beggars. (July 2008)

The views expressed in the literature on street children address different dimensions associated with streetism, including poverty and civil strife. Much remains to be understood about the everyday lives of such children on whose behalf myriad NGO projects are launched. Furthermore, available information treats the street children as undifferentiated groups and delves into the children's street-based activities with minimal or no reference to home life / school life or life after the street. There is even less information about how they interact with one another, their families and mainstream society. In chapters 3, 4 and 5 I explore the social world of Ethiopian street children living at home and gangs of homeless girls and boys living in loose-knit social groups. The chapters include invaluable information about the role NGOs, teachers, church groups and the police play in their lives.

Methodology

There is still controversy over the most appropriate approach for conducting social and cultural studies of urban environments. Recent writings on research in the urban context affirm that attempts to establish single discipline–based, universal definitions of the 'city' and 'urban social behaviour' are misplaced. The trend is to use a multi-disciplinary approach combining ethnographic and mathematical analysis or a family of methodologies and insights involving comparative analysis, case studies, situational analysis and social network (see Sanjek 1974; Nestmann and Hurrelmann 1994; Andranovich and Riposa 1993; White 1993; Rogers and Vertovec 1995; Smith 2001; Wang and Hofe 2007). This is in accordance with Clyde J. Mitchell's (1966) conclusion that analysts from various disciplines are likely to select, from the total set of diacritical features of the city, those that are theoretically pertinent for analysis in terms of a specific discipline.

Questionnaire interviews may be invaluable for need assessment or to make a brief socio-economic survey of a targeted group of people. They are less useful when it comes to extracting information on the role of culture/nurture/environment in explaining streetism or the origins of street children in Ethiopia. Besides, the bias and error of needs assessments and brief socio-economic surveys and other quantitative procedures are sometimes more subtle and therefore more troublesome to spot because the overall perspective they reflect is often that of a global view. My quest was further complicated by the fact that I did not have a firm idea of what I should look into. My original interest was influenced by what is generally written about street children and non-street children. It was aimed at securing information about what I, at that time, assumed to be important to their way of life in the street. These were the so-called 'rule-governed cultural world' created by children (see Opie and Opie 1959; Stone and Church 1968; Glassner 1976; Spier 1976; Goode 1986; Fine and Standstrom 1988); their secret lore and language (see Opie and Opie 1959; Hardman 1973a, 1973b); as well as their social networks (see Aptekar 1988; Swart 1988; Ennew 1994a). Since I did not have a prior experience or knowledge of youth gangs I was able to just observe their actions and record their narrative free of any assumptions.

Narratives tell us much about culture and the nature of culture, but narratives have no meaning without reference to their sources. Besides, as Alan Bennett (1997: 41) so succinctly put it, 'One cannot overstate the untidiness of human speech or reproduce it accurately on the page.' This is because people interact with one another not only in accordance with their position in the social space but also with the mental disposition through which they apprehend this space. People respond to other people and to their environment based on their definition of the situation. Since the children's actions did not always accord with the idealized worldview found in their narratives, I soon realized that the type of narrative I required could neither be derived from answers to specific questions nor extracted from questionnaire-based data. Even an insight into the above-mentioned issues called for a thorough understanding of the social meaning behind any sort of account the street children might give about their personal experiences. In order to analyze the problem of streetism, I needed to establish the necessary background knowledge about their social, work and leisure activities at home and in the street. I would also have to delve into the reality behind the contemporary social constructions of childhood within their social environment. In other words, I had to acquire an insight into the activities, attitudes, habitual practices and basic axioms of the street children and their families.

There were numerous methodological implications and differentiating elements to take into account when carrying out field work amongst youth gangs and the street children coming from heterogeneous, multi-ethnic and/or mixed backgrounds (see Aptekar and Heinonen 2003). Faced with a multi-site approach to participant observation in an urban setting, and in order to obtain qualitative responses to my queries, I was obliged to consider the street children and their families that I was to work with as a group for all practical purposes. I had to search in their life styles and narratives for common features that might comprise a shared stock of social norms and customs. In other words, I had to establish 'their common culture' without blurring their ethnic essence or diminishing the significance of their diversity. A common determinant of this 'common culture' was the strong sense of *yilunta* or honor, shame and family pride which permeated their narratives and actions that I define and discuss in chapter 2.

My experience in choosing a field site, identifying and making contact with the families of street children, was far from idyllic. It was exacerbated by the fact that there are no settled, stable reference populations of street children in any one location of the city. They can be found in practically every part of Addis Ababa. Besides, the street children and their families do not form a homogenous group where each individual's social position is defined by age, gender or birth position. As in most capital cities the world over, the population of Addis Ababa, as opposed to its rural counterpart, is heterogeneous. The street children and their families live in socially diverse communities, scattered about the city. They come from different backgrounds, with differences in ethnicity, norms, social values, languages and a multitude of household compositions. Apart from a brief history of the city, chapter 1 includes a methodological account linked to urban based multi-site field work amongst destitute children and their families.

Far from creating social tension, urbanization has encouraged the intermingling between the various ethnic and religious groups. Inter-marriage across ethnic, and even religious lines, is common. Some street children's mothers have several offspring from different fathers coming from the various regions of Ethiopia. The above-mentioned diversity notwithstanding, poverty and the overcrowded living conditions found in Addis Ababa bring about some kind of uniformity to the way the poor live and socialize their children. I found that economic and social factors if conceptualised in terms of occupation, habitat, language, religion and eating habits create uniformity in their lives and life styles. Midway through my field work, I identified three themes, which encapsulated their 'common culture'. These were the concept of *yilunta* (shame, honour and family pride). This promotes hegemonic masculinity within the 'wider Ethiopian' culture and accounts for the gendered nature of how Ethiopian children are socialized and how gang members operate. Central to my analysis on youth gangs was also the concept of reciprocity, because what mattered most in their interaction with one another was what they did for each other and not what they said about each other. I used Michael Carrither's (1992) sociality theory as a method of enquiry in order to shift the emphasis from the intractable nature of culture and explore the context in which the children experienced girlhood, boyhood and streetism. Finally, research with vulnerable children, especially one dealing with the sensitive topics of gang life, sexuality, theft and violence requires the researcher to face up to the ethical, practical and moral issues in carrying out field work. Throughout the book, I have addressed the issues of reflexivity and positionality including the moral and ethical dilemma I faced working with the children and their families as well as their reaction to my presence in their midst.

Participant observation meant following the children around in the streets and visiting them at home. In short, it was more like a continuous form of chit-chat and loitering with intent than a series of question and answer sessions. I have therefore concentrated on their real life experiences by giving a voice to the children and parents, mostly as first person narratives and/or by contextualising matters narrated by others. This was in addition to observing what they actually do and how they go about doing it. Clifford Geertz's (1973) 'thick description' method made it possible for me to provide the details of the complex facets of streetism and avoid giving a too superficial snapshot of the children and their families. That is, an ethnographic method, which privileges engaged listening and descriptive writing in order to represent the enigmatic and shifting nature of social existence.

Culture

According to anthropologists, our understanding of the symbolic notion of culture is that of a human construct, which is based on the most insubstantial and refractory of bases: the inter-subjective and shared world of meaning of a particular population. The implication is that a multitude of diverse cultures exists worldwide. Culture matters. This is expressed through the dilemma still facing scholars writing culture (Clifford and Marcus 1986), working with (Appadurai 2008), against (Abu-Lughod 2006) or instead of (Carrithers 1992, 2009) culture as a concrete concept embodying our lived-in experiences. Notwithstanding the many definitions or the various ways it is used, there is no escaping the confines of culture. Its enduring strength is in its role in helping us distinguish between cultures, the difference between the self and the others, and even as an explanation of how people function. Furthermore, culture provides us with the framework that enables us to project the existence of a commonly held worldview. It facilitates the use of terms such as beliefs, values, norms, custom, tradition and even religion interchangeably or as a clear demarcation. In short, it allows us to shift convincingly from the conjectured to the positive thus turning what is socially constructed into a 'reality'.

The Amharic word for culture is *bahil*.[2] Further exploration of culture by Dr. Girma Getahun, an Ethiopian lexicographer and researcher, shows that this definition limits itself to one of several definitions of the same term in English. He sent me an e-mail explaining that '*bahil*' generally refers to traditions, customs, habitual practices, ways of life, etc. It does not convey the meaning of cultivation, erudition, refinement of taste and manner, or that of nurturing or breeding (bacteria, cells, etc.) as the English term does. Moreover, unlike the English term *culture*, *bahil* may not be used as a verb or adjective. In other words, one needs to provide contextual meaning in Amharic to convey the various nuances of *culture*. For instance, 'a cultured man' can only be translated as *yetemare sew* or *yeteraqeqe sew*,[3] and not as *yebahil sew* or *bahlawi* sew. Similarly, 'the culture of cells' may

---

[2] I have written Amharic terminologies in simple English in the way one would hear the words instead of using transliteration to make it easier for the non-Amharic speakers to pronounce the words. *Bahil* is the Amharic word meaning culture.

[3] *yetemare sew* means an educated person; *yeteraqeqe sew* means a refined, sophisticated person.

only be rendered in Amharic by such phrases as *yehiwasoch rbata*,[4] or *hiwasochin marabat*. Culture referring to the arts as manifestations of human intellectual attainment, may be conveyed with such phrases as *sine-tibebawi bahil, sine-tibeb inde bahil*, etc. In short, there is no simple Amharic equivalent for the English term (18 February 2010).

My informants, including members of my Ethiopian family, do not speak of culture as discursively neutral but culture as simply 'fact'. Speaking as insiders, without any pretence of objectivity, they talk of culture in terms of behaviour, social practice, customs, traditions and the socialisation of children or as a way of differentiating the way they do things from other cultures, e.g. 'Western culture'. The inference is invariably that 'Ethiopian culture' is superior to other cultures.

The above notwithstanding, there *is* nevertheless a 'wider Ethiopian culture'. The narratives and life stories of the multi-ethnic parents and children I worked with were invariably embedded in diffused perceptions of *yilunta*. This idea formed the basis of a masculine hegemony-based ideology regarding male/female and adult/child relationships. *Yilunta* provided one of the culture protocols, which gave significance to their acts since it was pivotal to the intentions and meanings that organized their experiences. The interaction between the two sexes was thus a very gendered and subjective process. This was continually affected by unintentional distortion, intentional manipulation and/or selective amnesia, thus creating a degree of change, modification and continuity. Chapter 2 provides a definition of *yilunta* and delves into how this gendered process unfolds. It also details the manner in which gender shapes the lives of children and youth gangs in Addis Ababa and affects their lives and actions, beginning with their socialization at home.

The task of explaining the 'common culture' of a disparate group of street children in an urban setting is not as straightforward a task as it might seem even for a 'cultural insider'. As a 'cultural insider', I fall into the category of those Lila Abu-Lughod (2006: 153) calls '*halfies*', 'people whose national or cultural identity is mixed by virtue of migration, overseas education or parentage and whose situation neatly exposes the most basic of those premises surrounding the notion of culture'. Abu-Lughod further asserts that the problem facing halfies is that of gaining enough distance from their subject of inquiry, since the 'other' is in certain ways the self and the researcher is likely to slide into subjectivity (ibid.: 155). Abu-Lighod answers the question of positionality and reflexivity in relation to the researcher in the research process by quoting James Clifford (1986: 154) 'that ethnographic representations are always partial truths and this needed the recognition that they are also positioned truths'. In my case, it took me another six years after six years of field work, to find the right words to articulate what I wanted to say.

---

[4] *yehiwashoch rbta* is derived from *hiwas* = cell (biology); *hiwasoch* = cells; *ye-hiwasoch* = of cells and *rbta*, marabat = breeding.

In the literature on gangs and street children there is much reference about such youths having subcultures. Clive Glazer (2000: 7) states that 'in order to protect their realm and status, youth subcultures insulate themselves from the outside world and create exclusivity through style'. Scott H. Decker and Frank M. Weerman (2005: 23–27) mention the role of ethnic culture in terms of ethnic minority migrant parents attempting to raise their children as they were brought up in their native land and the influence of global youth culture on group dynamics amongst gang members in Europe. Apart from providing an overview of Addis Ababa since its foundation in 1887 and the setting in which street children live and operate in, I have explored in chapter 1 the complexity of the ethnic scenario in Ethiopia and its urban aspect and its lack of influence on youth gang formation.

Lewis Aptekar (1994) explored racial and cultural factors in connection with street children worldwide but the results were inconclusive. This is not surprising. In my experience, the street children of Addis Ababa cannot be said to be, or to have, a sub-culture, if by this we mean that they form a rule-governed, static social entity that functions separately from the rest of the community. Besides, childhood being but a transitory phase to adulthood, they do not form a homogenous group. Furthermore, giving an account of Ethiopian culture, let alone its variations, is a far more complex exercise than at first appears. There is little or no secondary data about Ethiopia on which to base an understanding of the cultural norms affecting street children's and youth gangs' social lives. Formulating a hypothesis based on previous ethnographic research on the 'wider Ethiopian culture' would have been tantamount to resorting to cultural reductionism.

The research for this book is concerned with the relationship between the telling of a life story and disclosing a culture in order to help understand the social world that the narrator shares with others. It is also the ways in which culture marks and shapes people's narratives including how they make use of cultural resources as reference points and struggle with (or manipulate) its constraints in order to effect change and continuity. The operative themes I employed to delve into the notion of culture are custom, habitual practice and way of life. By including my informants' voices in the discourse and depicting how they actually live, I was able to make aspects of the 'wider Ethiopian culture' visible not merely as a set of habits and traditions but as a lived experience.

Sociality Theory

In his book *Why People Have Cultures,* Michael Carrithers (1992) states that anthropologists work on the premise that man is a social animal. Human beings do not gain their livelihood individually but collectively. People are inextricably involved with one another in a world in continual metamorphosis (ibid.: 199).

Carrithers proposes a novel way of dealing with the intricacy of culture as well as its variation and mutability. He suggests that, if there is diversity, this must depend on it being a diversity of something. We must therefore look into traits that all humans share in order to be able to create such diversity (ibid.: 5). He concludes that one set of universals that unifies our species is the interactive character of social life (ibid.: 10). An intense awareness of self and other, combined with creativity and narrative thought, are abilities that are common to all populations. Carrithers designates these capacities as 'sociality', which, he says, forms the basis of cultural and social variability. It is this sociality with its incessant mutability which unites our diversity. He therefore proposes that we shift our emphasis from culture to sociality because human relationships are slightly more important, more real, than those things we designate as culture (ibid.: 30). After all, people react to other people, not to an abstraction called culture (ibid.: 35).

Carrithers (1992) defines sociality theory as the human capacity for immensely varied and complex social behavior, asserting that we are not just passive animals who are moulded by our respective societies and cultures but actively make and remake society into new ways of life. Carrithers does not propose replacing the notion of culture with that of sociality. He aims to give us a theory that allows a metamorphic view of society, a concept that would permit us to see that people actually create, manipulate and transform the connections between them (ibid.: 35 and 199): 'According to the culture theory, people do things, because of their culture. ... According to the sociality theory, people do things with, to and in respect to each other, using means that we can describe, if we wish to, as culture' (ibid.: 34). Sociality theory provided me with the means to transcend the abstracted nature of culture using the more tangible idea of sociality. It also enabled me to capture the distinctions between ways of life in an unambiguous manner, without diminishing the vigour of cultural effects. It gave me a methodology that could accommodate continuity, change, creation and re-creation in social life, while allowing an accessible form of analysis that resides in the concrete. This is because sociality theory concentrates not on how culture says people ought to live but on how they actually live.

In the literature on street children in Ethiopia, they are always 'the object', never 'the subject'. They are the observed, the talked for and/or talked about. I have provided their life stories in order to avoid writing about them as an undifferentiated, abstracted, faceless and nameless group of people. In order to include the children's voices, and that of the related and non-related adults in their lives, into the discourse, I have opted to depict their lives through the prism of their actions and narratives. After all, narrative practices interweave to shape the self and its many identities as well as constituting and guiding social action. They can refer to psychological processes in self-identity, memory and meaning making. They are also one of the elements in a broader cultural and linguistic 'turn' through which recognition is given to the shaping effect of cultural environment and to subjective experiences (see Andrews et al. 2000). There still is a paucity of information about youth gangs in Ethiopia and street children's families, let alone details about the give and take of their everyday lives over a long period. This book strives to encode personal experience narratives in order to transform lines of cold print into almost audible speaking voices and fill this lacuna.

Street children in Ethiopia, as elsewhere, do not form a homogenous group. Besides the natural transition from childhood to adolescence and adulthood, their life circumstances do not remain unchanged but show much variety. As a methodological tool, sociality theory was particularly suited to capturing the inconstancy of their life experiences. I have used sociality theory to look into aspects of their social life that homogenise key aspects of their social world and explore the context in which they experienced their childhood and streetism. In other words, find ways of locating contemporary (urban-based) social norms connecting the children to each other and to the wider adult world. Consequently, sociality theory has enabled me to go beyond collecting and reporting the facts of their lives in this difficult street-based social setting.

The Book

This book is an anthropological account of the children's home, school and street lives. It contains personal case studies of the children and their families. The unusually long period of field research made it possible to provide a rare and significant picture of how youth gangs come into being and disintegrate. The long-term post-field data has enabled me to give an account of their post-street life as adults and as parents in their own right.

Although I talked to more than two hundred children and adults and visited fifty-two homes, I have focused my writing on two households: one with both parents living together and the other a female-headed household. The book tries to evoke the texture of life, not just for the children, but for their mothers, sisters, brothers and fathers and shows their extraordinary devotion to each other. It offers a clear analysis of how gender shapes the lives of street children. It uses their own words to highlight their experiences of girlhood and boyhood at home, in schools and on the street. Based on long-term empirical investigation, this work gives an insider's knowledge about the painful process by which street children make varied attempts to disengage themselves from street life and search for supportive socio-economic alternatives as post-adolescent boys and girls.

The underlying theme throughout this book is the central contribution played by *yilunta*-based discursive identity formation and hegemonic masculinist ideologies found in the 'wider Ethiopian culture' affecting their lives. Socialisation is understood to be an essentially passive process on children's part. It takes for granted the active role of adults in the socialisation process. A less gendered and less commonly observed phenomenon is that at times the children themselves end up parenting their parents. Such role reversal occurs when, occasionally, street children subvert the adult/child socialization process and play a corresponding part in socialising their mothers and siblings. Chapter 3 provides empirical data showing how this process unfolds.

Throughout the six years I was in the field, I kept almost daily contact with three all-male and one mixed-sex youth gang. I have chosen to depict the lives and times of one all-male and one mixed-sex gang. This was because some boys from the all-male gang eventually joined the mixed-sex gang when their former group disintegrated. This facilitated my entry into this new group and thus gave me a way of furthering my understanding of the effects that age and post-pubertal sex had in their lives. The details provided in chapters 4 and 5 shatter the myths that gang life provides an alternative to home life and that such groups form a close knit and harmonious social group. While blaming lack of amenities and welfare provisions for such children, including the abuse they suffered at home before entering street life, it shows how at least some of the suffering is the direct result of the children's own attitudes and behaviours. The street is a world in which children are powerless and must use their courage and wits to make the most of the few choices they have. Using the children's voices as a first-person narrative makes it possible for them to be the observing eye. The narratives include invaluable information about the role religion, NGOs, teachers, church groups and the police play in their lives.

The book also tackles the seldom-discussed issue of children's sexuality and child-on-child sexual abuse. The issue of child sex abuse is a sensitive and difficult subject. Life on the street means an increased risk of gender-based violence, especially for female gang members. There is much written about the need to protect children from sexual abuse by adults, but very little is known about child-on-child sexual exploitation. Chapter 5 explores the extent to which intra-gang violence, especially violence against female gang members in mixed-sex groups, is the result of masculine ideas of male-on-male and male-on-female relations. This includes child prostitution and occasionally the gang rape of the girl child as well as physical and verbal assaults on boys by other boys, by boys on girls and by girls on other girls.

The books I had read prior to carrying out my field work did not capture the difficulties and complexity of embarking on an anthropological investigation amongst street children and their families. The overall picture was that group life provides such children with the emotional, social and economic security they need thus providing what the adult social world was unable or unwilling to secure for them (see Aptekar 1988; Swart 1990). The only long-term study was Aptekar's (1988) two years of psycho-social research on the street children of Cali, in Colombia. Apart from in times of ill health and bereavement, amongst those I worked with, group life meant yet another hurdle they had to face alone.

The lack of information about youth gangs in Ethiopia is probably because such children are loath to give an account of their lives or the road they have traveled to end up homeless on the street. It took me years of contact, even long after I had established a rapport with them, to earn their trust in order to provide the case studies and life stories in chapters 4 and 5.

Finally, nothing had prepared me for the emotional baggage that goes with the field work, or with the degree of social involvement I have ended up with. Nor for the heat, the cold, the dirt and the sickening smell related to trudging around the back streets of Addis Ababa. The alarm I felt with all sorts of fleas crawling up my legs was mitigated by being overwhelmed by the kindness and hospitality of the community. I did not expect to be irritated at being constantly accosted by beggars, rude men and even the street children themselves or the boredom I had to endure while waiting for a child, a parent or just something to happen. However, these were minor inconveniences compared to the abject misery and poverty my informants lived in. There were times when I felt that I ought to give up my research and do something about helping them. Several times, I had to stop going anywhere near the children or their parents for a week or two, in order to be able to continue helplessly witnessing their plight. I often found it impossible to remain impassive and not get involved in the children's quarrels. The girls I liked most seemed to have an uncanny ability to transfer to me their dislikes of other people and involve me in their squabbles. It was emotionally easier for me to work with boys than with girls. Most of the fights I have had with parents have been in defence of daughters.

I do not feel that I have betrayed the trust of my informants by giving details of their sexual proclivity, including the nefarious aspects of gang rape and child prostitution, because I was never sworn to secrecy. I have never asked or encouraged them to divulge anything about their sex life or criminal activities. I made it plain from the start that I was researching their lives and that I would be writing about it. I never offered any kind of monetary or other rewards for information, nor was I asked to give by the children or parents I worked with. By the time I had recorded their lives, I had become yet another adult in their lives, but one they could confide their pain to. I have indicated throughout the book the type of material help I was occasionally able to contribute.

In April 2010, I went back to Addis Ababa for a family reunion. As I write these words, beggars, street children, unemployed youths and youth gangs, some as young as six years old are still sleeping on pavements and verandas and are a ubiquitous sight in Addis Ababa. The government has decreed that peddlers and beggars refrain from selling or begging from cars and have started penalizing motorists who give alms or buy from them. Many of the houses where my informants lived have been raised to the ground and new high-rise buildings are being erected. Most of those who were expelled have lost their means of livelihood and network. The building boom has provided employment to unskilled labourers.

The rest still beg and hawk at night or away from the main road. Many young girls have taken up shoe shining in what has become an increasingly overcrowded profession. It is still difficult for me to reconcile myself to the poverty, ill-health, malnutrition, high unemployment and squalor that the great majority of the people of Addis Ababa live in. I hope that the more intimate details revealed in this book will provide an eye-opener and offer a fresh approach for policy makers, development professionals, politicians, academics, students and people involved in grass-root initiatives to help children and families living in difficult urban circumstances. This book gives testimony to their suffering, exploitation and helplessness but also to their humanity and innate intelligence.

1

ETHIOPIA

The Country

Ethiopia is situated in the northeast corner of the Horn of Africa. It is bordered by Djibouti and Somalia in the east, by Kenya in the south, by the Sudan in the west and by Eritrea in the north. The country is as large as France and Spain combined and covers a total area of some 1,221,000 square kilometres. After the establishment of the newly created State of Eritrea in 1992, Ethiopia lost its nine hundred kilometres of coastline along the Red Sea and is now a land-locked country.

The geography of the country is characterised by a variety of reliefs, ranging from 90 metres below sea level in the Afar Depression to the elevated central plateaux varying in height between 2,000 and 4,600 metres above sea level. It is a land of great geographical diversity with high, rugged mountains, flat-topped plateaux, deep gorges, incised river valleys and rolling plains. *Abbay* or the Blue Nile, its most famous river, flows a distance of some 1,450 kilometres from its source in Lake Tana to join the White Nile in Khartoum. Apart from the brief Fascist Italian occupation of 1935–1941, Ethiopia has maintained its unity and independence by successfully defending itself against a succession of Arab and European foes.

Ethiopia's population has grown from 33.5 million in 1983 to 75.1 million in 2006, out of which half are under the age of fifteen. The crude birth rate stands at an average 47.3 per 1,000 of population. Total fertility rate was 7.7 children per women in 1990–2000. Infant mortality rate stands on average at 86.0 per 1000 with rates for under age five reaching 145.2 per 1000. Civil strife and famine have inevitably affected Ethiopian children. Throughout the past two decades, children and their families have been on the move in large numbers in search of a secure way of life. One result has been that the capital, Addis Ababa, has experienced enormous population growth through the influx of migrants as well as an increased birth rate (United Nations Population Division 2008).

Ethnicity

Ethiopia has a rich well-documented cultural past, which dates back to pre-Christian times. It has its own written script, Amharic, with its unique alphabet, which is the official language. Its ethnic composition is as diverse as its topography. Even though the numbers are often in conflict, it is estimated that it has as many as seventy ethnic groups speaking over two hundred and fifty languages and dialects and many religious communities, which include Christian, Muslim and Jewish as well as a myriad of traditional religious beliefs (Central Statistical Authority 1999).

Modern Ethiopian culture is the product of many millennia of interaction among people in and around the Ethiopian highland and lowland regions. Varied ethnic, linguistic and religious groups have influenced its evolution. The country's political history was shaped and is still dominated by intense intra-ethnic and religious conflicts. Wars, insurrections and rebellions were and still are common occurrences. There is an abundance of scholarly work on Ethiopia and the Ethiopians. Historically, Ethiopia used to be divided into the Northern Highlands, the core of the Old Ethiopian Christian Kingdom and the Southern States, most of which were brought under imperial rule by conquest. In recent times, writings about the social, ethnic, economic and political forces that helped determine the nature of Ethiopian history, ancient and modern, is surrounded by intense debate and controversy. Ethiopian and foreign authors vie with one another to put forth their own perspectives on the subject (see W. James et al. 2002, especially articles by Christopher Clapham, 'The Political Framework, Controlling Space in Ethiopia', and Alessandro Triulzi, 'Battling with the Past, New Frameworks for Ethiopian Historiography'; see also Ezekiel Gebissa 2009, *Contested Terrain: Essays on Oromo Studies, Ethiopianist Discourses and Politically Engaged Scholarship*).

Research suggests that ethnic identities tend to attain their greatest importance in situations of flux, change, resource competition and threats against boundaries (see Gellner 1983; Anderson 1983; Eriksen 1988; Banks 1996). Ethnicity in Ethiopia is an enormously complex concept and is not amenable to simple classification. The ethnic composition of Ethiopia is as diverse as its history and topography. No ethnic entity has remained untouched by others, even among groups who think of themselves as unique or are considered by others to be different. This is due to migration or conquest and assimilation in earlier times and forced resettlements (see A. Pankhurst 1992) and urbanization in more recent times. Intra-ethnic marriage and ethnic mixing has occurred in the past and is common in urban centres. These mixed-up past boundaries between ethnic groups are now being 'remapped' – with at times an uncategorisable present. Furthermore, Ethiopian Christian Orthodox Christians and Muslims each make up approximately 40 per cent of the total population. They are found among most if not all the ethnic groups. Protestant and Catholic converts and adherents of traditional local faiths of different persuasions make up the rest and live interspersed among Muslims.

The usual ethnic markers, namely territorial demarcation, mythical origins, linguistic association, physical appearance, ways of being and doing, religious affiliation, shared oppression or forced assimilation by dominant groups or even the extent of ethnic mixing are still being used by separatist movements, politicians and scholars and rearranged as facts to project new or old realities. Even though ethnicity is at times a subjective response to historical experience and current situations, traits based on ethnicity, much like those based on language and religion, are still deeply ingrained and have not been susceptible to elimination by politics or conquest (see Turton 2006).

The population of Addis Ababa comes from mixed and varied ethnic backgrounds even though some people often express their political loyalties in purely ethnic terms. This may be partly influenced by the fact that in order to be registered in *kebeles*,[1] and acquire the much-valued identity cards, they are obliged to declare their ethnic affiliations. It is exacerbated by the perception that the Tigray, the ethnic group from which Prime Minister Meles Zenawi stems, benefit unduly from the economic, developmental and political power they derive from his rule. Nevertheless, most if not all the street children families, migrants and city-born residents of Addis Ababa I knew had little or no contact with their places of origin. The only street children where ethnicity may have a bearing on being street children with regular contact with their families are the Gurague, who account for 2 per cent of the population of Ethiopia.

The Guragues are a singular example of rural/urban continuity, even though their traditional way of life has been disturbed by migration and external influences. Shared geographical origins and language as well as myths of common ancestry define them as a group. They are a prime example of a community of people bound by a common interest. Gurague living in Addis Ababa are academics, civil servants, rich merchants, peddlers, shoeshine boys and labourers. Seifu Ruga (1976: 203) asserts that urban-rural links are kept alive by migrant urbanites avoiding making a complete break with their rural socio-economic roots. Christian Guragues return to their villages for *Meskel*,[2] every year. The Muslims go during *Arefa* after the Ramadan ceremony.

I have met many Gurague shoeshine boys who live communally with older siblings or relatives. They draw lots in order to decide who will be going home that year if they cannot all afford to go back. Those unable to visit their families due to financial constraints make all sorts of sacrifices to send presents to their relatives. The Gurague have transplanted and moulded several traditional social

---

[1] *Kebeles* are urban dwellers associations.
[2] *Meskel* is the 'Feast of the finding the True Cross'. It is celebrated by followers of the Ethiopian Orthodox Christian faith.

self-help schemes to meet 'modern' urban demands (Seifu 1976: 204–217). This is done though membership of several kinds of associations at tribal, agnatic or village level in Addis Ababa and back in their homeland (ibid.: 205). They all aspire to own or maintain a small farm of *ensete* (false banana plant). 'This is reinforced by the Gurague attitude that a person who does not maintain his farm (back in his village) is usually considered by his neighbours as rootless and "hopeless" even though he may have no use for the farm' (ibid.: 209).

Marcus Banks (1996) considers that ethnicity is such a difficult concept to define that it is becoming a less useful form of analysis. Nevertheless, for social anthropologists, the focus is on the group's definition of their culture and differences from other groups. Banks describes the primordial approach to ethnicity as derived from blood and origin, as well as religion and language. In contrast, instrumentalist ethnicity is concerned with personal outlook of the subject; here ethnicity is to realise a particular outcome, and is often related to particular historical or socio-economic circumstances. Hiranthi Jayaweera (1991) adds perceived common origin and experience to the above. He also introduces situational and symbolic forms of ethnicity, which are used to assume an identity that aids a group in relation to particular territorial, political or economic circumstances. From the above discussion, it seems that ethnicity is best defined as a composite concept. Besides, ethnicity and allegiance to ethnic groups can change through assimilation, marriage outside the group, acculturation, and conversion to another religion or even due to geographical circumstances. In the literature of youth gangs, 'race' and ethnicity play a significant part among such street groups (see Glazer 2000; Schneider and Tilley 2004; Poynting and Noble 2004). Christopher Adamson (2004: 143) writes: 'The effects of racial and class structures on the behaviour of American youth gangs have been so profound that scholars who have sought to develop race-invariant theories of gangs and delinquency have been stymied.' As I shall argue in chapters 3, 4 and 5, shared lifestyle and circumstances were more important than ethnic identity or class affiliation in the urban setting of Addis Ababa. Furthermore, most town dwellers, migrants and non-migrants alike, had 'to learn to live with each other' and therefore conform to an urban way of behaviour regardless of ethnic origin.

Consequences of Famines in Ethiopia

Ethiopia's principal resource is its land. Its population is predominantly rural. Agriculture provides the major part of national production, exports and employment. It is estimated that over 90 per cent of the population live in the rural areas, mainly as subsistence farmers. The principal exports are coffee (the most important cash and export crop), followed by grains, pulses, fruits and vegetables and cattle on the hoof and hides and skins. The country's mineral resources include oil, gold, platinum, copper, potash, iron and natural gas. However, at present, mining contributes less than 1 per cent of GDP.

The country's proximity to the Equator and its great altitudinal ranges have combined to form three distinct climatic zones. The *dega* (temperate zone), the *woine dega* (sub tropical) and the *kola* (tropical), or hot zone, include desert and semi-desert lowland areas to the east and southeast of the country. There are three seasons throughout most of the country. These are the *belg* (small rains) from February to May, the *keremt* (big rains) from June to September and the *bega*, the dry period from October to January. The two rainy seasons enable the cool and temperate regions to produce two harvests a year under normal conditions. Some of the southeastern and most of the lowland areas have much shorter rainy seasons; sometimes no *belg* rains at all. Because Ethiopia's agricultural economy is based on subsistence farming, when the rains fail to arrive on time, famine ensues.

Amartya Sen (1999: 192) puts forth a powerful argument for the close link between political freedom and famine preventions, namely that 'no substantial famine has ever occurred in any independent country with a democratic form of government and a relatively free press'. He states that democracy and a free press provide the political incentives for governments or authorities to prevent famines. In an earlier book, Sen (1983: 757) compares and contrasts famine situations in India and China. He concludes that while the situation of regular malnutrition and hunger was far more severe in India than in China, as reflected in the difference of life expectancy (between 66 and 69 years in China, but only 52 years in India), India did not have any famines after independence. This was due to the pressure of newspaper and diverse political parties. On the other hand, in spite of the professed commitment of the Chinese Communist Party to eradicate regular malnutrition and hunger through an equal access to means of livelihood, the regime's lack of democratic transparency and inadaptability to sudden changes resulted in their lack of response to request for food distribution in affected regions. This was a major factor leading to the 1959–1961 large-scale famine, which resulted in millions of deaths. Sen's postulation is instructive for explaining famines in Ethiopia.

Drought and famines have been striking Ethiopia for centuries (see R. Pankhurst 1961, 1968; Relief and Rehabilitation Commission report of Addis Ababa 1986 report, *The History of Famine and Epidemics in Ethiopia prior to the Twentieth Century*). This is due to a combination of low productivity, absence of developed infrastructure, and rapid population growth, as well as adverse climatic conditions. This has not been helped by political repression and armed conflict. In the post–World War II period, the problem was exacerbated by civil strife and political and economic mismanagement. In more recent times, the world's attention has been focused on Ethiopia mainly due to three famines of biblical proportion. The most devastating one was the 1964–1966 famine in the northern provinces of Tigray and Wello. This was followed by the 1973–1974 famine in which about a quarter of a million people died and 50 per cent of the livestock were lost in the same region. Another famine occurred in 1984–1985, and for the third time in two decades, the televised pictures of a starving mass of people in the highlands of Ethiopia triggered an unprecedented response internationally (see W. G. Dawit 1989). The Derg's solution was to put in place a massive forced resettlement, which caused massive rural urban migration in subsequent years (see A. Pankhurst 1992). I knew many street children whose parents were part of that exodus, and who had ended up trapped in a cycle of poverty and joblessness.

During the latter part of the 1960s there was a drive to establish a viable tourism industry. Posters showing the beauty of the land and its cultures were displayed in every hotel and restaurant. The ubiquitous accompanying English language caption read: 'Ethiopia: thirteen months of sunshine and three thousand years of history.'[3] University students and other dissidents made it a sport to deface the posters by changing 'thirteen months of sunshine' to 'thirteen months of hunger' and 'three thousand years of history' to 'three thousand years of misery'. The world reportage of the latest famine in the making (May/September 2008) continues to affect Ethiopia's image as a land of hunger and misery.

In 1974, mounting pressure for a more open political system, coupled with the disclosure of the 1973–1974 famine, led to the overthrow of Emperor Haile Selassie. Colonel Mengistu Haile Mariam's so-called Marxist-Leninist regime (commonly known as the Derg)[4] that followed ruled the country for seventeen years. Ethiopia was proclaimed a socialist state on 20 December 1974. The nationalisation of land, banks, insurance, commercial and industrial companies followed. Thousands of Ethiopians were killed during what is now known as the 'red terror' unleashed by the Derg against its opponents. The end of the Derg was due to several factors: a Somali-backed civil war in the Ogaden in 1977; drought, forced resettlement and the use of hunger as a weapon to subdue uprisings in rural areas; the mismanagement of human and material resources as well as the demise of the USSR. Mengistu Haile Mariam was found guilty of genocide but never put on trial. He now lives in Zimbabwe in relative comfort with his wife and children. I was often told that there were less beggars and street children during the Derg's reign due to their social policy of helping the poor first.

---

[3] The Ethiopian Calendar Year (E.C.) is in many ways different to the Gregorian Calendar Year (G.C.). It contains 12 months of 30 days each, followed by 1 month of 5 days. Every 4th year is Leap Year when an extra day is added at the end of each year. The first day of the year is *Meskerem* first, which falls on 10 or 11 September of the Gregorian calendar. The Ethiopian Calendar Year is seven years behind the year according to the Gregorian calendar, thus 1997 G.C. is 1989 E.C. Christmas usually falls on 7 or 8 January G.C.; accordingly Easter 1997 was celebrated in Ethiopia on 27 April G.C. and not 30 March 1997 G.C. The Ethiopian Millennium was celebrated on 12 September 2007, seven years behind the G.C.-based year 2000 Millennium.

[4] Hereafter, I shall use *Derg* to refer to this Soviet-backed Marxist Military regime.

The current government came into power in 1995. It is the successor of the interim government set up by the Ethiopian People's Democratic Front (EPRDF) during the transitional period to the 1995 multi-party elections. Prime Minister Meles Zenawi is the leader of the Tigrean People's Liberation Front, the largest group within the EPRDF. His government aims to decentralise power and has established a market economy, although land remains State-owned property. Land-locked Ethiopia maintained cordial relations with Eritrea until the latter started a border dispute in May 1998. Since then, Ethiopia and Eritrea, two of the poorest countries in Africa, have spent millions of dollars financing this border dispute. In spite of the loss of thousands of their citizens, they have yet to resolve their differences. On top of this cross-border war, Ethiopian soldiers were stationed in Somalia for two years and embroiled in an intra-clan war taking place in the Horn of Africa and were only withdrawn in January 2009. Separatist movements are still a great concern to the present government. Rural urban migration due to poverty and joblessness continues unabated. As Muhammad Yunus (1998: 215) so succinctly put it, 'Poverty is not created by the poor; it is created by the structures of society.' The effects of urbanization, over-population, rural-to-urban migration and especially political and economic mismanagement by successive governments are the causes for the emergence and proliferation of the street children population.

Addis Ababa

Addis Ababa was founded in 1887. In spite of the present government's decentralising efforts, it is still the political capital of the country and its economic and administrative centre. With a population of 3,627,934 in 2007, it is a mosaic of social and ethnic mixing and diversity. Its altitude ranges from 2,500 to 3,000 meters. It has a surface area estimated to cover 21,000 hectares. It lies at the foothills of the Entoto hills and is cut through by numerous fast-flowing streams and rivers. The city was not properly planned. Just over a century ago Addis Ababa started out as a garrison town for Emperor Menelik II's army. It then 'grew as an agglomeration of *sefers,* following the contours of nature rather than the dictates of man' (Proceedings 1986: 5). *Sefer* means neighbourhood and in modern times it also refers to certain areas of the city. The system of *sefers,* that is military camps and settlements, was established in medieval Ethiopia: 'Chieftains with their retinue used to settle around the Emperor's compound. The imperial quarter was usually located on the highest place in the garrison and the *sefers* were scattered over a large area around it, each chief taking his specific place herein. ... The area between *sefers* was filled in as more residences got built' (Bahru 1986: 43). Some *sefers* were originally populated by migrants from other parts of Ethiopia and are still known as such: *Welo sefer, Dorze sefer* and so on. Other neighborhoods are named after past trading or other activities, such as *Serategna sefer* (workers' neighborhood), *Sega Tera* (meat place) or *Kera* (abattoir). In the course of time the city 'continued to sprawl from a camp into a metropolis', hence 'the bizarre juxtaposition of luxury and squalor that has been noted by more than one observer'. (ibid.: 45). It has defied numerous urban-planning programs, initially by the Italian Occupation Force during the Second World War and by successive Ethiopian Governments since then.

Addis Ababa is now an autonomous chartered city known as Region 14. It is divided into five major administrative zones that include twenty-eight districts referred to as *weredas*. It has over three hundred government-controlled urban dwellers associations, called *kebeles,* which serve as the smallest public service unit similar to a ward. They serve a *sefer* (neighborhood) comprised of a localized or delimited group of people.

Kebeles, or urban-dwellers associations, were first established in July 1975 by the Derg. A *kebele* is the smallest administrative unit of Ethiopia similar to a ward, a neighbourhood or a localized and delimited group of people. It is part of a *woreda,* or district, itself part of a zone, grouped into ethno-linguistic regional zones (*kililoch*). They impacted heavily on the children and families I worked with. Originally, *kebele* officials were responsible for the collection of rent, the establishment of local judicial tribunals and the provision of basic health, education and other social services in their neighbourhood. By late 1976, their powers included the collection of local taxes and the registration of houses, residents, births, deaths and marriages. Initially, mid- and lower-level bureaucrats and teachers were elected and filled *kebele* jobs. The Derg soon purged most of them for opposing its 'revolutionary regime' and put trusted party members to run *kebele* business. During 1976–1977, at the height of 'Red Terror', peasants, officials and students, thought to oppose the Derg's regime, were branded enemies of the people and summarily executed, jailed or tortured. *Kebeles* were responsible for ensuring neighbourhood defences and for forming militia groups to carry out the terror (see Chege 1979 and S. Dawit 2002). These *kebele* officials and militia members were, as John Markakis and Ayele Nega (1978) put it, persons of dubious character, indeterminate occupiers, busybodies and opportunists of all sorts. The militia units in charge of local security were the perennially unemployed, the shiftless and hangers-on, young toughs and delinquents who transformed themselves into revolutionary proletarian fighters. Most took this opportunity to perpetrate crimes and conduct vengeance against people they disliked or disagreed with.

After the overthrow of the Imperial Government in 1974, the Derg nationalised land and houses. People who had more than one house had to choose the one in which they wished to live in. The rest of their properties were expropriated. *Kebele's* were set up to administer nationalised properties. The Derg placed trusted party members in key positions and put them in charge of building more houses and distributing the expropriated houses to the poor. Since there was no significant public funding for such housing projects, the end product was the proliferation of sub-standard houses and makeshift shelters as well as the dilapidation of the nationalised houses and apartment blocks.

Housing

Approximately 75 per cent of the sub-standard housing and makeshift shelters found in Addis Ababa are owned by the present government, and are administered by the State-controlled *kebeles* (see Solomon 1993; Solomon and Aklilu 1993; Ministry of Works and Urban Development Addis Ababa 2006 Annual Report). Many of the *kebele*-run houses are single rooms with an occupancy rate of six to ten people. In 2001, monthly rent was as cheap as two *birr* or as high as two hundred *birr* (£1 Sterling = 20 *birr*). Low-income households, and this includes the majority of the families of street children, constitute the bulk of Addis Ababa's population. They rent or share such houses and are subject to *kebele* housing rules (see Ottawa 1976; Ministry of Works and Urban Development Addis Ababa Report 1996). Less than half of the fifty-two households I visited had secured *kebele* houses. The rest either sub-rented corners of one-room houses or floor space by the week. Sub-letting a corner of a one-room house or renting floor space for the night is a common phenomenon among migrants and non-migrants alike. Because of the over-crowding, proprietors who owned some of the dilapidated properties and those who rented out floor space by the night, charged rents that were four to ten times higher than the *kebele*'s. Twelve out of the twenty-two families I visited were not able to meet the monthly rent and owed considerable amounts of money to the *kebele* or to their landlords. Chapter 3 provides details of the importance of housing to street children's families.

The poorer segment of society (this includes street children's parents) need to belong to a *kebele* to be able to live in rent-controlled *kebele* houses to acquire the necessary address and therefore an identity card in order to be part of the *sefer*. A *kebele* address means access to some kind of free education for their children, rudimentary health services, jobs, citizenship and so on. It is very difficult for jobless poor people to acquire a new *kebele* membership when they move residence. Due to the perennial housing shortage, *kebele* officials refuse to register newcomers. Even people with secure jobs are obliged to retain their original *kebele* membership and identity cards long after they have left the neighbourhood. This is because of the difficulty they encounter in having their new address and status entered into the *kebele* register where they subsequently go to live.

The housing crisis is exacerbated by the influx to the city of poverty-stricken rural-to-urban migrants and internally displaced people who arrive due to civil unrest and government-forced resettlement policies. This has resulted in severe overcrowding, shortages of housing, a drain on the already insufficient social amenities and high youth unemployment. *Kebeles* are unable to accommodate these newcomers because they lack the means to build new houses (see Ottaway 1976; A. Pankhurst 1992; Ministry of Works and Urban Development Addis Ababa Report 1996). Some in-migrants are able to use the social network of long urban–established kith and kin to find jobs or temporary shelter in town (see Ephrem 1998). However, the over-crowded conditions, and the abject poverty their town-based relatives live in hinder the proliferation of such social support systems.

Apart from some isolated housing estates, the substandard type of houses, normally found in shanty towns or squatter settlements, are scattered in a hap-hazard fashion within the city itself. Plastic-, mud- or cardboard-walled houses are built and extended adjacent to each other or near and behind tall buildings and modern villas. Unlike the metropolis of many other developing countries, Addis Ababa has no marginalized squatter settlements in which the poor are iso-lated en mass. Hovels, shacks, mud-plastered houses, palaces, churches, superb villas and skyscrapers can be found in the same *sefer*, often in the same street. Very few neighborhoods are free from such a mixture of rich, poor, middle-class and low-class housing. This often creates a feeling of several 'villages' dispersed helter-skelter within the precincts of the city. Although some areas are less crowded and are relatively free of extensively built poor housing, there is no social homogene-ity. Prostitutes, beggars, street children, day laborers, street vendors, diplomats, civil servants, rich merchants and academics live side by side or rub shoulders as they go about their daily lives. However one chooses to define them, street chil-dren can be found in virtually every *sefer*. Therefore, there are no settled, stable reference populations of slum or squatter children and their families allowing the construction of a representative sample.

My informants lived in some of the densest settlements in the city, in cramped one-room dwellings, with no privacy and few possessions. Most of the houses lacked basic amenities such as toilets, water, electricity or paved roads. They are considered locations of poverty, squalor, destitution, insecurity and danger. Out of the fifty-six houses I visited, only four did not have leaking roofs or gaping walls. The dwellings consisted of a room covering at most an area measuring two by four meters. In this room between four and ten people ate, socialised and slept. The majority of the street children I knew lived in wattle and daub, mud-plastered walled houses, with leaking corrugated iron roofs and beaten earth floors. The rest survived in wind-blown hovels crawling with lice, fleas and flies. None of the houses had windows; many had cracks in the roof or walls. The poorer houses were separated by walls through which neighbours could hear each other breathe. The only daytime light filtered through cracks in the roof, walls or an open door, increasing the lack of privacy. Fetid rainwater full of feces and human detritus flowed through the slum community housing, spreading putrid smells and disease. During the rainy season, barefoot children and adults alike had to walk through the filthy shallows to reach their homes.

Very few households had access to a shared or individual outside kitchen. The great majority of those I frequented cooked inside their one-room homes. Furniture typically consisted of a bed or straw mattress, a wooden box and kitchen utensils such as a *jebena* or a clay pot for brewing coffee, which is found in most Ethiopian houses, one or two aluminum pots and dishes, some coffee cups and glasses. A few families had a *metad* or clay pan for baking *injera*, a flat bread made from *teff* and indigenous Ethiopian wheat and a *messob*, a hand-woven grass basket for storing *injera*. Those who could afford it usually acquired the much-treasured Chinese kerosene stove. Otherwise, they used wood, charcoal, dung, leaves or waste paper as fuel for cooking.

Rain often meant flooding, inside and outside the buildings. An early morning visit during the rainy season revealed the beaten earth floor had turned into a pool of mud. All human belongings would be piled up on top of a single bed or box, wet through and through. The inhabitants usually sat on any available bed, box or the corner where the roof leaked least and waited for the rain to stop. If the floor got too wet during the night, they just sat where they were until morning. Most, if not all, the children I visited slept on the floor, fully dressed. They covered themselves with skimpy, tattered and filthy blankets and whatever they could lay their hands on, to ward off the all-season cold nights. Many did not have a second outfit. Those under ten years of age were obliged to sit naked while their siblings or parents washed and dried their clothes. During the rainy season, homeless adults and youth gangs slept under trees, near church walls or on shop verandas.

In spite of their proximity to luxurious houses, many poorer dwellings lacked water, electricity, sewage or latrine facilities. When families had no piped water in their compounds, children were usually sent out to buy water from public water points. Where electricity was available, a group of houses shared a meter and paid the bill according to the number of bulbs in each house. Those without an electricity supply used a locally made kerosene lamp that emitted noxious black fumes, which at times turned the children's spittle black. The sanitary conditions were appalling. Most if not all the pit latrines I saw were over-flowing. The alleys separating the houses turned into small fetid rivers during the rainy season. Stagnant pools of human and domestic waste glided into the open sewers surrounding houses and hovels alike when it rained. A 1996 study revealed that 3.9 per cent of the housing units in Addis Ababa had flush toilets, 16.7 per cent had shared pit latrines, 20 per cent had private dry pit latrines and 59.3 per cent had no facility whatsoever (see Ministry of Works and Urban Development 1996, Addis Ababa Report). In some places, NGOs have built pit latrines that are much appreciated by adults and children alike. Those unlucky enough to be without a latrine either defecated in the vicinity of their dwellings or went far away near riverbanks or woodlands to relieve themselves. Chapters 3 and 4 reveal the extent of privation and squalor that surrounded the families I worked with.

Street People and Others

The population of Addis Ababa is said to be growing at an average annual rate of approximately 3.8 per cent. It was said to be 2,112,737 as of October 1994, and by 2006 it had reached 3,147,000 of which 1,636,000 were males and 1,511,000 were females. Nearly half (47 per cent) of the total population are migrants. The proportion of children under the age of fifteen amounts to about 32 per cent of the total population. The 1994 census result indicated that there are 410,443 households with an average of 5.1 persons per household. At the time of the census the rate of unemployment was 35 per cent of the economically active population aged fifteen to sixty-four. Almost all ethnic groups are represented in Addis Ababa. The major ethnic groups are Amhara (48 per cent), Oromo (19.2 per cent) and Tigray (7.6 per cent). The same statistical source gives the population of Orthodox Christians as 82 per cent, Muslims 12.7 per cent, Protestants 3.9 per cent, Catholics 0.8 per cent and the remaining 7.6 per cent follow other religions (Central Statistical Agency 2002).

As already emphasised above, there is no settled, stable population of street children families in any one location of Addis Ababa. They live among diverse communities, scattered about the city, in numerous back streets and in houses similar to those depicted above. The areas where such families live are not difficult to find. One has only to step out of the main road and follow any of the many footpaths or side roads to be faced by the glaring misery in which the majority of Addis Ababans live. As far as my research was concerned, it was not geographical location per se but where I was able to engage with my informants, which was of crucial importance to me. The children took me to their homes. I did not pick out a specific neighbourhood for special attention. I did not operate in any one area, but in a multitude of areas.

None of the twenty-five street children families I ultimately targeted for intensive study were neighbours. Most of them lived miles apart from each other, in similarly dilapidated houses. This was mainly for practical reasons. Within six months into my field work, I realized that if I wished to operate freely among the street children families I was working with I had to create the necessary space to avoid offending or upsetting my informants. If I visited one house, I felt obliged to pay a call to the other house. Some mothers assumed that the other mothers were more concerned about giving me information about them than about their own families. The children, who had first taken me to the neighbourhood, would complain that I had talked to their friend's mother and not theirs. I felt pressurized into spending more time trying to appease their sensibility than concentrating on what I was trying to do. It was easier for me to convey to the children that they were all my friends and that I was not there for a particular child. The rare times I was confronted by a particularly persistent child, all I had to do was avoid the street for a few days, walk away or ignore her or him. In chapters 3, 4 and 5, I explain the circumstances which enabled me to establish rapport and remain in the lives of those I have selected to include in this book.

There are a multitude of churches and traffic lights and as many spots in front of commercial premises where the street children operate. The only fixed street-based location I frequented intensively for a longer period was a church propitiously located near a traffic light where one of the three gangs of homeless boys I worked with had made their home for more than three years. I have given a detailed description of the area in chapter 4. Street-based fieldwork meant roaming from street to street. Location-based research entailed going from neighbourhood to neighbourhood. In other words, 'field-site' in my case refers to people and multi-sites not areas, neighbourhoods, homes or specific streets.

2

YILUNTA

Shame, Honour and Family Pride

In spite of the ethnic and religious diversity already described, there are shared cultural references in the 'wider Ethiopian culture', in which masculinity and femininity are powerful social-control mechanisms. Even though both concepts project complex, changeable, multiple and contradictory symbolic interpretations and lived-in realities, masculine identity is valued over feminine identity. This gender-based ideology is produced, shaped and maintained by social conventions and habitual practices. The subordinate status of Ethiopian women is based on deep-rooted traditional values and beliefs, which transcend ethnicity and religion. This endorses a form of sanctioned domination of men over women because qualities deemed masculine, such as rationality, independence, assertiveness, protectiveness and physical strength, are valued over female 'traits', like docility, submissiveness, irrationality, dependence and physical weakness. The key terms here are values and belief systems, since the sharing of values is one way of defining culture. This is because values and belief systems connect us to each other, to the community, to morality and to the moral self. They help us to recognise how the lives of men and women are shaped more by socially defined values and perceptions, than by biological differences. They improve our understanding of how socially constructed roles, which are based on traditional values, lead to experiences, needs and choices that are different, diverse and unequal between men and women.

In *The History of Sexuality*, Michel Foucault (1981: 86) postulates that 'power is tolerable only on condition that it masks a substantial part of itself. Its success is proportional to its ability to hide its own mechanisms.' He further affirms that 'power comes from below; that is, there is no binary and all encompassing opposition between rulers and ruled at the root of power relations' (ibid.: 94). In other words, for masculine power to work, both men and women must use the same system of knowledge that naturalise this power and adhere to it. In short, it must become part of society's norm. Feminists' quest has been to deconstruct and eliminate this knowledge power base by demonstrating that it is socially constructed and not genetically determined or divinely inspired. This chapter explores aspects of the discourse that naturalises this gendered knowledge power base in Ethiopia and its influence on the socialization of children in Ethiopia.

Masculinity

The above assertion is not an attempt to limit the category 'man' to a specific predetermined set of ideals with strict boundaries, so that even the most dis-enfranchised Ethiopian man is seen to have more access to power and privilege than any Ethiopian woman does. Masculinity is not valued per se unless it is being 'performed' by a biological male and underpinned by gendered social values, which have marked effects on male and female consciousness. The model of domination I am referring to is in keeping with Michel Foucault's (1981) model of power, which challenges the monolithic notion of male power and domination over women including its association with physical strength. Foucault places power per se as inscribed in discourse and belief systems where it is less legal or formally sanctioned in character and where it is not always easy to identify actual agents. For Foucault, power is present in the defiance of the subject as well as in its exertion by the initiator. He concludes that rather than a repressive system of law and order, power may actually function as the source of all our knowledge. Therefore, one of the prime effects of power is that certain bodies, gestures, discourses, desires come to be identified and constituted as that of the individual's. Such normalized 'truths' permeate people's beliefs and dispositions, thus making them acquire a certain way of seeing society. In short, Foucault is interested in systems of rules that put aside meaning and truth in order to focus on the condition in which normalized 'truths' can be seen as legitimate. Accordingly, subservience need not be a lack of power inasmuch as it represents a different form that power might take. 'Power relations are both intentional and non-subjective' (ibid.: 94). A relation of power does not constitute obligations or prohibitions imposed upon the 'powerless' by the 'powerful', rather the rules and responsibilities governing both are internalized and transmitted by and through the 'powerful' as well as the 'powerless'.

Similarly, Pierre Bourdieu (1977) asserts that people's knowledge of their culture is very subjective and therefore culture can only be observed subjectively. For example, his notion of habitus emphasises the idea that individuals, though they often do not think of their actions as intentional, behave in an intentional manner. This is because people acquire patterns of thought, behaviour and taste which links social structures with social practice. The driving force is not some abstract principle, still less a set of rules, but a disposition inculcated in early years of life and constantly reinforced by calls to order from the group. As Anthony King (2000: 420) succinctly put it: 'Individuals do not solipsistically consult *a priori* rules which then determine their actions independently, but rather individuals act according to a sense of practice, which is established and judged by the group.' Accordingly, male power over women in Ethiopia rests primarily on the deep structures provided by socially constructed 'traditional' forms of masculine and feminine identities. There are no chains or bars helping to endorse a form of sanctioned domination of men over women or parents over children, just the restrictions of convention and social expectation derived from a broader cultural context that is imbued with a communal sense of *yilunta* or shame, honour and family pride.

Modern cultural forms contain older cultural beliefs and practices. As David Heinige (1982: 129) puts it, 'The past has happened and cannot change, but the interpretation and understanding of it continues and will never stop changing.' All stories have a cultural locus, and personal narratives are constructed within a wider social context; they both reproduce and are produced by dominant cultural meta-narratives (see Andrews et al. 2008). In fitting with the above assumptions, I found that gendered identity formation and gender-based attrition among the street children and members of youth gangs I worked with were amenable to analysis and interpretation in terms of masculine ideology and masculinity. This is because my informants merged essentialist ideals of maleness found in the 'wider Ethiopian culture' with social practice in their narratives and actions. *Yilunta* was pivotal to the boys' personal conception of masculine dignity and the rationale behind many of their actions. The Ethiopian ideal of masculine power was mostly out of reach of members of the youth gangs because they did not have the class advantage to offset the poverty and powerlessness they endured.

Yilunta

The 'wider Ethiopian culture' is shame-based. The ideal Ethiopian child, male and female, is one that has been inculcated with and internalised a deep sense of *yilunta*. Roughly translated, *yilunta* means having a heightened perception of what others may say or even think about what one does in private or in public. Most importantly, *yilunta* means having a deeper sense of shame in personally knowing that one has done something shameful regardless of what people may think or say or even whether anyone knows about it. The nearest but not equivalent Western notion of *yilunta* as a sense of shame is the Italian concept of *vergogna* (see Sciama 2003).

The value of *yilunta* is not in its truth as fact, but in its truth as meaning making. It is the rationale or justification behind the act rather than the act itself. All the parents and children I talked to, irrespective of class or ethnic background, associated *yilunta* with shame, honour or family pride. More often than not, children and adults alike drew on, recycled, negotiated and merged essentialist ideals of maleness and femaleness derived from their sense of *yilunta* with social practice. The proof that it was a socially constructed notion is that children and adults alike were able to continually manipulate, distort and even intentionally or unintentionally re-arrange its meaning to fit in with the truth they wanted to project or to achieve their goals. This might be pressurising daughters or sons to subject themselves to certain culturally ill-defined norms – whatever these may be – and behave as expected by their parents or for a child bride to go back to an abusive husband in order not to shame her family by abandoning her marital home.

The inherent meaning of *yilunta* also incorporates being alert to public op-probrium and being constantly conscious of society's 'gaze' on the self. In terms of family pride, this involves a deeply rooted concern with status and family honour. For girls and women this means that regardless of economic circum-stances or social status they are supposed to appear respectable. For example, the constant bickering between a mother and her daughter was not because the girl spent her days working and trading in the streets but because she 'showed face' to everyone and associated with undesirable men. This is how it was expressed: 'My daughter shows face to one and all. All sorts of vagabonds and street children are her friends. She goes trading, eating, and fighting with them. I told her to "snub" them,[1] but she will not listen. Which man would want to marry her unless she changes her behaviour? She has no *yilunta,* she has no regards to what people may say or for my feelings as her mother.' The daughter's retort was that either she frequented with such people or they starved. Chapter 3 provides details of how this unfolds in real life.

For boys and men, *yilunta,* in association with their concern with status, means not losing face, protecting and honouring the family including financially helping relatives if necessary. Sensitivity to and concern about the opinion of others and a strong sense of propriety in dealing with friends and family alike is key to having *yilunta.* Among the youth gangs I worked with, the expression they used to justify their disapproval of an unpopular comrade was that he had no *yilunta,* meaning 'he is unscrupulous, he has no shame'. For upper and bet-ter-off middle–class males, *yilunta* meant being conscious and taking pride in the knowledge of one's class position. This precluded certain types of work and other social activities, which ranged from housework, accepting lower-status jobs like portaging, or marrying beneath one. On 29 June 2001, I recorded a destitute Ethiopian mother talking about her 12-year-old son in reference to housework: 'What will his future wife say about me if I let him mess around in the kitchen? That I turned him into a woman! What will his friends say of him? That he is *yeset lij* [i.e. son-of-a-woman].' I have heard many young Ethiopian migrant men living in London and Manchester saying how relieved they were to finally break

---

[1] The word used in Amharic was '*kuribatchew*'.

free from the shackle-like crown bestowed on them as males by *yilunta* and thus be able to take on any kind of menial jobs to survive in the West. There is a paradoxical tension between such freedom in the West and its shackles at home. It is reflected in the fact that all the Ethiopian men I met at universities abroad or in the Diaspora, who were happy enough to cook, clean, and even care for their babies in the UK, automatically reverted back to type and were never seen in the kitchen when they returned to Ethiopia.

Yilunta also incorporates the introspective self-analysis of one's motives, behaviour and actions. Someone who has internalised a sense of *yilunta* can be said to be *ainafar*. *Ainafar* can also be translated as shy, a greatly valued female trait. *Ain* means eyes and *afar* means shame or ashamed. *Atafrem* and *atafrim,* the masculine and feminine versions of 'have you no shame?', are often used to stop a child or an adult from infringing accepted codes of behaviour. The alternative is the ubiquitous '*ende!*', an interjection that has no equivalent word in English. Women use it to deflect unwanted attention from men or to indicate that they are offended. Parents use it to stop a child in its tracks before it misbehaves. It can be used with humour or aggression. Depending on inflection, context, or facial expression, the recipient is able to interpret whether the expression is meant in jest or anger and react appropriately.

Yilunta is a very powerful and prevalent sanction. It is feared and hated by children and adults alike. It generates shyness in children, thus making them loath to confront any kind of adult authority, parental or otherwise. It touches on the child's (especially a girl's) identity. It influences their self-image and life-long comportment in private or in public. This includes respect and complete obedience to parents and elders for both sexes plus for girls acting demure and submissive towards men and all adults. The educated urban elites are aware of the implication of inculcating too deep a sense of *yilunta* in their children. They try to avoid this pitfall by encouraging their children to explain themselves, voice an opinion and even discuss 'adult' matters within the family. They nevertheless expect their children to conform in public to most, if not all, the behaviour expected of children in the 'wider Ethiopian culture'. Accordingly, they are not averse to chastising their children verbally and physically, in order to inculcate total obedience and respect for their elders.

Even though the sense of *yilunta* was mostly evoked in terms of female sexuality and morality, the emphasis for men was centred on being fearless alpha males, protecting family honour, achieving financial or social success and being seen to help family welfare. It was above all else not being seen as 'a female' and thus losing face in public. *Yeset lij* or 'son of a woman', inferring that the male it is addressed to is not a 'real' man, was a typical insult and *ende set ashenahalew,*[2] was the type of offensive female referencing threat hurled at a boy by another boy.

---

[2] *Ende set ashnahalew* means 'I shall make you sit down and urinate like a woman', the inference is that women are inferior and weaker than men are.

Above all else, *yilunta* for men of all classes is striving to become a man among men, or better still a man above other men and female members of one's family. Having *yilunta* involves aggression as a means of saving face when their 'manhood' is brought into question. It is like a character context in which opponents seek and maintain face at the other's expense by remaining steady in adversity. The overarching consensus among the boys I knew was that backing down or failure to retaliate (or at least be seen as likely to retaliate) might be construed by witnesses as evidence of cowardice. Since they had little or no outlet for masculine assertion, the posturing, bravura, bravado and violence among members of youth gangs, including aggression towards female gang members, was a continuous attempt to at least be seen to be manly. Chapters 4 and 5, provide insights about the way this process unfolds.

The kind of supporting evidence I give below validates my definition of *yilunta* and makes my contention of the existence of a 'wider Ethiopian culture' which is imbued with a common sense of *yilunta* more convincing. I asked Ethiopian academics and other friends whether there was an equivalent word for *yilunta* in their mother tongue or 'native language' and what *yilunta* meant to them. Eshetu Chabo,[3] a Gamo, began by warning me that 'language is a dictionary of a culture. It is a challenge to try to convey some fundamental thought patterns from one language-culture community to another.' He nevertheless described what *yilunta* meant to him as follows: 'It was *yilunta* that obliged me to leave the drinks party where I met you even though I was enjoying the conversation because I came there with another guest who wanted to leave. The equivalent expression for *yilunta* in Gamo is "*assi ay ganne gene*", which literally means "shouldn't" what others might say/feel not to be taken into account?' In other words: '"*yilunta/assi ay ganne gene*" is striving to avoid disapproval by others, which may lead to ostracism. You like someone … but are too ashamed to say it. Someone offers you food, but you say that you have just eaten when in fact you are starving. You hold back and refuse to be offended, choosing to see the best in other people. It is also operating within societal norms … avoiding any or all actions or words that would engender disapproval by others … polite reservation might cover part of it' (27 and 29 January 2009).

Dilu Shaleka, a Sidama anthropologist, gives two equivalent words for *yilunta* in Sidama language: '*fokkifata*' and '*saalfata*'. According to Dilu Shaleka both words mean

> to be ashamed, or to feel respect for public opinion, to exercise a restraint against a temptation or an urge to do something indecent or inconvenient. *Fokkifata* is used for adults. *Saalfata* is the root word *saala* and literally means shame and another word *Waawu* or shame. They are both used to socialize children. Another more practical expression in association with *yilunta* is *manu mayáe*, which literally means 'what would others say?' People in difficult circumstances use this expression to explain that what

---

[3] Eshetu Ghabo is a professional Amaharic-Gamo-English translator based in London.

made them hesitate to pursue a certain course of action was the fear of public opinion and opprobrium. (27 January 2009)

In another e-mail communication, Kelemework Tarefe, a Tigray anthropologist, wrote: '*Yilunta* is known as *elunta* in Tigrigna. With regard to your question, *elunta* for me means a tendency to conform to others' demands and suppress your own feelings and motivations because of the fear of rejection by others. It is something inside my mind but somehow planted by friends, family members and the social environment at large. I want to be integrated with others so I don't want to behave differently, especially in a way that society does not like' (31 January 2009). All the Guregue street children and families I knew had a heightened sense of *yilunta*, which they called *qemet*.

Various writers have eloquently illustrated the central role that masculinity plays in the 'wider Ethiopian culture'. In her article 'The Hagiographies of Ethiopian Female Saints', Selamawit Mecca (2006: 153–167) writes that the stories surrounding saints' lives are intended to convey a moral message rather than provide historically accurate information. Their objective is to provide doctrines and correct values intended to guide the behaviour of the community. Out of the 202 hagiographies written in *Ge'ez*,[4] only 9 are about women saints. They invariably portray women as lacking wisdom and unable to perform miracles without supernatural intervention and the help of men. In comparison to the life stories, teachings and practices relating to male saints, those dealing with female saints usually focus on the women's bodies, especially their beauty and fertility. Male saints are categorised as priests, administrators, powerful men and defenders of the faith or teachers. Their characters are infused with masculine power, fearlessness and the ability to perform miracles on their own. Female saints show fear when faced with danger and difficulty. Instead of confronting evil head-on like 'men', they cry and pray. Selamawit notes that the lives of women's saints are there to highlight and give prominence to male characters. She concludes that the parables have less to do with women and more about creating a correct perception of men and by association confirm what women are not.

The Aari live far away from the highlands dominated by the Ethiopian Orthodox Christian faith.[5] Commenting on the cult of masculinity among them, Alexander Naty (2002: 59) writes that 'the Aari rebelled in situations where the

---

[4] *Ge'ez* is an ancient Ethiopian script and language. It is the precursor of Amharic, the lingua franca and modern Ethiopian language. It is still used in liturgy by the Ethiopian Orthodox Christian Church.

[5] The Aari people are agriculturalists. They number around 160,000 and live in the South Omo region of Ethiopia. Aari is a Omotic language and has nine dialects: Gozza, Biyo, Bako, Galila, Laydo, Sayki, Shangama, Wubahamer, Zeddo and Sido the central dialect. Even though some Aari have converted to Evangelical Christianity and Islam, most are followers of traditional religions that include the veneration of ancestors. They attribute their clan origin to certain rivers, mountains and trees. See Hayward 1990 and Central Statistical Agency of Ethiopia 2005 for a detailed expose.

State was weak and unable to exert any control. Acts of violence often followed their rebellion. They justified their violence by articulating a cult of masculinity. In reclaiming old notions of masculinity, the Aari used a variety of metaphors to describe their powerlessness vis-à-vis the State, the old imperial regime as well as the *Derg* i.e. "becoming women", "castration", "penis-shortening" and "becoming sheep"' (ibid.: 62). In short, masculinity was used as a collective self-expression, agency and self-assertion for Aari men.

The writer Eisei Kurimoto (2002) uses female and male narratives among the Anywaa,[6] to describe their fear and alarm at the erosion of their traditional way of life due to urbanization, Christianity and modernity brought about by development and State interference. His female informants speak with nostalgia, and lament the loss of the old order with its own political system, when everyone, especially women, knew their places and their utility: 'Anywaa generally understood that the (1974) revolution brought on the age of commoners. "People became one" ... "oneness" implied "equality" ... "People began to stand up". To stand or get up (*oo maal*) in contemporary Anywaa language has two important implications. One is that now people do not have to kneel down in front of *nyiye* or *kwaari* (chiefs) and that women do not have to do the same in front of men' (ibid.: 227). This book's contribution to the discourse is its support of my contention that aspects of this 'common culture' are imbued with a sense of *yilunta*. This shared cultural reference creates and sustains an idea of women in association with object/utility/dependency and men with subject/action/agency in the Ethiopian cultural psyche. Women are classified according to what they are for, while men are looked at in terms of what they can do. The shared view encapsulated within *yilunta*, which I want to project below, is one that links children to family and community values. According to my informants, family, friends and the community inculcate *yilunta* and other belief systems into children but adherence to these values is largely the individual's responsibility.

Socialisation: A Girl or a Boy?

The inculcation of children with a gendered identity begins at birth. This could be as soon as someone exclaims 'It is a girl' or 'It is a boy'. The tone of voice ad-

---

[6] Anywaa are a Nilotic people, two-thirds of the Anywaa population live in Ethiopia and one-third in the Sudan. According to the national population census of 1994, there are 44,581 Anywaa living in Gambela. The Anywaa are agri-pastoralists. Even though Christian evangelism is making a fast inroad into their culture, most follow tradition religions beliefs. They believe in God and use trees as a symbol for their God. Arranged marriage and polygamy are common. Having many daughters is considered a blessing and good fortune because of the heavy bride wealth payment involved. Nevertheless, traditionally, Anywaa women were expected to crawl in front of their husbands while serving them food.

opted by Ethiopian men and women in front of a baby boy or girl differs. A soft, high-pitched 'tchi, tchi, twii. Wui, wui. Wui, look how pretty she is; look at her slender fingers' and so on is usually earmarked for girls. A deep-throated 'Ho, ho, ho, ho, look at him, how strong he is. The little lion cub!' and so on is reserved for boys. The initial answers I received regarding the merits of having male or female children from poor mothers were inconclusive. Some of them declared a preference for girls, 'because she will take care of me'; other mothers preferred boys, 'because he will take care of me'. Most fathers preferred to have sons. Subsequent discussions revealed that both fathers and mothers wished to have as many male children as possible and that girls were less welcome than boys. Girls were generally considered trouble because of the danger of the 'male gaze' and associated female sexuality. Ideally, in order to overcome her sexuality and frailty, a girl would have to become an 'ideal' Ethiopian woman: virginal, chaste, modest, submissive, respectful, domesticated, serene and, of course, beautiful!

In *Women the Longest Revolution,* Juliet Mitchell (1966) wrote that the acquisition of gender identities and roles explains why women accede to their own oppression. She omitted to add that it is women, more so than men, who inculcate this gendered identity to their children. There was general agreement among my informants that mothers as a whole are in sole charge of socialising children. The process of helping a girl child internalise *yilunta* or the subjective self-knowledge of the 'ideal' Ethiopian female is said to be assured through the constant vigilance and the formidable 'female gaze' projected by mothers and female relatives.

The onus of conforming to idealised femininity rests upon the girl. This is because the intended and projected meaning behind becoming a woman is not of the girl as a potential victim of male sexuality, but of the girl who does not conform to type, as a potential victimiser of the entire family. Much like the ideology behind so-called 'honour killings', it is the girl who brings 'shame' to the family and pays the penalty, and not the man who seduced or raped her. For example, the reaction to a fourteen-year-old girl impregnated by her 35-year-old teacher was: 'What was she doing in his house?' He had lured her with promises of private tuitions and monetary remuneration if she cleaned his house, and then raped her. The response to a 15-year-old girl who was raped by a university student in his mother's house was: 'Who forced her to go there?' He had promised to give her his old textbooks, which she was too poor to buy.

Arguments for chastity or at least a sense of *yilunta* or shame or guilt regarding sexual matters in men and boys generated guffaws or dismissed derisively. The most memorable ripostes I received were, 'Why should a man worry? *It* is not soap, *It* does not wear out; A girl's virginity is priceless, until she loses it.' Accordingly, among the population of street children and their entourage, as soon as a girl child lost her virginity or gave birth, no matter how young or how far under the age of consent, she was automatically considered a woman and treated as an adult. Worse still, most boys scoffed at the idea that rape is rape if the victim was no longer a virgin. As put by a 14-year-old boy: 'They couldn't have raped her. She was no longer a virgin!' This was in reference to the rape of a 13-year-old female gang member by three of the boy's comrades. The great majority of boys and girls from the mixed-sex gang I knew considered the gang rape of a female gang member to be equivalent to beating her up for infringing gang rules such as withholding money she earned from prostitution or refusing to be the 'wife' of an assigned comrade. Chapter 5 provides vivid illustrations of this assertion as narrated by the children themselves.

The above may be a reflection of the still-prevalent tradition of expecting a girl (usually a child bride) to be a virgin on her wedding night and it being her husband's 'duty' to forcibly take her, i.e. literally rape her. Spousal abuse in Ethiopia may thus start as marital rape on the wedding night. The bride is supposed to resist her bridegroom's attempts to rape her, thus demonstrating her innocence and modesty. The day after, the groom's best man and friends carry the blood-stained bridal sheets to her parents as proof that their daughter was a virgin and has upheld her family's honour. Child marriage is still prevalent in rural Ethiopia. In fact, practically all the rural-to-urban migrant mothers I knew told me that they had been given in marriage to men they did not know already, either before they reached puberty or by their fourteenth birthdays.[7] All the boys and men I worked with were emphatic in their wish to marry a virgin.

For boys, patriarchal ideology demands that this same 'female gaze' ensures that they are raised to become men. The 'ideal' Ethiopian man is sombre, quiet, reflective, rational, brave, fearless, handsome, respectful and submissive to his family and to none other. He may be obsequious to elders or towards the chosen few he deems worthy of his respect but he is master in his house. A potent insult hurled at a cowardly or shiftless boy or man is *yeset lij*. Although *yeset* means woman and *lij* means child, the insult is invariably directed at males. *Yarogit lij*, meaning an old women's son, a mama's son or a weakling, is another affront directed mostly at boys. Mothers' role in the enculturation of sons, with the occasional help from fathers or male relatives, involves not sparing the rod or the child. More often than not, violence among and between youth gang members was initiated by a boy trying to command respect, honour and prove his physical strength or fearlessness, embroiling his comrades in his quarrels. Boys are therefore victims and victimisers of the same patriarchal and masculine, ideology-driven, gender-based violence in Ethiopia.

---

[7] A UNICEF 2003 report indicates that in Ethiopia and in parts of East Africa, West Africa and South Asia, marriage at the age of seven or eight is common. In Ethiopia 60 per cent of girls are married before they are eighteen years old. In rural areas many girls aged eleven or twelve are given in marriage by their parents to men they have never met. Early marriage can have harmful consequences for the girl child. They include health problems, spousal abuse and the denial of education. Once married, girls often do not go back to school. See also Heinonen 2002.

Parenting among the Poor

Anthropological studies on parenting assume that there are cultural variations in child rearing. The conceptual framework is the interpretation of parental behaviour in its local context. It is assumed that child-care is mediated by cultural scripts, which may be affected by economic factors (see Le Vine and New 2008). There were similarities between the ways poor mothers raised their children and how family members interacted with one another. All the street children and parents I have interviewed maintained that raising and socialising children is a woman's job. Girls and boys were supposed to be guided, disciplined and trained into womanhood and manhood by their mothers or other female members of their families. Mothers' roles in socialisation involved inculcating children with the idea of blind obedience and deference towards all adults, especially parents. Children were expected to learn to behave in this way through effusive praise, strict discipline, physical or verbal chastisement, sound parental advice and the good example set by adults, rather than internalised convictions. Mothers' contribution to child rearing involved ensuring that children fulfil the role expectations and the behavioural patterns found in the 'wider Ethiopian' cultural context, especially a deep sense of *yilunta*. Ideally the proper parent/child (or even non-kin adult/child) relationship is based on ritual forms of demeanour by the child, which may be construed as abject servility towards adults.

Fathers said that their contribution to child rearing began after the child, especially a boy, reached the age of seven and began to 'know his soul' *liju nefsun taweke behuwala*. Their role was usually restricted to guiding and disciplining troublesome children, especially boys, when mothers were unable to cope. Mothers and fathers interpreted 'knowing its soul' to mean: when a child is aware of right and wrong; when one can talk sensibly to the child; when a child realises that she or he has a mortal soul; when the child starts being aware of other people's feelings; when the child stops being gullible and childish; when she or he is able to hide her/his feelings and begins to manipulate people. Devout Christian and Muslim mothers pointed to a spiritual and emotional consciousness in the child 'knowing its soul' and added the associated significance of seven being the age at which Christian children are expected to fast at Easter (Lent) and Muslim children during Ramadan.

As a rule, after the age of five, children and parents, especially mothers and sons, had an 'aloof' relationship. Although not very demonstrative physically, the emotional ties among members of street children families were very strong. The feelings parents and children had for each other were made apparent not through kisses and hugs, but by what they did for each other. Feelings also were vocalised through what they said to each other and by what they said about each other. Effusive blessings might reward a child's accomplishment or endeavour: 'my master', 'my angel', 'my life', 'brave boy', 'my little lion' or 'my beauty', 'may

God bless and protect you'. Conversely, misconduct unleashed a torrent of verbal
abuse that would make even an adult cringe: 'may God take your eyes out', 'you
filth', 'you monster', 'you cancer'.

The most common mechanisms of inculcating appropriate behaviour and
yilunta included insults, criticism, public humiliation and finger pointing or corporal punishment. There was also the matter of the children's remarkable sus-
ceptibility to all the legends about demonic and saintly influences. They did not
treat lightly a curse delivered in the name of a saint. Many children said that they
preferred a beating to verbal abuse, because the mental pain they suffered from
being insulted, cursed or publicly shamed haunted them and lasted longer. Physical punishment could be a slap in the face, punching, pinching, or fumigating
children by covering their heads and sprinkling *berbere*[8] on hot embers or even
assaulting them with sticks, stones, belts or anything that fell into the adult's
hand. *Kurkum* was a favourite method of corporal punishment. This is the use
of a clenched fist, with a protruding middle finger to hit the errant child on the
head. It is the most common form of physical attack on children by parents,
teachers and even the police. Most, if not all, the street children and non-street
children's parents assured me that it was no use reasoning with or physically punishing children under age five, since they soon forgot why they were chastised. In
real life, this belief did not stop many parents from slapping, pinching or hitting
even toddlers for being unruly, loud or disobedient. I have seen mothers pinching the thighs of their 3–5-year-old daughters in order to teach them not to sit
on the floor with their legs apart and to act demurely in public, while boys of the
same age were encouraged to flaunt their physical strength and manhood. It is no
wonder that traditionally raised Ethiopian women seem to take up so little space
in a crowed room, while the men appear to suck up most of the oxygen!

As Tedla Diressie (1999: 14) puts it, '[Ethiopian] … society believes that the
family has the right to do anything with their children and corporal punishment
is considered to be essential to make children behave and internalise the norms of
society.' The parents' sense of *yilunta* precludes apologizing to a child or admitting that they are wrong, no matter what. Whenever I pleaded with a mother or
father to let their child know that they were mistaken and should not have punished her/him before making sure of their guilt, I was told that the child knows
what is what and it is a shameful thing or *yilunta* for an adult to apologize to a
child. Some even claimed that such a gesture might embarrass the child, and that
it was best not to discuss the matter further.

Dependency, blind obedience and total deference to parents and all adults
were associated with the ideal child and childhood. This was a heavy task to
achieve for the street children I worked with since they were expected to be an-

---

[8] *Berbere,* red-hot chillies infused with garlic and herbs, is part of the staple of condiments in Ethiopian cuisine.

swerable adults, workers and bread-winners in the street, but instantly turn into dependent, malleable and voiceless children when at home. The street-working, trading, law-enforcing and begging fraternities held street children and members of youth gangs responsible for their actions in the street and treated them as adults for all practical purposes. The same presumed 'adult' children in the street were expected to be dependent and voiceless at home as well as in the neighbourhood they lived in. Their parents, especially their mothers, were made accountable for their behaviour within their community. The constant shift between their adult (street) and child (home) identities created a sense of *anomie* in many of them. The street children who had a home to go to at night and a family they could call their own lived in a kind of hopefulness that they would be loved, approved of or praised for being obedient, working hard and handing their meagre earnings over to their parents. The members of youth gangs and older street boys I knew had lost this hopefulness and with it a sense of belonging. More often that not they were quick to challenge, insult or even assault adults, including the police, and were considered feral, dangerous to society and lacking any sense of *yilunta* by most urbanites.

Yebet Moya (Domesticity)

Another aspect of socialisation is related to the notion of domesticity or *yebet moya*. This involves all sorts of domestic and other skills imparted to a girl child by female members of the household in order to equip her for adulthood and motherhood. The abject poverty poor mothers live in precludes them from having the time or means to impart culinary or other domestic skills to their daughters. Boys from poorer households usually help out and do 'women's work' in the home. However, they seldom continue to clean, wash, cook or serve food for the family after the age of twelve or at the onset of puberty. Unless they are ill, their mothers' sense of *yilunta* makes them reluctant to 'turn their sons into girls'. They seldom expect their teenage boys to help with housework. Chapter 3 contains passages which illustrate the incompatibility of this idealised worldview and the conflicting reality facing poor mothers and sons. Boys from better-off families were spared having to help out, since even secretaries, sales girls, teachers, chauffeurs and taxi drivers could afford to hire a full-time live-in maid. These housemaids were expected to do all the cleaning, washing, cooking and serving until everyone had gone to bed, with hardly a day off during the week. It was common for servants working for expatriates living in Addis Ababa to hire their own servants to take care of their homes and children, while they catered for foreigners. The present government has instituted a minimum wage for domestic servants and a few NGOs set up projects to train young women in domestic work in order to improve their chances of getting better-paid jobs. Most of the trained girls end up as domestic servants in the Middle East.

Among families of street children, girls as young as five were expected to gracefully and automatically take up any domestic duties asked of them. Many become adept at anticipating adults' needs and seeing to their comfort by the age of eight. Actually, this behaviour is not class, education or status based. Hosting parties or serving guests, especially men, with decorum becomes second nature for most Ethiopian women. The difference is that, due to their abject poverty, girls from poor families are often burdened with the child-care of their younger siblings, domestic chores and adult-like responsibilities before they reach puberty, and continue to toil the rest of their lives.

Kesewgar Menor (Living with Other People)

One of the basic concerns of urban-based poor parents is to establish and maintain good neighbourly relations and contain enmity. The socialisation of street children includes inculcating them with the vital art of living with other people. This homogenises the way poor people raise their children. After the age of seven, all children are expected to learn to live with other people (*kesewgar menor*). Parents, especially mothers, are expected to inculcate this ideal in their children. The dos and don'ts associated with knowing how to live with other people are varied and many. They include not fighting with neighbourhood children and adults; not loitering around people's houses in the hope of being offered food (tell that to a 3- or 5-year-old child who had not eaten anything all day!); not touching other people's property and not discussing family matters with outsiders. Ideally, a good child does not answer back, contradict or insult an adult in public or private. He or she is expected to agree to run errands for neighbours, family friends and relatives alike and refrain from causing any kind of friction with neighbours. In short, she or he has developed a strong sense of *yilunta*.

Members of their communities expected mothers to be answerable for their children's misconduct. In the highly diversified and over-crowded urban context of Addis Ababa, migrants and city-born people encounter large numbers of expectations governing social relationships, which they have to adhere to. The customs and values migrants practise in rural-based ethnic enclaves are part of a particular social context. These cannot be replicated in an urban-based markedly dissimilar geographical, cultural and economic setting. Rural-to-urban migrants are therefore obliged to relate to the sort of social situations that existed in town before their arrival. Ritual practices and relationships with affines used to arbitrate marital and other disputes within the community are taken over, and depersonalised, by the state machinery in the *kebele* courts or at police stations.

In the poverty-stricken and over-populated urban context, there is a breakdown of traditional forms of adult behaviour towards all children. Customarily all adults, especially family friends, relatives and neighbours, are supposed to protect or even remonstrate with an errant child. Urbanites cannot count on the customary rights afforded to all adults, neighbours and friends to scold or even physically chastise a child who misbehaves. Urban residents, rich and poor alike, prefer to grumble and keep out of other people's business. Occasionally, children who caused discord, no matter how trivial the misdemeanour, ended up receiving severe beatings or being verbally abused by their mothers. The overtly public demonstration that accompanied disciplining children in such instances helped mothers convince their neighbours that they were indeed strict disciplinarians and therefore raising their children properly. It also defused any tension that may have been created by the children's behaviour.

From time to time poor mothers sided with their children and got embroiled in their sons or daughters' disputes with neighbours, adults and children alike. Apart from encountering the ire of offended or offensive mothers, there was the occasional risk of provoking the guilty children into retaliating. This could be by attacking or constantly bullying the neighbours' children, throwing stones or even destroying anything left outside. Enmity caused by children's bad behaviour was one the major causes of rifts between neighbours.

Children Parenting their Parents

Socialisation is understood to be an essentially passive process on the children's part. It takes for granted the active role of adults, especially mothers, in the socialisation process (see Mayer 1970; Fortes 1970; Hardman 1973a, 1973b, 1974; Le Vine and Williams 1974; Whiting and Whiting 1975; A. James 1979; B. B. Whiting and Edwards 1988; A. James and Sprout 1990; Shieffelin 1990; Mandel 1991). Interestingly, a role reversal occurred among my informants, when occasionally street children subverted this process and played a corresponding part in socialising their mothers and siblings. As already mentioned above, a common theme running through the street children families' lives is the gendered aspect in the socialization of such children by their parents. A less-gendered and less–commonly observed phenomenon is that at times the children themselves end up parenting their parents and siblings. Unlike their mothers, rural-to-urban migrant children learn to speak Amharic, the *lingua franca,* within weeks of arriving in the city. They then proceed to teach their mothers. Seven-year-old or even younger children replace the eyes their blind parents have lost and guide them to lucrative begging spots. Destitute children also learn the intricacies of begging and trading in the street with an alacrity that belies their tender age and they socialise their mothers into street life. City-born and barely-literate children often become the interpreters of officialdom and its bureaucracy for their illiterate mothers. Since many mothers had no one to turn to or with whom to discuss family or emotional matters, children as young as eight would be roped in as their friends and confidants, so that the line of authority between parent and child was blurred. Girls were more adept at coping with this additional 'adult' role expected of them than boys were.

Due to their dependency on their children for survival and the position of power this afforded their children, many mothers were obliged to reluctantly accept a 'diminished' child-like role of dependency upon their children. In other words, they were obliged to adopt new strategies and assume new identities in order to accommodate their reversed economic position and social importance within the household. This subversion of the socially constructed and taken-for-granted comportment appropriate to parent/child interaction in the socialization process generated contradictory and at times disruptive role expectations and responsibilities from mothers and children alike. In chapter 3, I explore the changing socio-economic position of parents and children and the cultural articulation of this in generational terms.

Finally, *yilunta* was one of the repositories of information about the 'wider Ethiopian culture' that I used to unravel the cultural context in which the children were socialised and operated. This is because it permeated my own childhood and adulthood. More importantly, *yilunta,* as part of their collective memory, was the cognitive map my informants used, through their narratives and actions, to make sense of their lives, their self-identity and achieve their goals, especially in adversity. A collective memory they often produced in the present in response to contemporary and situational demand. This served me as a guide to both the symbolic complexity of *yilunta* and the often-ambiguous relation between my informants' narratives and the practice or behaviour it supposedly justified. The rest of this book is an account of the ways in which change is negotiated and continuity effected in their intimate interaction with one another and in their relationships to cultural forms and material practices.

3

SON OF A WOMAN

There is still a lack of consensus about the definition and classification of street children (see Swart 1990; Cosgrove 1990; Barker and Knaul 1991; Rosa et al. 1992; Oritz et al.1992; Lucchini 1993; Tyler 1997). The phenomenon has in fact become one of those controversial issues where everyone's argument seems to be valid. Lewis Aptekar (1993), for example, contends that there are no street children in the USA or in the developed world. This is because the degree to which children, particularly school-age children, are left to fend for themselves is greatly restricted by the State interceding to care for them. Aptekar writes: 'What the developed world has, is a large delinquent population most commonly found in the poor urban slums' (ibid.: 3). The terms ON the street, OF the street and ON *and* OF the street are commonly used to classify street children in Ethiopia (see MOLSA/Radda Barnen 1988; Molsa et al. 1993; UNICEF/TGE 1993; Heinonen 1996). The main criterion for children ON and OF the street is the children's sleeping place. Children ON the street refer to those engaged in street life but with regular contacts with their families. Children OF the street denote those who live, work and sleep in the street. As will be shown in this book, the above classification is too rigid and does not correspond to the realities found in Ethiopia. This is because the street children of Addis Ababa do not form a homogenous group; some live with their families, others live apart from their birth parents as part of the numerous homeless youth gangs found in Addis Ababa. Besides the natural transition from childhood to adolescence and adulthood, many alternate between home, school and street life.

The children's public image in Ethiopia reflects the ambivalent picture their presence in city streets conjures up in popular imagination and people's reaction to them. Addis Ababa is not a tourist town. Street children and their families live off the charity of Ethiopian people or by trading in the informal economy. Nevertheless, the public does not approve of children roaming around the streets apparently free from parental control and adult supervision. Pedestrians and motorists alike find being constantly accosted by such children irritating. Shop owners hire guards to keep them away from their doorsteps, even though many end up patronising a select few. The police harass them constantly in order to get them out of the streets. Even street children's mothers hold contradictory or ambiguous perceptions of the street. Some maintain that streetisim makes their children unmanageable and unprincipled. Others claim that children left at home to fend for themselves get bored and cause mischief with neighbours. A few are convinced that idle children pick up baneful principles from neighbourhood children but learn to be useful from street work. The children themselves are aware that engaging in street work is the only way they can increase their own and their families' well-being.

In Ethiopia, street children used to be called *duriyotch* (vagabonds). The modern, politically correct equivalent to street children in Amharic is *godana tedadari*. Roughly translated, it means 'street dwellers' or 'those who live off the street'. The word child is not included: *godana* (street) and *tedadari* (living off). They are also known as *berenda adari*. Here again the word child is not included: *berenda* (veranda) and *adari* (sleeping at night). Although *godana adari* usually refers to street children, *berenda adari* can be used to refer to homeless adults. The children themselves usually refer to their street-related activities as 'work', even when they are begging. Those living at home and attending school invariably call themselves students. This chapter is an ethnographic account of home-based street children and their families.

I have chosen to focus on two families to describe how street children's families live and interact with one another because both families were dependent on the income generated by their children's street-related activities for their survival. Furthermore, they were afflicted by most of the factors related to poverty and streetism, which I observed among twelve other street children families and twelve control-group poor families with no children involved in street life. This was for practical reasons. Due to the number of families I worked with, I wanted to avoid presenting them in an abstracted and de-personalised form in the text by attempting to include all their voices into the discourse. Instead, I strove to identify the underlying trends related to streetism from which I could extrapolate and present general laws of social behaviour, while allowing the children and their families to speak for themselves.

Lemlem was a city-born female head of household with two daughters and a son. Mulu was an in-migrant mother with five sons and two daughters and a live-in partner. Although the mothers knew each other, when I met them they lived in different parts of the city, had different social networks, neighbours and sets of friends. By the second year I had became 'part of their families' and could come and go as I pleased. I knew their neighbours, the children's teachers, friends, family members and business associates. I also knew how much they earned, what they spent their money on, and the hardships they endured. They fought, argued or praised each other, oblivious to my presence – the ultimate goal of an ethnographer wishing to establish complete rapport. If I did not grasp the meaning of an act or a reflection, I could always discuss it with other members of the family, my control group or bring up the subject another day. Below, I discuss the economics of street life, housing, parenting and street work. I shall begin by providing the life stories of the two mothers and their children.

Mulu's Story

Mulu claimed to be twenty-nine years old when I met her in May 1995, four months into my field work. She had four sons: Isaac (fourteen), Bereket (twelve), Abraham (eight) and Dojo (two), and two daughters: Abeba (ten) and Tutu (five). She gave birth to Hennock, her last-born son, in 1997. Her partner, Fikru, was away from Addis Ababa. He reappeared early in 1997, two years after I had befriended the family. He was the father of four out of her seven children.

I met Mulu by accident. I chanced to stop at her pavement stall and asked her the price of a cup full of grilled peanuts. She was the first street seller who did not try to over-charge me. She was breastfeeding Dojo, Isaac was changing coins for minicab drivers, Abraham was playing with the shoeshine boys surrounding her. Later in the week, I met her on her way home; she told me that she was going home to brew coffee and invited me to share it with her. I followed her.

Mulu was born in Harrar. Her father was an Amhara civil servant and her mother an Oromo.[1] Her parents divorced when she was six years old. Her mother re-married and moved to Addis Ababa leaving her children behind. Her father brought a 15-year-old bride home. Mulu did not get along with her stepmother. She went to live with her child-less godmother. Mulu never learnt to read and write either in childhood or during the adult-education campaign set up by the Derg. She spent her younger years helping her godmother in her trading activities and acquiring domestic skills. She was indeed a very good cook. The few occasions when she was able to prepare her own spices and bake her own *injera,* she would cook delicious *shuro wat* or *gomen wat,*[2] and invite me to eat with them. She eloped with Isaac's father when she was fourteen and went to live with him in Assab, now a port city in Eritrea. The man was a civil servant. He died less than a year after Isaac's birth. Mulu said of this time:

> I was very happy with Isaac's father. I went out of my mind with grief when he died. We never even had time to get married. His best friend was an officer in the army. He helped me financially. I moved into his house. He is Bereket's father. That is why my two first-born sons look physically different. I did not know that the man was very

---

[1] The Oromo ethnic group represents approximately 40 per cent of the population. They are primarily concentrated in the southern half of the nation. The Amhara and Tigrean groups, who constitute approximately 32 per cent of the population, have traditionally been politically dominant.

[2] *Shuro wat* is spiced sauce made from chickpeas; *gommen wat* is cabbage sauce.

violent and jealous. I was scared to leave him because I had two children by then. The only time I had any peace was when he was ordered to go somewhere to fight against the Eritrean rebels.

On one of these occasions, my older brother sent word that he was in Asmara on business. I picked up the kids and went to see him. I told him about the man's violence. My brother was going back home the next day. He suggested that I go with him. I did not even collect my belongings. That same year Bereket's father died on the battlefield. Since we were not married and I had abandoned him, I was not able to claim a widow's pension or anything from the Derg. Isaac and Bereket were both born in Assab two years apart.

Mulu returned to Harrar in 1984 and stayed less than six months. Since her godmother refused to have anything to do with her and her two sons, she moved in with her father and his latest teenage bride. She did not get along with her second stepmother. Her father told her to live peacefully with his new wife or move out. Mulu had no money and nowhere else to go. She met a married man who helped her financially, but she got pregnant again. The man gave her enough money to go to Addis Ababa in search of her mother before anyone noticed her condition.

According to my calculations, Mulu arrived in Addis Ababa towards the end of 1984. She stayed with her mother for less than a month because her stepfather did not approve of her or her children. Her mother asked relatives living not far from where Mulu now lives to give her daughter and grandchildren temporary shelter. Mulu says her relatives resented her being pregnant as well as having to house and feed her and her two illegitimate sons. Besides, they could hardly feed themselves, let alone take on a young family without any resources. She chanced to meet Lemlem, a woman she knew in Assab, who suggested that Mulu move in with her until she gave birth and found her way round town.

Lemlem had a lodger named Fikru who was then a civil servant working as a clerk in a military barracks. Soon after she moved in, Fikru and Mulu became lovers. In spite of the fact that Fikru was legally married with two sons in Mekele, his birthplace, he and Mulu declared that they were married and set up house. Abeba was born in 1985 in the same house they were living in when I met them in 1995. Fikru claimed her as his child, even though he knew that she was the daughter of the married man whom Mulu had left behind in Harrar. Abraham, Tutu, Dojo and Hennock were Fikru's children. He had grey hair and looked much older than Mulu when I met him in 1997. Mulu said that he was old when she met him. He was tall, well groomed and kept his threadbare suit clean. I never managed to find out how old he was. He was a silent, sombre character and did not welcome intrusive questions. The story goes that Fikru lost his government job and his right to a pension in 1990 after the fall of the Derg. He was unable to find any kind of work. He decided to go to Mekele, where he hoped to find employment and send money to help Mulu and the children. Mulu had already given birth to Abraham, her fourth child, and was expecting another. Mulu fed her children by working as a day labourer on various building sites until she gave birth to her daughter Tutu.

Less than two weeks after giving birth to Tutu, Mulu joined Lemlem in gathering and selling firewood from the nearby forest. Isaac, her first-born, and Lemlem's eldest daughter, Mimi, spent their time either helping their mothers gather firewood in the forest or roaming around town selling peanuts, boiled eggs or anything else their mothers gave them. Both families made barely enough to make ends meet. Mulu's health deteriorated mainly due to the fact that she had very little to eat. She had had no medical attention before, during or after giving birth. She told me that she had had a very difficult pregnancy and had tried to abort the child unsuccessfully several times. Like many other destitute and illiterate women, Mulu often resorted to abortion as a form of contraception. Rather than beg in the streets, she went back to work on building sites during the day. That is until poor health drove her to join Isaac in full-time trading in the street to feed her family.

Lemlem's Story

Lemlem was monosyllabic, quiet, sombre and reflective. She was not easy to talk to. She was often in pain and moody. She was tall, well-groomed, dark-skinned and very beautiful. She paid particular attention to her appearance. Unlike Mulu, Lemlem hated working in the street. She was born in Addis Ababa. Her parents were from Tigre. She spoke Amharic and Tigrinya fluently. Her children could only speak Amharic. Her daughter Mimi was also very pretty and very coquettish. Contrary to her mother, she was vivacious and outgoing. Her sister was very shy and did not even try to imitate her. She merely followed her around and willingly did whatever Mimi asked her to do. As they grew older and physically mature, both girls had to contend with lurid comments and sexual harassment from unfamiliar men and policemen. Their little brother was small for his age, very shy and a silent presence in their midst.

Lemlem's parents arranged her marriage to an Amhara soldier when she was fifteen. After his promotion to sergeant, the Derg transferred him to Assab where he joined a garrison fighting Eritrean insurgents in Assab. She joined him and gave birth to her two daughters at age sixteen and eighteen. Mimi was fourteen years old when I first met her. Although Lemlem claimed to be twenty-six years old, according to my calculations she was thirty when I met her in 1995, but she looked much older.

Lemlem was repatriated to Addis Ababa after her husband died in action. The Derg assigned her a *kebele* house and provided her with a small widow's pension. This was the house where Mulu and her family now live. At the time she met Mulu again, Lemlem was also expecting a child from a married *kebele* official.

The man used his influence to help her acquire a bigger *kebele* house in another part of the same neighbourhood and transferred the registration of the existing house to Fikru, her lodger. After the demise of the Derg in 1990, Lemlem's married lover, the father of her then 5-year-old son, lost his house and his job. He left without a trace. With the change in Derg government, Lemlem lost her widow's pension. She was obliged to find alternative means to feed her children. She joined other women who gathered firewood in the nearby forest on the hills surrounding Addis Ababa and where Mulu eventually joined her.

The Economics of Street Life

Mulu and Lemlem's children, like many street children living at home with their families, had extensive emotional and economic gender- and age-based ties with their mothers. The many reasons that spur children to enter street work vary but bore some similarity to how Mimi and Isaac entered street life.

Mother and Son

The turning point in Isaac's relationship with Mulu, his mother, began in 1991, after the birth of Tutu, when Isaac was barely ten years old. He told his mother that he would stop going to school altogether and work full-time in order to feed the family. This is how he expressed it: 'I have never been scared or ashamed to work in the street. After Tutu's birth, we were desperate. We had no food at home, mother was not very well and Tutu was dying. I told mother to stay at home and take care of herself and the baby and that I would take care of all of them.' Isaac says that Mimi, Lemlem's daughter, showed him everything there was to know about street life: where he could buy or even beg for leftover food or sell this and that. Mimi even gave him and their mothers the initial idea of asking street hawkers and merchants to hand over their small change in the evening so that the two of them could exchange it with minibus drivers for a small profit.

Isaac had a pivotal role in initiating his mother's career in the street and teaching her the fundamentals of street life. Prior to this, Mulu had worked as a casual labourer on building sites or gathered firewood for sale. Both were back-breaking activities and she barely managed to feed her children. Looking for firewood meant going eight kilometres up the nearby hills surrounding the city before dawn and braving the dangers of being beaten, or even raped, by the forest rangers. She then had to spend the rest of the day trying to sell the wood. When she realised that she no longer had the physical strength for working on building sites or carrying firewood, and no hope for a cure for Tutu, Mulu joined Isaac on the street full time. Isaac was by then ten years old and an accepted member of the street-trading fraternity, selling whatever was profitable. All she had to do was build upon the goodwill established by her son. Mulu proceeded to expand his network to include traffic-police officers, minicab drivers, street traders, shop owners and a coterie of shoeshine boys. This was an easy task. She was very friendly, liked to chat and had a kind word or a smile for everyone.

Isaac worked exclusively with and for his mother. The two had more of a mother/daughter than a mother/son economic link. Mulu had the final say in how they spent the money. She discussed every major expense with her son. Whenever I compared notes about finances with either of them, Isaac referred to their communal earnings as 'their' money or 'his' money. Mulu always claimed that it was all her money. When I pointed to the difference, she retorted:

> You have finally realised that he is a male child. He is just asserting his manhood. I let him talk and say what he likes. I do what is good for everyone. If he whinges and complains, I pretend not to hear. Abeba or Mimi would never dare say it is their money. It is easier to deal with girls. One need not cajole or fool them. They are easily cowed. All you have to do is make them feel ashamed and guilty. They have more *yilunta* than boys do. Anyway, if the girls do not realize that there is barely enough to feed and clothe everyone at any one time, they ought to be ashamed of their selfish behaviour. Boys are different. They need to show off and assert their manhood from time to time.

Mulu and Isaac's makeshift pavement stall was situated away from the main thoroughfare, but near enough for pedestrians, motorists and university students to use on their way up and down to the city centre. They operated at a crossroads, adjacent to a long stone-built wall and flanked by a well-attended church. The two roads opposite led to dilapidated houses surrounded by crudely built makeshift shelters and shacks, a bakery, two cheap teahouses, a shebeen and a garage. Since there were no public toilets around, children and adults alike urinated or defecated behind the few shrubs growing along the wall. Minicab drivers, their assistants or even male motorists and passengers often stopped their car in front of Mulu's stall and urinated against the wall while chatting with her. The shoeshine boys surrounding Mulu did the same. From time to time, even women caught short would squat behind one of the shrubs. At certain times of the day, the stench emanating from the mixture of fresh and stale urine, new and old feces was overwhelming. Mulu just covered her lower face with her shawl (*netela*),[3] and stoically waited for the stink to abate.

Mother and son jealously guarded their territory against all newcomers. They harassed, shamed or even solicited the help of friendly traffic policemen to move other traders away. The only competition they tolerated consisted of the numerous shoeshine boys of *Gurague* origin. As well as being their customers, the boys

---

[3] *Netela* is a hand-spun and woven traditional Ethiopian cotton shawl.

willingly ran errands for Mulu. They left their money with Mulu for safe keeping out of fear of being robbed by youth gangs or older street boys while they roamed around looking for customers. Mulu and Isaac did a brisk trade up to about ten in the morning. Isaac ran up and down changing coins for minibus conductors, selling cigarettes and matches to motorists or pedestrians on their way to work, to the town centre or to the university. Shortly after 10:00 AM, Isaac took over the stall during the dry season when his mother went home to have breakfast and a coffee break or followed her home during the rainy season.

By the time I met them in May 1995, Mulu and Isaac were operating full-time on the street. Depending on how much capital they could raise, Isaac collected coins from other traders and changed them into notes on their behalf with minibus assistants for a small fee. Mulu was in charge of the stall and sold peanuts, oranges, bananas, cigarettes, pens, matches, lighters and sweets. She was in charge of the money. She took her youngest child everywhere with her. She constantly bought him bread and all sorts of food to keep him quiet. She breastfed him until he was three years old. She eventually weaned him off by smearing her nipples with bitter *tchat*[4] juice. Two-year-old Dojo looked strong, happy and healthy. Five-year-old Tutu was half his size. She was left to roam around the neighbourhood they lived in. Mulu was convinced that her neighbours were kind-hearted and that they would come to Tutu's rescue if she were in danger. The only time they did anything for her was to send a child to call Mulu because Tutu was lying comatose on the asphalt road after being run over by a car in a hit-and-run. She was seven years old and had followed neighbourhood children who had wandered off to the main tarmac road to play. She recovered without medical treatment. Abeba and Abraham went to school in the morning or afternoon, depending on their school's schedules, and they ran errands and did small jobs for Bereket or Mulu the rest of the time.

Mulu and Isaac had an invariable routine. Mulu woke up at dawn, put Dojo on her back and walked a mile down the road to where she set up her pavement stall. Isaac followed her carrying their merchandise. Throughout the years I worked in the field, I saw police officers regularly harassing street vendors by either destroying or confiscating their goods. That is unless they circulated among the crowds. Mulu carried the minimum amount of supplies she could gather and run with towards the churchyard around the corner when she saw danger coming. At times, her shoeshine friends would leave their work and rush down or up the street to alert her that there was a police patrol. This meant that she had to send Isaac, or

[4] *Tchat*, also known as *Khat* (catha edulis), *qat*, *chaad* and *miraa* pronounced *tchat*, in Ethiopia is used by adults and children alike. It is an amphetamine-like stimulant which causes excitement, loss of appetite and euphoria. Although the World Health Organization has classified *khat* as a drug of abuse, Ethiopia exports it all over the Middle East, Europe and America. It is regularly consumed by many Somali and Ethiopian migrants living in the UK. See Ezekiel's 2004 book, *Leaf of Allah: Khat and Agricultural Transformation,* for an in-depth study on the subject.

one of the shoeshine boys plying their trade from the same spot, to her house to fetch supplies when they ran out. Between 1995 and 2001, she had her supplies destroyed four times. The first and second time, two police officers trampled on her oranges, cigarettes, peanuts and pens. The third and fourth time, policemen confiscated her lighters, matches and cigarettes, which they quite rightly claimed to be contraband goods. It took her months to recuperate from the loss.

Once or twice a week, Mulu bought fresh supplies for her store from the *Mercato*,[5] and paid nearby traders she owed money to or contributed to one of her rotating saving schemes (*iqub*) or burial associations (*idir*) after her mid-morning coffee break. She was perpetually in debt and short of money. She constantly panicked about being in arrears with her membership to burial associations, rotating credit schemes, creditors or rent. It was not as if Mulu did not have long-term plans. The problem was that in her circumstance, all her plans were little lessons in tragedy. As she succinctly put it, '*kejib terfo le woosha*'.[6]

Home Life

The bulk of what Mulu and her son made in the street went to feed the family. Meat and other non-vegetarian treats on the family menu were rare, or only at Easter after the traditional forty days' fasting kept by pious Orthodox Christians or at Christmas. Milk was unheard of. Butter was acquired only for cooking the traditional *doro wat*[7] at Easter. Mulu's only luxury was her mid-morning coffee break. I occasionally helped carry Dojo and stayed for a chat. She roasted green coffee beans, pounded then brewed the coffee three times in a traditional clay coffee pot and drank it black. Delicious! Even better in her view, was when occasionally Lemlem or other female neighbours joined us. Children, even toddlers, were banished outside. Brew after brew, cup after cup, we chatted about everything that came to mind. We talked about men in general. We interpreted our latest dreams and nightmares. We laughed out loud about the age at which and how we lost our virginities. Occasionally, the conversation included the joys and pains of childbirth, or of being a woman in a man's world. Even though her friends and neighbours came from different ethnic groups, they had invariably been subjected to one form or another of female genital cutting in infancy and were more or less child brides. We read each other's coffee cups and worried about our children's future. We discussed life under the Derg and the present government's indifference to the plight of the poor. After clearing the coffee cups, Mulu

---

[5] *Mercato* is a word borrowed from the Italian *mercato*, meaning 'market place'. It is the name of the central market in Addis Ababa. It is said to be the biggest open-air and covered market in Africa.
[6] 'What is left from the hyenas will not feed the dogs.'
[7] *Doro wat* is chicken stew.

usually ate whatever was left over from the night before or, more often than not, a small bun bought that same morning. If Bereket, Abeba and Abraham were not at school, they would wait for her to bring groceries back from town.

Mulu went back to the stall at about one in the afternoon during the dry season or later in the afternoon during the rainy season. She either brought food from home for Isaac or gave him money to buy a glass of strong sugary tea and a bun, a cake or a samosa from the teashops across the street. They then worked, slept, socialised and generally lounged around until four, when business would pick up again. They usually closed shop at about five or six in the evening. From time to time, Bereket helped Isaac carry their goods and/or Dojo home. Isaac often bought sweets for Tutu. She always ran towards him and checked all his pockets and would get very upset and hit him repeatedly when he did not have a treat for her. He invariably let her vent her anger. The entire family was usually home by seven and asleep by nine. There was a happy, care-free atmosphere in the house until Fikru came back to stay with them for good.

During the six years I knew her, Mulu bought herself two dresses, three shawls (*netelas*) and several headscarves. She wore cheap plastic sandals or flip-flops. She purchased trousers and T-shirts for Isaac whenever his clothes were in tatters and showed his naked body or private parts. Whatever she bought him looked tattered or dirty within days. He was slovenly and forever running after customers, piling coins in his pockets, lying or sitting on the pavement or mock wrestling with the shoeshine boys surrounding his mother. As soon as he started feeling the lice roaming around his hair, he bought a brand new razor blade and asked his mother or brother to shave his head. He went barefoot until he began working as a minibus assistant at the age of seventeen.

Mulu bought the other children second-hand imported clothes called '*salvage*' as and when she spotted a bargain and felt that it would fit one of them. Abeba, Tutu and Abraham were unkempt and dirty. They walked barefoot, wore everything they could get their hands on and rarely changed or washed their clothes. Abeba was very clumsy. She had been told often enough that she was too black, too kinky-haired, and therefore not pretty. Unfortunately, she believed it and had very low self-esteem. She had flawless ebony-black skin, beautiful white teeth and big brown eyes and looked exquisite on the rare occasions she had a new or second-hand dress on, washed her face and braided her hair. Mulu bought Bereket new clothes and decent-looking shoes just before school resumed or whenever she saw second hand salvage clothes that would fit him. She adored talking about how handsome and elegant he looked. Bereket was indeed good-looking and well groomed. He was a head taller than his brother and mother. He washed his and his mother's clothes regularly. He kept his face, hair and hands clean. His siblings loved him. He was gentle and patient with everyone. They all believed that he would finish school, and help the family.

Mimi and Lemlem

As mentioned earlier, Lemlem's daughter Mimi taught Isaac everything to do with street work. She recalls vividly her first trading activity. Her mother bought contraband cigarettes from a neighbour, gave her a few open packets and told her to sell single or multiple cigarettes. She was eight or nine years old. She did a brisk trade and subsequently added other products to her merchandise. She preferred this to helping her mother around the house or gathering wood for fuel.

When I first met them, Mimi was fourteen years old and her sister twelve. They spent most of their mornings selling processed food prepared by themselves or their mother as well as cigarettes and sweets. The girls returned home around lunchtime. If they had not managed to sell enough products, they would find a shady place to rest and continue to ply their wares until they had got rid of most of the perishable food they were selling. Mimi supplemented their income by looking after other street vendors' makeshift stalls for a small fee or changing coins for minibus assistants. She was an anomaly since changing coins for minibus drivers was a male activity zone. She was expelled from school for non-attendance shortly after her fifteenth birthday. Mimi stopped changing coins within a year after I met her. Minibus conductors, their assistants and male passengers as well as older street boys started grabbing her breasts, groping her or pinching her bottom.

Lemlem took in laundry from bachelors living in the surrounding area and prepared spices for sale and processed food for her daughters to hawk. She suffered from constant stomach pain. She was often impatient and irritable. She relied on her daughters to assist her with the washing as well as fetching and taking laundry from and to customers. She expected them to help prepare food for the family and for sale. Both girls loathed any kind of housework, especially cooking and hand washing men's clothes. They preferred to work on the street, away from the critical eye of their mother. The atmosphere at home was often tense.

Lemlem and Mimi had a typical mother-daughter economic relationship. Lemlem knew the price of everything and expected her daughter to hand over all the money she earned. She considered it as part of family income, with her having the final decision on how it is spent. They bickered constantly because Mimi withheld some of the money she made on the side. She often bought herself or her sister pretty things (at times on credit) or had their hair straightened. Inevitably, the mother would notice and beat both of them.

Mulu's Home

Mulu's family house was a one-room shack built against the wall of a dilapidated big stone villa. It had no window, was dimly lit and airless, with no electricity, no water and no sewerage. The family used a locally made kerosene lamp at night.

They purchased water by the jerry can and carried it back home from a water tap situated about three hundred metres down the road. At three metres by four, it was fairly large in comparison with the adjacent similarly badly constructed shacks and no worse than the numerous other poor people's houses I visited in Addis Ababa. Like practically everyone living in such surroundings, Mulu and her family had no privacy.

> My neighbours can even tell you, which one of my children has farted, and what they have eaten that day by the smell. You wonder how people manage to procreate in such crowded conditions. Some do it during the day when the children and/or other tenants are out. The others do it before dawn or at night. Everyone in the room, including children, pretends to be fast asleep. That is why it is important to know how to live with other people. There is no other way. You learn to keep your grievances to yourself and pretend not to know or understand what is going on. Children are innocent and gullible. When adults gossip or discuss matters in front of children who are not taught to keep their mouths shut, disaster can ensue. Whenever a child unwittingly disclosed sensitive family secrets, my godmother used to say: 'An adult speaks evil through an angel's mouth.' She inculcated me with a strong sense of *yilunta*. I know when to speak or not to speak of delicate matters in public. I have tried to teach all my children when to shut theirs.

The walls of Mulu's shack were made of flimsy eucalyptus wood poles covered with wattle and daub. There were gaps in the wall due to years of neglect and disrepair. The family covered parts of the inside walls with newspapers and various coloured magazine pictures of fashion models, film stars and footballers. These decorations were supposed to cover the holes in the wall and hide the sections where the original paint had faded. I was warned not to lean against the wall because of the bedbugs Abeba called *tuhan*, which hid their blood-bloated bodies, ready to come out to gorge themselves on the entire family at night. The house had a corrugated iron roof, an ill-fitting wooden door and a beaten earth floor, which was often muddy during the rainy season. They had a couple of three-legged wooden stools and a big stone where they could sit.

The family shared an unimaginably filthy pit latrine with six other households. The over-flowing toilet facilities meant that the whole neighbourhood went to the nearby shrubs or open spaces to defecate. The only time Mulu used the wind-blown hovel that was supposed to be the communal kitchen was when she had enough money to bake her own *injera*. Since she did not have her own *metad*,[8] she borrowed her neighbour's and gave two or three *injera* as a thank you. Until they eventually bought a charcoal burner, they cooked over three strategically placed stones. They bought small bundles of firewood or charcoal from the market as needed. Whenever they could buy food in bulk, they stored it in a corner with their cooking utensils and crockery.

---

[8] *Metad* is a flat clay dish for baking *injera*.

Mulu's entire family slept on two urine-soaked foam rubber mattresses, which they shared when I first met them. Abeba often dragged one of the mattresses to dry outside in the morning and dragged it back inside in the evening. Mulu bought a cheap mattress in 1997 after Fikru came back to live with them. She bought another one when his sons visited from Mekele a year later. She eventually bought a wooden bed a year after her two older sons had left home. Abraham, Abeba, Dojo and Tutu continued to sleep on the beaten earth floor. I never saw them changing or washing the blankets and assorted clothing material they used to cover themselves at night. When Fikru was with them, Isaac, Abeba, Bereket and Abraham made a makeshift bed for themselves and slept on the floor near the door. They piled the beddings on the two mattresses before going out in the morning. Depending on her mood, Tutu curled up under either Bereket's or Isaac's feet. Mulu did not like Tutu to share the mattress with the babies because she got stressed and scratched them when they cried. In spite of its limitations, Mulu and her children felt very privileged to have such a centrally situated home of their own.

As mentioned earlier, Mulu had entered the housing network in 1984 via Fikru, her partner and eventually the father of four of her seven children. Mulu's house was originally registered in Fikru's name. She grabbed every opportunity, including Fikru's long absences from the city, to assert her right to live in the house. In May 1996, *kebele* residents were asked to re-register themselves and their children. She claimed that Fikru was her legal husband and that all her children were his. She told the newly appointed *kebele* officials that he had abandoned her when she was pregnant with her sixth child. She did not know where he was and feared that he might be dead. She managed to have the house registered in her name and Fikru's name taken out of the register.

Mulu originally paid six *birr* per month rent. The rent was raised to sixteen *birr* per month in 1997. The same house could fetch at least one hundred *birr* a month on the open market. All those owing rent money to the *kebele* were asked to settle their accounts or face eviction. Mulu was told that she owed two hundred and fifty-two *birr* rent arrears. She joined a rotating saving scheme (*iqub*) worth two hundred *birr,* borrowed the rest and paid the bill. She also acquired a *kebele* identity card, without securing the mandatory official clearance letter from the *kebele* in Harrar, her birthplace, and last place of residence. She made sure that all her children were included on the residents' register. Isaac and Bereket were thus able to have their own identity cards before they left their mother's house. Even though they went to live in another *kebele,* they kept their name on the same register in order to avoid the enormous bureaucratic hurdle they would have to face in order to be registered in the *kebele* they had moved into. Until then neither she nor her children had had any kind of identity card. Fikru was the only one with any form of identity card. This was a great achievement for Mulu and an almost insurmountable feat to accomplish without a lot of money or the help of influential people.

Isaac was constantly by her side, reading and interpreting relevant documents, writing letters, telling her what to do and what to say. He also accompanied her to every meeting and gave her moral support whenever she despaired. Although Fikru was living with them, neither Mulu nor Isaac let him know what they were up to. Isaac's excuse was that since Fikru had never contributed to the rent, he had no right to be part of it. Mulu was afraid that if the house was put in his name, he might decide to bring his sons or in-migrant homeless relatives to live with them.

In May 1998, after one of their quarrels over her sons' attitude towards him, Fikru threatened to throw her out of the house and take away his children. The following sums up her reaction and the vital importance of housing to social connectedness and city-based poor women's empowerment.

> Let him talk! He does not know anyone at the *kebele* office. The house is now in my name. The *kebele* officials know who has been paying rent and living here for the last fourteen years. Besides *Abbay maderia selelew, gend yezo yizoral.*[9] Where will he take them? He has nothing of any worth that he can call his own. His other children and family do not want him. He does not even belong to a burial association. If he dies, he will have a decent burial thanks to me. No one will lend him money or give him credit. He cannot enter a rotating credit scheme because he does not know whether he will still have a job from one day to the next.

As long-time residents of the neighbourhood they lived in, Mulu and her children had achieved a sense of belonging, continuity and even permanence. It had taken her almost four years to achieve this precarious sense of security. This was not the case with many of the households I worked with. Only twenty-two street children families out of the fifty-two I visited had secured *kebele* houses. Twelve out of these twenty-two were not able to meet the monthly rent and owed considerable amounts of money to the *kebele*. The others rented corners of one-room houses or floor space by the week. Besides, many of the families of street children I knew had relocated at least twice. Some families had moved houses because they could not pay the rent; the *kebele* or property owners evicted others.

In June 2000, the *kebele* told Mulu that due to the housing shortage, she had to share her house with a newly wed young couple. They left after three weeks because of the lack of space and privacy. Mulu told me that they had had a proper bed, which took up half the space. They could not cope with the fact that Tutu was not only mentally retarded but looked it. They did not know how to behave towards her when she sat on their bed touching her private parts or stared at them while they ate. Mulu felt elated to have her house back. In June 2001, she was again in despair because the *kebele* had informed them that they would have to be re-housed on the outskirts of Addis Ababa. The original owner's children had successfully reclaimed their family house and the surrounding land. They planned to

---

[9] 'Because the Blue Nile lacks a home of its own, it roams around carrying tree trunks.'

build an apartment block. Fikru, Mulu and their four children (Tutu, Abraham, Dojo and Hennock) were still living in the same house in 2005. The heirs of the original land and house were in dispute with each other and fighting a court case on how to dispose of the land and main house. Those living in the Diaspora in the West wanted to sell up and cash in the money. Those who had never left the country during the Derg's reign wanted to develop the land and live in the big house. None of them had enough money to buy out the others.

Lemlem's Home

Unlike Mulu, Lemlem entered the housing network by virtue of her status as a soldier's widow with two children, sometime in 1982. Her subsequent affair with a high-ranking *kebele* official had enabled her to acquire a two-room house with a shared kitchen and latrine. It had a sturdy wooden door they could lock properly and an opening separating the two rooms. Lemlem hung a bed sheet as a curtain to separate the rooms. There was no proper sewerage but residents had dug a gulley around their houses to facilitate the flow of water and human waste when it rained. They carried their garbage to the skip on the main road, which municipal trucks emptied from time to time. They had access to a communal water tap and intermittent electricity. Residents paid for electricity by the number of light bulbs they used and water according to the number of people per household. Lemlem had one light bulb strategically placed between the two rooms. She paid for water as a single adult occupant because children were not included in the count. They had two single beds with fairly clean blankets and bed sheets. Lemlem slept with her son. Mimi and her sister shared the other bed. They slept head to toe. They had room to store their cooking utensils, crockery and a charcoal burner. There was space for washing material, a wooden box to store their clothes and the laundry Lemlem took in for washing. They also had three wooden stools, a chair and a coffee table. The house had a cement floor. They kept their house spotlessly clean. It was a poor household and the family made a precarious living, but relatively speaking they were better off than all the other poor families I had visited.

During the six years I frequented them Lemlem took in three temporary lodgers to supplement their meagre family income. A young girl learning hairdressing stayed with them for two months. She finished her course but could not find a job. Her father stopped paying her rent and since he had paid for her course, he did not think it fit to continue supporting her. She moved back in with her hated stepmother, half-siblings and father. The other two were bachelors. One was a university student from a rural area and another was a trader in the small market nearby. They both left after a few months. Mimi said that it was difficult to have them around because they took up most of the space and wanted to keep food and to cook in the house. The trader wanted to bring a bed into the house and the student kept inviting his friends in the evening.

Lemlem's family house was located very near the main road and was surrounded by better-off households. Shortly before they were evicted, Lemlem had
been selected by an NGO and was receiving food aid and financial help towards
her 11-year-old son's education. She had secured this by pretending to be a displaced widow from Eritrea,[10] and by promising to keep her daughters and son
out of street life. In 1997, Lemlem and many other families who were allocated
kebele houses by the Derg were forced to move out because the rightful owners
were able to claim their properties back. As mentioned earlier, after the change
of government in 1991, many *kebele* officials were fired and replaced by entirely
new people. Lemlem's family's fortune changed for the worse because they were
given one week to move out of their house.

Unlike Mulu, Lemlem had never been obliged to network among *kebele* officials to legitimise her right to government housing. However, the fact that she
was already on the *kebele* residents' registration list, allocated a *kebele* house and
had a *kebele* identity card legitimised her right to alternative accommodation.
Since her ex-lover, and *kebele* official, was her only link to the *kebele* housing
network, she had no other recourse but to accept whatever was on offer. Mimi,
her daughter, spoke for many others when she summed up the effect of the forced
geographical relocations on her family:

> You can see how bad this new place is. We do not have access to water or electricity.
> We have to live in a room with a couple and their 4-year-old son. We share a filthy pit
> latrine and kitchen with four other families. These people do not want us here. I do
> not blame them. We are too far away from the main road. This is a poor neighbour-
> hood. There are no streetlights. We must get back home before dark because we cannot
> see our way home at night and we fear being bitten by stray dogs.

> We have lost more than our beautiful house. We have lost our friends, our custom-
> ers and our credit facilities with shop owners. My little brother has stopped going to
> school. It is too far for him to walk there and back. He is now twelve years old. He
> has started selling things on the street like the rest of us. He does not mind. He hated
> school. The teacher often beat him for being unruly, not having school supplies or
> just about anything. Besides, we all prefer to be out of the house all day because the
> other people are always in. The food aid from the NGO has stopped, since they were
> focusing on poor families in our old neighbourhood. They provided jobs for several
> women in the neighbourhood. Mother was hired to bake *injera* and was either given
> food for work or money. This place is too far away from the main road and too muddy
> for them to bother. Besides, the NGOs have stopped selecting those they wish to
> help; they now work through *kebele* officials. You know how wicked and corrupt these
> people are. They usually put forward their own friends and relatives, including those
> who are not so poor. We do not know anyone here, official or otherwise. There is no
> one to help us.

---

[10] When Eritrea got its independence, they expelled persons who they deemed to be non-Eritrean,
including those of mixed parentage. Shortly after, the Ethiopian government retaliated by expelling
persons who they considered Eritrean nationals.

Housing affects children's education and well-being in terms of physical space and comfort. In Addis Ababa, the sort of supportive social networks poor mothers could count on affected their ability to provide a loving, caring and materially supportive environment for their children. The poorer segments of society needed to belong to a *kebele* to be able to live in rent-controlled, government-owned cheap houses and acquire the necessary address and therefore an identity card in order to be part of the neighbourhood. As far as poor mothers were concerned, being on a *kebele* residents' registration list meant some access to housing, some kind of free education for their children, rudimentary health services, childcare, information about jobs and a much-valued *kebele* identity card. The State does not have welfare provisions for the poor. Poor parents' coping mechanisms were dependent on the social resources they could access. These were determined by the type of personal ties they had with *kebele* officials, teachers, the police, health care workers, friends, relatives and neighbours. In other words, it was the mothers' relationship with those in a position to facilitate their entry into various social network systems, which accounted for the most consequential diversity of experience among children on the street. This relationship was embedded in where such mothers were located within the existing social network and support systems. Apart from its socially integrating experience, housing was one of the best indicators of whether a poor mother was able to form a supportive social network. As I shall demonstrate below, membership in burial associations, rotating credit schemes and religious associations were also good signs of social integration.

Social Networks

Studies of social networks among street children are primarily focussed on homeless children and are centred on peer-group relationships,and friendships (see Aptekar 1988; Swart 1990; Ennew 1994). Those concerned with the subject of home-based street children concentrate their inquiry on such children's ability to cope with the hardship they face in the street and/or their survival strategies. The emphasis is on child-child encounters, with minimal information about the influence of the presence of adults in their lives or their parents' social networks (see Baker and Knaul 1991; Lusk 1992; Richter1992; Lucchini 1993; Campos et al. 1994; Rosa et al. 1994; Hecht 1995).

Social relationships do not exist in isolation; they are embedded in social networks. The kinds of social systems in which urban-based parents operate significantly affect the nature of their community networks. Among other things, the sort of supportive social network poor parents can count on affects their ability to provide a loving, caring and materially beneficial environment for their children. Furthermore, the composition and structure of the personal set of ties with friends, relatives and neighbours that female heads of household, with dissimilar life experiences, take for granted differs. This is because it is related more to where such mothers are located in the various networks than on who they are as individuals. This last element accounts for the yet another diversity of experience among street children living with their natal families. It is therefore apt to analyse such children's life circumstances not only in terms of their street-related activities, but also in terms of their mothers' social support and social networks. The intimate community networks explored below document the configuration and the way different women and men are differently and uniquely situated and its effect on their sense of belonging to the community.

Idir (Burial Associations)

The majority of poor mothers I met responded to the diversity of demands and conditions of urban life by participating in or striving to belong to at least one community-based voluntary association. They attached considerable value to their membership of *idir* and did everything to pay their dues. Those who did not belong to any association were either homeless or truly destitute. The following are two examples of the significance of *idir* in the social world of poor women and its effect on their self-esteem. The first example is based on Mulu's experience and the second on that of a homeless mother.

Mulu belonged to two *idirs*. The one she referred to as her big *idir* had men and women members. The fees were four *birr* fifty a month. Bereaved members could access one thousand seven hundred *birr*. The money was used for funeral and related expenses. Mulu also belonged to a female-only *idir*, for which she paid one *birr* fifty per month. In addition, she contributed free labour, such as cooking and serving for the funeral repast. The female-only *idir* was worth two hundred *birr*. Mulu explained:

> Lemlem helped me join the women's *idir* soon after I arrived in Addis Ababa. Fikru belonged to the other *idir* before I did. Since he was often away and had ceased to pay his dues, they removed him from the list. As soon as I could afford it, I begged them to put me on the big *idir* list as well. They asked me to pay eighty *birr* joiner's fee and they wrote in my name where his used to be. I pay one *birr* fifty a month for the women's *idir*. I sometimes have to additionally contribute *injera* or other foodstuff towards the burial feast. I never fail to contribute my share of food or money, even if it means depriving my children. At the worst time of my life, when I did not know where our next meal was coming from and when I thought that Tutu was going to die, it made me feel that we were still human beings.

Even though Mulu's women's *idir* was very small, it was very practical and affordable. Bereaved members were given ninety *birr* for the death of a man in the family, eighty *birr* for a woman and sixty *birr* for a child towards funeral and related expenses. Whatever money was available from the membership was used to buy a coffin and pay for the church service. If the mother was very poor, members contributed coffee and groceries for the meal and during the customary three-day mourning period. If the bereaved was extremely destitute, members consulted the person's best friend or a neighbour on how best to use the money and made the necessary arrangements. If, like Mulu, the woman was a member of two *idir,* i.e. a mixed-sex *idir* and a female-only *idir,* she could dispose of the money from the female-only *idir* as she saw fit. Most women bought mourning attire with it: a black scarf, shawl (*netela*) and dress.

The best example I have of the integrating experience of *idir* is the story of a homeless rural-urban migrant mother and her 4-year-old child. The woman told me that she had run away from an abusive husband in a rural area and taken her then 1-year-old daughter with her. She had no network or relatives in town. The little girl had suffered most of her life from some kind of skin ailment. Mother and child slept on the pavement outside a church wall. They both begged not far from where Mulu sold her goods and had gradually become part of her entourage. The child died suddenly early one morning. Since the woman was homeless and was too destitute to belong to a burial association, Mulu asked her female *idir* group to help. Lemlem agreed to let the woman use her house as a temporary home to mourn the death of her daughter and receive visitors.

Lemlem and Mulu secured the money from the *idir* to buy a coffin and pay for the church service. In accordance with Ethiopian Christian Orthodox rites, they buried the child the same day she died. Members of the female *idir* and those of the street-begging fraternity contributed food and money towards the after-burial ceremonies. Even though the woman went back to sleep in the street four days later, she was grateful to Mulu and Lemlem for, as she put it, 'making her feel like a human being and giving her daughter a Christian burial'. In 2001, many NGOs were trying to incorporate burial associations and other indigenous associations into NGO-related entrepreneurial or other projects. Mulu and her friends thought this was sinful on their part, saying that it would destroy the symbolic significance and autonomy of the association. In Mulu's words: 'It is not just the money, which matters. We know that we are part of the community through such associations.' They were convinced that, as soon as outsiders interfered with any association, its control would be lost to its members. They also thought that NGOs should give them money and help, not the other way around.

Iqub (Rotating Saving Scheme)

In all the six years I roamed the back streets of Addis Ababa, I never met anyone who did not belong to at least one *iqub*. There have been times when Mulu simultaneously belonged to two or three *iqub*. The smallest was worth seven *birr* and took seven days to complete. The highest amounted to two hundred and forty *birr* and lasted a year. The organising principle behind all the *iqub* was the same. Mulu's seven-*birr iqub* had seven members: Mulu, a 20-year-old street trader and five shoeshine boys all under the age of fourteen. Each member paid in one *birr* per day. Whoever needed the money most on the day asked could claim the seven *birr*. Otherwise, the names of those who had not yet received their *iqub* that week would be written on pieces of paper and a non-member asked to pick out a name. As soon as everyone had received his/her entitlement, another *iqub* would begin. No one defaulted, and no one found it amiss that adults and children belonged to the same *iqub*. Mulu liked to receive her *iqub* on Saturdays because she used the money to pay for another mainly adult *iqub* she belonged to and for which she paid out fifteen *birr* every Sunday.

Many of the street children I knew had their own *iqub*; some were as low as fifty cents per day and worth not more than five to ten *birr*. In addition, some children belonged to adult-organised *iqub* in their own right or had joint membership with their mothers or friends. Unbeknown to their parents, Mimi and other street children often started an *iqub* in order to buy themselves clothes or other treats. Boys usually got away with it since most worked independently of their parents. Their mothers had thus no way of knowing how much money they earned per day or how they disposed of it. Since Mimi, like many other girls, worked for her mother, any acquisitions not sanctioned by Lemlem created friction between the two. Mimi invariably tried to assert her right to spend some of the money she earned from her *iqub* on herself. Her mother always maintained that the money was needed for household expenses and at times physically chastised Mimi to make her point.

The following narratives encapsulate the gendered essence of street child–mother economic interaction as reflected in *iqub*. I told Mulu that Mimi always said 'my money' when she talked about her own or joint *iqub* she had with her mother and that Lemlem claimed it was hers and the two would fight over whose right it was to have a say on how it was spent. Mulu agreed with Lemlem: 'That girl has spent so much time in the street with all sorts of vagabonds that she now thinks she is a man and behaves accordingly. She has no *yilunta*. Lemlem is right to take the money away from her. She is a girl. What does she need the money for. … Lemlem gives her everything she needs. Mimi knows how desperately the family needs all the money they earn.' As he grew older and his relationship with his mother's partner soured, Isaac became resentful of the way the money they earned together, especially their joint *iqub*, was disposed of. In 1998, Fikru's oldest son came to visit his father. Mulu felt obliged to give Fikru the two hundred *birr* she received from an *iqub* in order to enable him to buy his son new clothes and send presents for the rest of his other family in Mekele. Isaac found out about it and for the first time in his life left his mother to lodge with other people:

We had a joint *iqub* worth two hundred *birr*. She has spent the money on that man and his family. I am going around with torn trousers and no shoes. She does not care about me; she cares about someone else's sons. Even if I work with her money, half of the profit is mine. I worked for it. I do not want to live with her any more. I will not work for her until she hands over the one hundred *birr* she owes me. Fikru has no *yilunta*. He is not a man; he lives off a woman and her children.

After this episode, Isaac and his mother bickered constantly about money and his hostile behaviour towards Fikru. Up to then, Mulu had got away with dispensing with the money they earned as she deemed fit. Isaac continued to rebel against Fikru's presence in their home and eventually left home, aged seventeen, taking Bereket with him. Unbeknown to his mother, he had by then discovered sex with a handsome mature woman. As Mulu's trusted son, Isaac used her much-expanded network to find himself a job as a minibus conductor and create his own network in order to access credit facilities, rent accommodation and live an independent life.

Mehaber (Religious Associations)

Mehaber are religious associations. Members meet once a month on particular saints' days. Individual members prepare a feast to celebrate their chosen saint at home and invite fellow members. Long before he met Mulu, Fikru used to belong to a *mehaber* devoted to the Archangel Gabriel. Since his legal wife was not domiciled in Addis Ababa, he used to pay Lemlem or other ladies to prepare the formal lunch when his turn came to celebrate his *mehaber*. His relationship with Mulu began when he paid her to prepare food and officiate at his *mehaber*.

Due to financial constraints as well as his frequent and long absences from the city, Fikru was not able to keep up with his *mehaber* obligations. Since many of his fellow *mehaber* members lived in the neighbourhood and were his friends, they regularly invited him to partake of the festivities. Fikru sought information about job opportunities on building sites and other such temporary jobs at *mehaber* gatherings. Members collected money in order to help him out when Mulu gave birth to Hennock in 1997. In 1999, they used *mehaber* money to buy him a second-hand suit and shoes before he went for a job interview as a night watchman. He did not get the job because he was too old. Fellow members considered their contribution to be a gift normally extended to a member facing difficult circumstances.

Mulu did not belong to a *mehaber*. She nevertheless helped other women prepare *mehaber* celebrations and readily accepted invitations. She also gratefully accepted any financial help her partner's fellow *mehaber* members extended to her family. She considered many of them her friends and occasionally asked the better-off ones for short-term loans. However, she refused to contribute to Fikru's *mehaber* because she considered it a luxury the family could ill afford. She also resented the fact that he invariably returned home drunk after attending a *mehaber* gathering and bemoaned the loss of his ability to afford to hold his own ceremony.

In conclusion, the above ethnography about the process involved in accessing social resources available and how parents cultivated and maintained personal relationships into social network systems demonstrates how these come to be supportive. This is relevant to parents and children alike, since as will be revealed below the children themselves often relied on their parents' networks to identify non-familiar adults they could call upon when faced with difficulties.

Motherhood

There is ample literature on motherhood as institution and social discourse in terms of balancing work and families, reproductive technology and single mothering including its social and cultural contours (see Basin et al. 1994; Miller 2005; Devasahayam and Yeoh 2007). Most feminists and anthropologists agree that mothering is culturally constructed (see Shari 1995). As explained in chapter 2, the socialization of children and shouldering the domestic sphere is considered a mother's job in Ethiopia. Accordingly, mothers of street children in Addis Ababa are expected to care for their family's material needs and for their children's moral formation. Due to the dominance of the ideology of femininity and motherhood and the changing family constellation, childbearing and parenthood have a strong impact on such women's daily lives. The abject poverty in which they live blurs the boundaries between the private and public sphere, the community and the individual. Since mother and child alike straddle the domestic and public spaces of family life, attempts to uphold the idealised and gendered aspects of household care and responsibility have negative consequences on boys' and girls' relationships with their mothers. In an effort to balance the conflicting demands of family responsibility that social and cultural norms define as their primary concern, such mothers negotiate, contest and reconfigure motherhood or write the script as they go along. The following depiction of family conflict and emotion management details mothers' concerns with ensuring their children's physical survival and maintaining culturally sanctioned forms of raising their children.

In spite of the constant physical and verbal chastisement which took place, the children and parents I knew showed immense affection and caring for each other. As Thurer Shari (1995: 6) so succinctly put it: 'Mother love, though it is vulnerable to environmental manipulation, seems to be a fact.' A very unsettling phenomenon was the singling out of one child among others for special punishment. What I did not expect to uncover was the amount of gratuitous punishment meted out by older full- or half-siblings. The most harrowing stories I have recorded were about stepmothers and stepsiblings. As depicted in chapters 4 and 5, these cruel acts had nothing do with socializing, love or caring.

Although violence against and among boys was more common in the streets, girls were more at risk of a beating at home. Street boys got away with it because mothers did not exert as much control over their movements or behaviour. They also had flexible economic ties with their mothers over which they more or less had complete control. More often than not, the girls' economic activities were related to that of their mothers'. Furthermore, mothers relied upon their daughters to hand over all their earnings and considered this money as family income which they could dispose of at will. They also expected the girls to help around the house from age five onwards. Asking daughters to act as surrogate mothers and nurses was common, even where there were several boys in the family. The reason I was given for this was that girls did not need to play all the time; they were more patient than boys were; they were less likely to disobey an order and they take their family responsibility to heart while boys do not. Like many mothers, Mulu and Lemlem often beat, insulted and cursed their children even in my presence.

Mulu's Case

I never saw Mulu hit or insult Bereket, Isaac or Tutu, her mentally retarded daughter. Until her two older sons left home, she always had the right words or gestures to make them conform or make them feel loved. Abraham and Dojo did not fare so well. She regularly hit Dojo around the legs and on the hands when he was a toddler because he was fighting with Tutu or trying to steal some peanuts from her stall or just wandered down the road when he was bored. She once sent Abraham to fetch the cigarettes and lighters she knew were contraband goods and had been hiding for a special customer who wanted to buy the lot. Abraham took too long and the customer left. She grabbed her son's arm and hit him around the head several times with her knuckles and collapsed in tears despairing about his laziness.

Mulu had an uneasy relationship with Abeba. She literally never spared the rod, or the amount of insults and curses, she meted out to the child. It was usually an on-the-spot slap, a *kurkum* on the head or hitting her daughter around the body with her shoe. She lost her temper very quickly and calmed down just as quickly. Reasons were varied but many and had began in Abeba's infancy. Soon after giving birth to Tutu, Mulu had no recourse but to go back to work to feed her family. Fikru had gone to Mekele in search of work. Mulu expected 5-year-old Abeba to care for the then 10-day-old Tutu and 3-year-old Abraham, rather than her son Bereket, then aged seven, while she joined Lemlem gathering firewood. She explained this by saying that Abeba was a girl and that, anyway, Bereket was in primary school. Tutu was a premature baby. Mulu soon realized that she was also mentally retarded and severely malnourished. Her neighbours said that, after she discovered that Abeba was drinking all the milk she left for the baby, she beat the child every time she came back from an unsuccessful trip to clinics, hospitals, faith healers, soothsayers, shamans, sorcerers and priests. The entire family still blamed Abeba for Tutu's fate. Abeba has no recollection of drinking the milk. She was haunted by her mother's reaction: 'I have tried very hard to remember, but I can't. I only remember mother's anger, the beatings and the curses. I preferred the beating to the curses. They still hurt. Perhaps my family and other people are right in calling me a glutton (*hodam*), because I am always hungry.' Unbeknown to his mother, Bereket asked all the adults in the neighbourhood to intervene lest his mother killed Abeba and went to jail and they all ended up in the street. They praised his mature foresight and adult-like action in family conflict resolution. It was common for neighbours to praise a child who showed a mature foresight in managing family-induced difficult situations by assuming the burden of a parent. Such comments and other remarks valorising street children's contribution to family income put paid to my original assumption that there was stigma attached to being a street child among the poor.

Abraham spent his days hanging around other people's houses in the hope of being given food. Although he was supposed to be in charge of disciplining Abraham, Bereket left it to Abeba to drag him away screaming from yet another fight with neighbourhood children, or beat him for being unruly or for refusing to carry out tasks expected of him. Even though Mulu expected Abeba to chastise Abraham and look after Tutu or Dojo, she often hit or slapped her daughter for beating any of them. She did the same if Abeba forgot to bring an item she had been instructed to bring to the street. She also blamed and chastised Abeba if neighbours complained about Abraham's or Tutu's behaviour. She often kept Abeba home from school to help with domestic work or nursing when she or any of the other children were ill. She never asked Bereket to skip school for similar reasons.

After Bereket refused to cook or cater for the house, Abeba was put in charge of making sure that Fikru's every need was met. She became adept at anticipating his wishes. She stood by ready with a jug of water for him to wash his hands before and after eating. If she poured the water too fast, or did not bring what he needed fast enough, all he had to do was silently stare at her and she would automatically react as he anticipated. She brought and took coffee cups, plates and glasses while he ate. She fetched water when he washed his clothes. This was not an exceptional case. Most adults, including Mulu and Lemlem, expected children to drop whatever they were doing and serve them. Parents did not need to say anything since the children had learnt how make to their parents' lives comfortable. Well-raised children automatically react to adults' needs. Girls, more than boys, become experts at reading adults' minds. They gracefully do as expected lest they incur a severe beating or curses and insults. Teenage boys carry out household chores with such ill grace that their mothers usually do it themselves or, where applicable, expect their daughters to take over. Boys thus learn to become men and expect their everyday needs to be met by their mothers, and later in life by their wives or other females, while continuing to show respect and deference to their fathers and male relatives. The difference in Abeba's behaviour was that she seemed petrified of Fikru. Her explanation was that although he had never raised a finger to her, she was scared of her mother's reaction if she displeased Fikru. Besides, 'He always remonstrates or defends his children to stop mother beating them. He never defends me even when he knows I have done everything to make his life comfortable.'

Lemlem's Case

Mulu's occasional rages against her children were short lived. It was usually an on-the-spot slap, hitting their heads with her knuckles (*kurkum*), throwing anything she could lay her hands on or hitting them around the body with her shoe. Lemlem ruminated on her grievances against her daughters and chose the time and place. Mimi was often the target of her ire. Two reasons were at the base of their mother-daughter conflicts: Mimi's behaviour in the street and their economic activities.

Lemlem knew the sale prices of everything and the values of the products her daughters sold. She also knew and disapproved of Mimi's other money-making activities, especially her temporary work with or for male street traders. Lemlem considered the girls' earnings to be family income. She also expected blind obedience, unconditional love and respect from all her children. She wanted to have the sole right to dispose of whatever money the girls earned. This state of affairs lasted as long as the girls were relatively young and malleable. As she grew older, Mimi asserted her right to some of the fruits of her labour, or at least to have a say in how they spent the money.

As mentioned earlier, Mimi had several activities of which her mother disapproved or did not know of. She was forever in debt because she could not resist buying a pretty jumper or dress from the stalls she minded for others. She liked going to the hairdresser and having her luxuriant kinky black hair straightened and paid for her sister to do the same. She regularly joined rotating credit schemes and just as regularly defaulted. She was often hiding from street traders, older street boys and shopkeepers she had insulted or owed money. Eventually, Lemlem found out, either because one of the traders would come to ask for their money back or someone would report that Mimi was quarrelling with someone in the street. She either 'grounded' her daughters by increasing their duties around the house or in the majority of cases used broom handles, sticks, shoes, her knuckles, bites and scratches to physically chastise them. She punched or cursed anyone who tried to intercede.

Whenever Mimi or her sister knew that a major beating was in the offing, they begged for assistance. This meant taking the traditional route of family conflict resolution. Either Mulu or myself followed them home, prostrated ourselves at Lemlem's feet, invoked the name of Lemlem's favourite saint, pleaded and begged her not to beat them. Lemlem would tire of the drama and promise to leave them alone. Usually, this method was a sure-proof way of ensuring that errant children would be spared the rod. It worked like a charm with Mulu and other parents but Lemlem broke her promises repeatedly. This meant staying on long after she had calmed down in order to make sure that she would keep her word.

Lemlem did not like the idea of her daughters working or socialising in the street. She disapproved of Mimi accepting money or any kind of gift or credit from the young men selling 'salvage' second-hand clothing. If they could dispense with the money the girls earned, she preferred to have them around the house where she could keep a watchful eye on them. At least once a day, she sent her son or neighbourhood children to find out where her daughters were operating. She panicked and was in despair if her daughters were late coming home or if her messengers came back saying that they could not find them. If this happened several times in a week, they were in for a beating.

Mimi was petulant and did not hesitate to punch, slap or insult any man who attacked her or refused to pay her for the work she had provided. Whenever she found out, Lemlem bristled with rage at her daughter's behaviour. Mimi insisted that she was only claiming what was rightly hers or calling a spade a spade. She was obliged to constantly lie to her mother and hide her money because of the misunderstandings and beatings. Lemlem's interpretation was discordant with this. Here is how she expressed it:

> I do not want to turn her into a liar or a manipulator. She just manages to tell what she calls a 'truth' the wrong way and at the wrong time. I do not want her to stop associating and fighting in the streets with these vagabonds and thieves because I may find out and punish her. I want her to stop, because it is wrong, wrong for a girl to comport herself like she does. She has no *yilunta* whatsoever. She does not care what anyone says about her or if anyone sees her behaving like a street whore. She should show some pride and dignity and not shame the family. Please make her understand before I kill her.

Mimi ran away from home twice. The first time she went to live with her god-mother in another part of town and stayed away for two weeks. The second time she hid herself with the family of a street vendor for four days. Lemlem nearly went out of her mind with grief both times. In spite of the constant quarrels, mother and daughter loved each other very much. Mimi did not wish to abandon her mother. She merely wanted to teach her a lesson. Just like all the physically abused street children I talked to, running away from home was one of the most powerful weapons she had against her mother. As depicted in chapters 4 and 5, many runaway children never return home and end up as members of youth gangs.

Fatherhood

Although there is ample literature on motherhood, there is scant academic writing about how fathers live up to or challenge strands of discourse that circumscribe their journey into parenting. In the literature on parenting, mothers' voices displace that of fathers. Available books and websites deal with single parenthood, child support, paternity leave and pay. They also delve into the trials and tribulations of being a new father, which are meant to reassure and mitigate any anxiety about impending fatherhood (see Newman et al. 1998; Berkman 2005). One such book will go a long way to rectify this gap (Miller 2011). Street children's fathers are indeed present in many such families. As shown below, fathers like mothers are bound by the cultural expectation of their roles and responsibilities as a parent. In Ethiopia, fathers are expected to present an indulgent but stern and authoritative male figure at home. The following depiction of fatherhood as experienced by Mulu's partner Fikru illuminates how fathers who are obliged to function in a radically impoverished social and economic context deal with the enigmatic and shifting nature of social existence. His case was compounded by his role as biological father and stepfather to Mulu's children.

Fikru's Case

Much of the discord between Mulu and her older sons Isaac and Bereket arose due to the presence of Fikru among them even though he never hit any of the children. Mulu's family harmony was disrupted when Fikru came back from Mekele to live with them permanently in 1997. After Mulu joined Isaac working full time in the street, Bereket had gradually taken over the running of the house, and most of the child rearing. This was in 1991 when he was eight years old. He attended school for half the day and did all the cleaning and washing. Apart from baking *injera,* he did all the cooking. Mulu either bought the groceries herself or left him enough money to buy a bundle of firewood and ingredients and condiments for cooking their dinner. He did not mind doing what he called 'girls things' because he could not stand seeing his mother disciplining Abeba for not doing the job properly. He carried on helping for a short while after Fikru came to live with them permanently.

Fikru was very clean and fastidious. He regularly washed his own clothes with Abeba or Abraham in attendance. When she did not have enough money, Mulu bought leftover food from poor university students, who smuggled it out of the main dining hall. Like many men in the neighbourhood, Fikru refused to eat bought leftover food. Most Ethiopians have a heightened sense of food pollution. They are loath to eat food or drink from a cup that has been touched by the hands or lips of strangers. Isaac bristled with anger at this because Fikru did not contribute to family income. Influenced by Isaac's hostility, Bereket refused to do any 'women's work' while his mother's partner lived with them. He rebelled against 'acting as Fikru's female domestic', as he put it.

When Fikru was with them, Mulu made sure that he had traditional Ethiopian home-cooked food at least once a day. This meant spending more money on food because she had to consider the resentment felt by her sons against her partner and make sure that the entire family ate the same thing. On the rare occasions that he earned money, Fikru handed over his entire wage to Mulu. Otherwise, he was more or less dependent on her for everything he ate or wore. Isaac and Bereket claimed to hate Fikru because he was not man enough to earn his living or pay the rent. Even though they did not have a father, they wanted to show him that they were men.

Fikru's presence and Bereket's refusal to cook for the 'man' added to Mulu's workload. Ababa was considered a bad cook and too dirty to be put in charge of the cooking. This meant that Mulu had to take over the cooking, while still working in the street. She stopped going back to the street after lunch and intermittently joined Isaac in the street late in the afternoon. Isaac resented having to work on the stall alone most afternoons. He considered Abeba too shy and inexperienced to manage their business. He only allowed her to sit and watch over their goods while he changed coins or ran to serve motorists stopping to buy a single cigarette or sweets. This and the fact that Isaac knew that his mother occasionally handed cash to Fikru created continual arguments between the two.

Fikru was not involved in the day-to-day activities of the family. This was primarily because Mulu would not even let him go the *Mercato* to buy supplies or carry her merchandise for her. She did not want to anger Isaac further and, more importantly, did not want Fikru to know how much money they made or how she disposed of their income. Fikru occasionally played with Dojo and Hennock but totally ignored mentally retarded Tutu. He once told me that there was nothing he could do for her because she was already damaged. Even though Abraham and Abeba were at his beck and call, he was a silent presence in their lives. He was uncomfortable with and hardly spoke to Isaac and Bereket. This was mainly due to their hostility to his presence. It is customary for mothers to enlist the help of fathers or male relatives to discipline unruly teenage boys. In desperation Mulu asked Fikru to help her discipline Bereket for refusing to cook and being rude to him, and Isaac for refusing to hand over the day's earnings. The two boys did not accept Fikru as a member of the family. When he eventually tried to discipline them, they left home for good. In Isaac's words:

I have moved out of her house. I am taking Bereket with me. His two sons came from Mekele. They thought their father was a big man and that he could find them jobs. Mother cashed in our two hundred *birr iqub* without telling me and bought them new shoes and suits. This is the second time she has done this to me. She bought Fikru a new pair of trousers. I am going barefoot and she bought him leather shoes. My brother and sisters are going in rags. She is feeding them meat practically every day. I have had enough. I told her to choose between him and me. All she has to say is: 'How can I abandon him now that he is poor?' As far as I can remember he has always been poor and has always lived off us. Let his sons feed him for a change. Can you believe this, I work and feed the man and she asks him to discipline me. The only reason that Bereket and I did not beat him to a pulp was out of respect for our mother. We did not want to shame her in front of neighbours. We did not want them to say that we have no *yilunta*. Do not worry, I will never abandon her; I love her too much. I shall help her pay the *iqub* and look out for my sisters and brothers, but I will not live under the same roof.

Mulu saw the deteriorating atmosphere in her house and her inability to discipline her sons differently:

Fikru left for Mekele when I was expecting Tutu. He came back to Addis Ababa sometime towards the end of 1992. He was unable to find work and became a burden to us all. He left for Mekele a few months later hoping to sell part of the land he owned in order to raise cash and start a business. I gave birth to Dojo in 1992 and he left again thinking that he could find a job or raise money in Mekele. You were with us when he came back empty-handed. His family had prevented him from selling any property. As soon as he came back, I fell pregnant with Hennock. The atmosphere in the house changed for the worse.

The last six years have been hell. Every time the man comes to stay with us, I fall pregnant and Fikru becomes an added burden. Isaac and Bereket do not hate me; they hate the man. That is why they have started quarrelling with me and finding fault with him. They are angry with me for getting pregnant again. They are scared that I might die giving birth. They want the man out of here. They also hate him because he keeps denying that Tutu is his daughter because she is mentally retarded. He was away for a long time when I gave birth to her. How can I throw him out? What will the neighbours say? They will say that I have no *yilunta* and that I chased him out because he has no job and is too poor! He has fathered the others after all. The whole neighbourhood thinks that he is Abeba's father. If it were not for him, I would not even have the right to live in the house we live in. He fed us when even my own mother refused to have anything to do with me, or my infant sons.

A few weeks after Isaac and Bereket left home, I took Dojo and Tutu home because they were quarrelling in the street and distracting Mulu, who was breastfeeding Hennock and taking care of her stall. Fikru was at home and his version was as follows:

I know that you must think ill of me. I did not drive her sons out of the house. They chose to go. She never allowed me to be their father. She did not let me discipline them when they were little. She let Isaac challenge me at every opportunity. By the time she asked me to discipline or talk to them, they were already men. They have never considered me their father or part of the family. They do not even think of me as a relative (*zemed*). They treat me worse than they would treat a stranger (*ba'ada*). They hate me and I have very little love for them. They look down upon me and consider me a burden. Mulu turned Bereket into a woman. He is forever sulking and going around with a miserable face, fussing around in the kitchen. She could have trained Abeba better. I will not allow her to do that to my sons. I gave her beautiful male children. Look how light-skinned and healthy they are. Abeba damaged Tutu. I dare not look at the child. I feel bad about her and do not know what will happen to her. I was not even here when she was born.

Fate dictated that I lose my job and could not find another, no matter how hard I have tried. Poverty and this government have turned me into her wife and a dependent of her son. The current government have refused to give me my pension. They say that I collaborated with the Derg. What else could I do? They fired thousands of civil servants and put their friends and relatives in our posts as soon as they took over power. Thousands like me were left to starve with our children. We served our country. We did not know any better. The Derg gave me a better chance in life than I would have had during the emperor's time. They were a government of the people and took care of the proletariat.

My family in Mekele have given up on me. They resent me as much as Mulu's sons resent me. I feel like a shunned leper at times. My older sons keep telling me to go and live with them in Mekele. How can I leave her and our children? People will say that I have no *yilunta*. She does not want to go to Mekele. She does not speak the language. In any case, she knows and I know that she would not be welcome there. I do not know what will happen to us. God has made us rich in children but he forgot to give me the means to feed them.

The above depiction of the gendered aspect of father's traditional role in disciplining and punishing children and father-son power relations is rare but of increasing interest to anthropological enquiry (see Perry 2009). Chapter 4 details the consequences of fathers' attempts to augment their diminishing household authority due to poverty through excessive physical abuse of their sons as an integral part of child rearing.

Playtime

There are numerous works on the importance of play in enhancing children's physical and cognitive skills, including developing their communications skills. Many touch on the gendered nature of this interactive activity (see Lancy 2008). Among street children's families, there were indeed gender-based differences in how much playtime mothers tolerated from their daughters and sons. Boys who had no connection with street life were encouraged by their parents to go out and play football and other games during weekends and school holidays. Girls aged eight and older were discouraged from playing in the street because it was conduct unbecoming for nice girls, as well as for fear that they would be bullied or sexually harassed. Mothers seldom approved of their daughters being outside playing and preferred them to be at home or in the neighbourhood where they lived. The following comments were common reactions: 'She is a girl; she does not need to play all the time. Boys need to spend their energy somewhere. It does them good to play.'

I never saw Mimi or her sister play. Their brother was too sickly and skinny to play with other boys. His mother and sisters were very protective of him and seldom let him out of their sight. A year after I met them, Isaac developed a passion for renting bicycles and riding up and down the street. Mulu disapproved of him spending money unnecessarily and the amount of time he began staying away from the stall. All he dreamed and talked about was becoming a minibus driver and helping his mother and siblings get off the street. Abraham and Dojo never ceased to josh each other or play. Bereket was a member of a football team and played football on Sundays. The team did not have proper equipment and most of the team played barefoot but they had a real football. Mulu had contributed half the money for the purchase of the ball. I never saw Abeba play with other children. She sometimes sat huddled with neighbourhood girls gossiping and giggling outside her house.

Education

Mass education is linked to the ideals of equality of opportunity for poor and rich alike. In practice, education in Addis Ababa reinforces existing inequalities rather than overcoming them. Most if not all government-run schools in Addis Ababa have poor facilities and over-crowded classrooms, with at times sixty to ninety pupils to a class. The teachers are under-paid and over-worked. There are not enough teachers or classrooms. Primary and secondary schoolchildren can only attend classes for half the day. The school schedules of all the children I knew were set up arbitrarily with unexpected changes mid term. Even though they were receiving 'free education', many destitute children and their families had difficulties buying uniforms and school supplies (see Tekeste 2006). The majority of street children I have met entered street life in order to earn money to buy school uniforms and/or school supplies during the long summer vacation and ended up permanent members of the street-begging or -trading fraternity (see Heinonen 1996). Some children appreciated the eventual relevance of a good education for their future life prospects. Just as many were discouraged by the glaring reality faced by the many jobless youths who had finished high school and were eking out a meagre existence portaging, washing or watching cars and doing anything they could to earn a living, including robbing other street children and members of youth gangs.

Due to the perennial ill treatment of schoolchildren by schoolteachers in government schools, many poor children come to see the school as a hostile environment. Throughout the years I carried out my field work, I was given graphic descriptions of the many ways teachers physically and verbally abused their pupils and got away with it. I also witnessed umpteen instances of six, seven and eight year olds being dragged screaming and crying to school. They invariably dreaded the ire of their teachers more than the corporal punishment that awaited them if their parents found out that they had skipped school. Mimi, like many other street children I know, still claims that her teachers' tyranny, more than anything else, precipitated her entry into street life and led her to quit school. This is how she explained it:

> I must have been nine or ten years old when I finally decided that I had had enough of my teachers' cruel behaviour. I used to attend school for half the day. I had a nasty teacher who used to beat me. Some days it was because I was late, another time because I was dirty or else because I did not have the proper school equipment. If I knew that he was going to beat me, I would hide my school equipment and join other children in the street. They were all neighbourhood girls and boys. We played together and sometimes they shared their sweets or food with me. I learnt more from them than I did from him. Mother beat me regularly for skipping school. I preferred being beaten by her than by the teacher. I was happy when I was finally expelled from school for non-attendance. She now oppresses my little sister and brother by forcing them to go to school. She does not know what it is like. She has never been to school. She believes that all the beatings and insults are worth it, as long as we can acquire a good education.

Like many poor street boys, Isaac quit school due a combination of things. These included what he saw as his teachers' inhuman behaviour towards him and his school friends, financial constraints and the demands made on his time by his street-related activities. He summed this up as follows:

> I failed every year. The teachers beat all the poor children who did not have all their school equipment. The last teacher I had used to pull my ears and hit me on the head for non-attendance, for coming in late or for being dirty. That is when I got in the habit of shaving my head. I could not help it. I had to help mother in the morning. I often had to skip school in the afternoon if we did not manage to change enough of the money the traders had given us for the day lest we lose their custom. After I was thrown out of a school for non-attendance, mother enrolled me in an evening class. I was too tired in the evening to pay any attention to the teacher. I preferred to rest and play with other boys rather than do my homework during the day. I often felt ashamed in class because I could not follow the lessons and the teacher made fun of me.

> Mother found out that I was skipping class most evenings and spending time playing with homeless boys. She threatened to beat me several times. In the end I threw all my school equipment at her and told her that if she forced me to go back to school I would leave her and I meant it. I was eleven years old. There is no hope for me. This

is the reason why I do not mind working hard to help Bereket finish school and lead a better life than I shall ever have.

Abeba did not mind going to school in spite of the horrendous experiences she has had with violent teachers. She once showed me a big bump on her head where the teacher had grabbed her by the hair and banged her head against the wall because she was late coming to class. She refused to let me tell her mother or talk to the teacher. She told me that the teacher would make life hell for her and her brothers if we complained. Abraham took the beating by teachers as part of his schooling experience. Bereket liked going to school and was seldom in trouble with his teachers. The only time he was in trouble at school was when he told a teacher that 'he had no right to keep beating his school friend for lacking school equipment when he damn well knew that the poor boy did not have the means to acquire any'.

Mainly due to the good relationships she has with *kebele* officials, Mulu was connected to the network that made it possible for her children to access health care and educational institutions. She seldom had difficulties in securing letters from *kebele* officials enabling her to have her children admitted to government schools or transferred to other schools. She even managed to have Abeba re-instated after she was expelled for absenteeism while looking after the family following Hennock's birth in 1997. However, she loathed leaving her pavement stall and spending a half a day or longer at the *kebele* securing such letters. It interfered with her ability to trade and to feed her children. She was never sure that the official who had the authority to issue the letter or the overall boss in charge of signing that same letter would be there that day, the next day or the day after. Isaac was always ready and willing to act on her behalf and usually managed to sort things out whenever her presence or signature was not required. In such instances, he told the officials that she was very ill and could not be present.

Mulu had a hard time enrolling Tutu in any kind of primary school because of her erratic behaviour and mood swings. Noise or children crying easily distressed her. Mulu made sure that she was never left alone with Dojo or Hennock because she would pinch and scratch them. Her mother and siblings were the only ones who understood what she was saying. Even though Mulu was told about NGO-financed institutions that were interested in helping mentally handicapped children whilst they were infants, she refused to do anything about it since they would only take care of Tutu until she was five. The place was too far away from where they lived. Someone had to make sure that Tutu was taken and brought back from the school. There was also the matter of feeding and clothing her. Mulu did not wish to waste her time doing the rounds of *kebele* and NGO offices getting this permit and that letter and letting her children starve. As is the case of many physically or mentally handicapped destitute children, the whole family assumed that they would either have to look after Tutu for the rest of her life or let her beg in the streets. In 1996 Mulu managed to enrol her in an NGO-financed school with the help of *kebele* officials and the influence of a female neighbour who had a job at the school. Her sister and brothers took turns taking Tutu to school and back. Tutu was eventually thrown out of the school. The teachers said that she was too violent and was hurting the other children.

Bereket, Abeba and Abraham had difficulties keeping their school equipment clean or out of reach of the curious hands of their younger siblings. Abraham was often in tears because Tutu or Dojo had managed to find his school exercise books from under the mattress and had been playing with them. Abeba had a filthy old cloth sack where she kept her school equipment. She beat the smaller ones mercilessly if they dared go near it and in return was slapped regularly by her mother for beating them. Since the room was too dark and they had no place where they study, they often sat outside or near the door to do their homework.

By 2001, Bereket had quit school and joined his brother Isaac as a minibus conductor. It was almost two years since he and his brother had left home and moved into another one-room shack with a young couple with an infant son. He told me that he quit school because he had been told that he had to repeat a class because he failed all his exams. Isaac still hoped that Bereket would go to evening classes and finish his education. In the six years I was in the field, I witnessed both boys and girls giving up their educations due to poverty, inadequate school provisions by the State and witnessing the fate of jobless young people who *had* managed to finish high school.

Health

Anja Krumeich's (1994) study of health, pregnancy and childcare details the dire consequences of inadequate health-care services on poor women. Available government-financed health care provisions for poor mothers and children in Ethiopia probably ranks among the worst in the world. Like many destitute mothers, Mulu did not expend much energy securing *kebele* letters giving her or her children access to health care. It was cheaper and more expedient for her to use soothsayers, faith healers, traditional herbal remedies and *tebel*[11] than modern medicine. Even when poor people were able to attend a clinic or admitted to a hospital with the help of a letter from the *kebele,* most could not afford the prohibitively expensive prescription drugs. Like other street children, Mulu's children suffered from skin, throat, ear and eye infections. More often than not, these ailments were left untreated due to lack of money. Those who used makeshift kerosene lamps and cooked inside their shacks often had sore throats and

---

[11] *Tebel* is holy water available free of charge from the church. Many Ethiopians believe in its curative powers.

constantly spat out dark brown or black saliva. Lighter-skinned children showed tell-tale marks of flea and bedbug bites around their necks. If a child had a fever or had any kind of stomach pain, they would be told to stay home until they felt better. Those who could afford it went to the chemist and asked the pharmacist to recommend a cure.

Mulu firmly believed in the power of Saint Gabriel to heal and ease her pain. If he failed her, it was because she was a sinner. Like most Ethiopians, she preferred to have a direct link with God or her favourite saint. She had a healthy disdain for priests and shamans. Her stepfather was a priest and dabbled in providing amulets for distressed barren or lovelorn women for a fee. We once opened an amulet he had given her to change her bad luck and stop her from having any more children. It was a piece of paper with a few Amharic scripts wrapped and sewn into a leather pouch. Thinking that the writing was in *Ge'ez*, an ancient Ethiopian language still used in the standard liturgy by the clergy instead of Amharic, I showed it to an expert in *Ge'ez* who could not make sense of the scripts either.

More than anything else, Mulu hated the time-consuming bureaucratic hurdles she had to go through to access any form of health care, even if it meant endangering her own health. Mulu had yet another difficult pregnancy when she was expecting her last child in 1997. She had swollen legs, her gums were bleeding and she often felt so tired during the day that she fell asleep in the street while trying to sell her goods. The following narrative explains her dilemma:

> I must have a letter from the *kebele* to get a place at the hospital. This means that I have to go there early in the morning and stay there all day. If the *kebele* official who writes such letters or the one who has the stamp is not there, I have to try the next day or the next. Once I have the letter, I have to stay outside the hospital all night queuing in order to get a registration card and an appointment to see a doctor. Otherwise, I have to queue all day to get the registration card only.

> Why should I waste my time? I know exactly what they are going to tell me in the end. Buy and swallow these very expensive vitamins, eat nutritious food, drink a lot of milk, stop work and rest until the baby comes. They will not tell me where I can find the money to eat meat and drink milk or better still who will feed my children while I sleep and rest all day. That is what they told me the last time I went near them when I was pregnant.

The above illustrates that whilst the *kebele* housing-network system enabled poor families to access a modicum of health care and education for their children, the bureaucratic and economic disincentives they had to overcome discouraged many of them from taking full advantage of it. Most if not all the government-run hospitals in Addis Ababa are in serious need of improvements in hygiene and building maintenance. The corridors and rooms are over-crowded and smelly. The private clinics and hospitals that have been flourishing since the demise of the Derg in 1990 are prohibitively expensive for ordinary citizens, let alone destitute families.

I went to visit Mulu after she gave birth to Hennock in 1997. Fikru welcomed me at their door and exclaimed: 'I only give her healthy male children!' He was referring to Dojo, Hennock and Abraham, his biological sons. The entire family was there and no one seemed to be celebrating the birth of yet another mouth to feed. In the 'wider Ethiopian culture' it is customary for women to stay in bed or at least around the house for forty days after giving birth. Mulu was obliged to stay at home mainly because she felt too weak and ill to resume trading in the street. For a while, their only income came from Isaac's efforts to change coins for minibus drivers. Since Isaac could not run their stall and change coins on his own at the same time, he began moonlighting as a minibus conductor.

By the time Mulu was well enough to go back to her trade four weeks later, they were heavily in debt. Isaac's relationship with Fikru had reached its lowest mark. He was no longer willing to help his mother on the stall or hand over the entire proceeds of his labour for his mother to dispose of as she saw fit. He preferred to work as a minibus conductor because he earned more money than he did changing coins. He hoped to save enough money to take driving lessons and become a driver. He spent most of his evenings and Sundays visiting his paramour. No one dared inform Mulu for fear she would go around there to pick a fight with the woman. After yet another quarrel with Fikru, because he had attempted to beat Isaac for being rude to his mother, Isaac and Bereket moved out of their family home. They found temporary accommodation with one of the minibus conductors about six kilometres away from where Mulu lived.

Mulu terminated her eighth pregnancy by drinking katikala[12] and asking female friends to jump on her back and stomach. It took her days to abort the foetus and she almost lost her life in the process. I was away at the time. I subsequently found out that, since abortion was illegal in Ethiopia, this was one of the many life-endangering methods poor expectant women and girls use to terminate unwanted pregnancies. In Asia, the Middle East and elsewhere, ultrasound technology, coupled with a traditional preference for boys, has led to mass female foeticide. The women I interviewed terminated their pregnancies regardless of the child's gender; they did so because of poverty or, if they were young unmarried girls, the stigma of having brought shame to the family. Most if not all of the destitute mothers I knew either were ignorant of birth-control methods or did not have adequate information or easy access to medical facilities. Many fell pregnant from a casual or temporary relationship. I have met ten women who were abandoned by their lovers as soon as they fell pregnant; they were left to raise their babies alone. Those who had a modicum of understanding of family-planning methods or modern reproductive technologies and attended the very few over-subscribed NGO-sponsored maternity clinics were either married or in long-term relationships. They were mostly literate, had regular incomes and were relatively young.

---

[12] A home-distilled, and very alcoholic, cheap beverage

Six months after her last pregnancy and unbeknown to her partner, Mulu had her Fallopian tubes tied. On hearing about the facilities sponsored by a UK-based charity and the fact that they could go back home within hours of the operation, two neighbours also had themselves sterilised. The over-crowded living conditions meant that their husbands found out about it. I was told that all the other men in the neighbourhood had warned their wives and partners of the dire consequences if they even thought about following suit without their permission. Fikru was inconsolable. He considered it an affront to his manhood and a personal betrayal that Mulu did not even have the decency to seek his approval. It was an unwritten but acknowledged fact, even among health practitioners of the charity, that women who wished to have their tubes tied had to have their husbands' permission. Mulu had made me write down that she was not married and she did not know the whereabouts of any of the fathers of her children. Since she could neither read nor write, she put a thumbprint signature on the declaration form. Although they were both married, the other two women did the same. They told me that it was pointless discussing it with their husbands and starting an argument. One of them said: 'All men are capable of doing is to take all the pleasure and leave women with the pain. All they think about is asserting their manhood and proving to other men that they are the boss in their house.'

Like Mulu, Lemlem had not received medical attention during her pregnancy or after giving birth to her son in 1990. She suffered from constant pain in her stomach. Whenever she was bedridden, Mimi and her sister forgot their dislike for housework and took care of their mother, their brother and their home. Lemlem's way of dealing with her ailment was to pray and attend church on the saint's day assigned to Saint Mary. She often sought the help of shamans or priests and wore several amulets they had prepared for her for a hefty fee.

All the mothers I knew, including Mulu, had submitted to a form of female genital mutation[13] which required having their clitoris cut out as part of the required traditional female circumcision. Quite a number of the teenage girls I interviewed did not know whether they had been circumcised or not. Mimi told me that her mother was against female genital mutilation. She had been part of the *cadre* while living in Assab with their soldier father, and had attended gender-awareness sessions organized by the communist regime which promoted the discarding of the custom. Mulu was in two minds about Abeba. She often thought that it would be better to have Tutu 'circumcised' just in case her innocence would make her a victim of some evil man's lust. She told me that she had contacted a woman circumciser and she was saving fifty *birr* for the operation. I went to see the woman and offered her a considerable amount of money if she refused to help Mulu. I received a slap and a torrent of insults and curses for my

---

[13] The most recent 'buzz expression' or 'politically correct' term for female genital mutilation, also known as FGM, is 'female genital cutting'.

effort. I told Mulu about the reception I received. She laughed and swore that she would never speak to the woman again. She also promised to leave both girls alone. That was in May 2000. Tutu was ten years old, two years older than when Mulu, her mother, was subjected to this barbaric, unnecessary and cruel ordeal, which is still part of the rite de passage for many girls in Ethiopia and elsewhere in the world (see Heinonen 2002).

Parenting the Parents

Ever since Margaret Mead published *Growing up in New Guinea* in 1930 and Dr. Benjamin Spock wrote his book, *The Common Sense Book on Baby and Child Care* in 1946, a multitude of books and websites on child rearing from every conceivable perspective – including medical, economic, cultural or even existential – have been available for public use or information. Anthropological field studies conducted at different times and in different settings focus on the dissimilar aspects of childhood and indicate the existence of cultural scripts that influence parental behaviour (see Levine and New 2008). Apart from children acting as carers to mentally or physically disadvantaged parents, there is little or no reference to children parenting their able-bodied parents. The emphasis is on adults' roles as parents. Street children often assume the adult role of homemakers and their mothers' mentors. They also teach their parents, siblings and other adults the tricks of street trading as well as are involved an all aspects of parenting their siblings and their mothers. The following details this reversed reality with children taking the role of parenting their parents. It shows how the subsequent diminishing parental authority faced by mothers meant that dependence on their children was not a question of whether, but at which stage and by how much.

Isaac

Until he left home, Isaac had a tremendous impact on how Mulu dealt with the outside world. She could not read or write and depended on him for anything official that came their way. She consulted with him about every aspect of her personal and social life from dealing with *kebele* officials or schoolteachers to her relationship with their friends in the street.

When I first met them, Isaac was clearly the favourite. Mulu never stopped extolling his virtues. He was 'my life, my soul, my father and mother'. She spent all her working days with him and admitted freely that he had taught her the intricacies of street trade and more. She conferred with him before joining yet another *iqub* or buying clothes for the children or meat during public holidays. He remonstrated with her whenever she picked a quarrel with other women or lost her temper with police officers. He was, as she put it, her 'friend, her confidant and definitely not a child'. This type of emotional bond was more typical of mother-daughter relationships rather than mother-son relationships. The only time I have seen it repeated was in four female-headed households where there were no daughters in the family. Although very close to their mothers, the two boys found acting as confidants to their mothers emotionally stressful. They used to plead with me to become their mothers' friend so that they could have someone to confide in about their emotional problems.

Until he left home at age seventeen, Isaac and Mulu nurtured each other and she protected him against violence in the street. As Isaac put it:

Mother is always panicking. She fears *kebele* officials, schoolteachers and even doctors and nurses. She is afraid of asking for information or anything even when it is her right to do so. I have to be there with her and push her to act on things. We would have lost our house if she had not listened to me. Mimi's mother is the same. We are still children but we have to act as if we were their fathers or husbands and advise them on how to react to things or what to do.

Mother is not afraid of policemen or street thugs, but I am. She often protects me and the other children from the many hoodlums who try to rob or beat us. She embarrasses me when she fights publicly with them or the police. She sometimes listens to me when I to tell her off and remind her that they could hurt one of us when she is not around. Ever since I can remember, I have been advising her on how to behave with neighbours and other traders, who she could trust and who she should avoid. Sometimes I feel that I am her mother.

Mimi

Much like Isaac, 12-year-old Mimi had been obliged to become a street vendor and her mother's confidant at a very early age, thus blurring the social adult-child boundaries between mother and daughters. Even though they fought constantly about money, the bond between Mimi and her mother were very strong. Although Lemlem claimed that she could read, she let Mimi read all official papers and interpret them for her. When they received their eviction order from the *kebele,* it was Mimi who convinced her mother that she had no other choice but to petition the *kebele* not to re-house them too far away from where they now lived. Mimi advised her mother on how to deal with NGO employees and what type of answers she ought to give them in order to be included in their projects. Mimi not only trained Isaac and Mulu for street work, but advised her mother on how to diversify her spice-making activities and who to target as potential clients. In time, she was to take over their trading activities and become the parent.

The Next Generation

Mulu's Family

Until 1998, Mulu's attempts at initiating Abeba into street work were unsuccessful. The poor girl was very shy and terrified of any type of duty outside their
house. Soon after Bereket and Isaac left home, Mulu gradually involved both
Abeba and Abraham in her street-related activities. A few months after her older
brothers left home, Abeba stopped going to school and took over her brother
Bereket's role around the house and part of Isaac's job in the street. She was
thirteen years old. She hated working in the street. She was very shy around
strangers and uncomfortable dealing with customers. She was scared of giving the
wrong change or failing to figure out the exact price of each item if left to fend
for herself. In time, she learnt to overcome her shyness and to do the work. By
2000, soon after Abeba turned fifteen, Mulu trusted her enough to leave her to
manage the stall and even sent her to the *Mercato* to buy supplies in bulk. Their
relationship strengthened. Mulu stopped beating Abeba. She told me that Abeba
is now a mature girl and that she could be trusted to understand how things were
in the family.

Mulu told me that she could not ask Abraham to do the washing and cooking because Fikru would not allow it. He would accuse her of turning him into
a woman, as she did with Bereket. She bitterly explained that the man did not
mind eating whatever Bereket cooked because he was not his son. Fikru would
not allow Abraham to work in the street. He wanted him to go to school. Initially, Abraham was put in charge of running errands for Mulu and Abeba as
well as taking and bringing back Dojo from school. By the end of 2000, he was
acting as Abeba's assistant in the street and missing schools regularly. Mulu took
Hennock everywhere with her. Isaac often stopped by to chat to his mother in
the street. He sometimes took a handful of peanuts and left ten or twenty times
more money than it was worth. After her brothers' departure, Tutu, now eight
years old, was more or less left to her own devices. She continued to roam around
the neighbourhood. She often went to play on the main asphalt road all by herself. Mulu's excuse for leaving her alone at home was that she could not work if
Dojo, Hennock and Tutu were with her at her stall because they never stopped
quarrelling. She did not have the means to hire someone to look after Tutu and
could not enrol her in a school because she was mentally handicapped and too
disruptive.

In June 2005, I was told that Isaac had a wife and a daughter. Abeba, now
aged twenty, had a child of her own and lived with the father a minibus conductor. Bereket was also married and had fathered a son. He did not finish his high
school. He failed all his exams and repeated several classes. Isaac still hoped to

become a minicab driver. He was saving money in order to pay for his brother's driving lessons before acquiring his own. The two brothers and their young families share a one-room house about two kilometres from where Mulu lives. Both are in constant touch with their mother. They often stop and talk to their mother when driving up and down looking for passengers.

In April 2010, while on a short trip to Addis Ababa, I visited Mulu and her Family. Fikru, Abraham, Dojo and Hennock still lived in the same house where I met them. Abeba and her daughter have moved in with them. I had difficulty finding her house because the government has bulldozed most of the houses nearby. Mulu lives in dread of being re-housed outside town or, worse, expelled once the developers come to build the planned high-rise flats. I also learnt that Isaac had been sentenced to five years imprisonment for rape. Mulu is convinced that it is a case of mistaken identity. The rest of the family says that he is guilty. They are not able to visit him since the place where he is serving his sentence is in another town, an expensive five-hour bus ride each way requiring an overnight stay to get the necessary permit to see him. Mulu reacted with anger and distress when I enquired about Isaac's presumed wife and daughter. She denied their existence and gave such a look to the rest of the family that I was unable to get anything out of them on the subject.

After the father of her daughter abandoned her, Abeba spent four years working as a domestic servant in the Middle East, sending money back to help her mother and paying the agent's fees. She left her child behind for Mulu to raise. She plans to go back as soon as the opportunity arises. Bereket did get his driving licence before Isaac went to jail. He lives in another town but keeps in touch with Mulu. Fikru has a day job as a security guard with an NGO. They all said that he spends most of his salary on drinks. I met up with him another day and he told me that he will not let Isaac or Bereket live in his house ever again. Mulu continues to trade. She depends on Abeba's daughter and Tutu to assist her in carrying her goods to and from the same spot near the university wall. She had lost a lot of weight. She looked unwell and defeated. She was constantly in tears.

Lemlem's Family

By June 2001, almost seven years after I had met them, Mimi, aged twenty-two, had a daughter by a street vendor she had known for a long time. They married and he moved in with them. The couple with a small child, with whom Lemlem's family shared their new accommodation, moved out. Mimi and her husband expanded his primary business of selling second-hand clothes by also lending money to street children and street vendors at high interest. Since Lemlem's health had deteriorated, she was restricted to preparing spices, which Mimi sold to other retailers. Mimi had also taken over the role of guiding and disciplining her brother and sisters. She made futile attempts to force them to quit street life and resume their schooling. I heard from Lemlem's family again in June 2007. I was informed that Lemlem had died. Mimi had two children of her own. She was looking after her younger sister's illegitimate son while the girl was working in the Middle East as a domestic servant. Their brother suffers from severe asthma attacks and is too ill to work. I was not able to find them in April 2010 because the entire area where they lived had been raised to the ground and a multi-story building was being constructed on the same site. Mulu confirmed that Lemlem has passed away but she had lost contact with them.

Summing Up

The universal picture emerging from the literature is that street children are more entrepreneurial than squatter or slum children, that they have more egotistic parents or that they come from dysfunctional families (see Aptekar 1988; Swart 1988; Ennew and Milne 1989; Boyden 1990; James and Sprout 1990; Ennew 1994; Hecht 1995). The general concept of the street is as a morally dangerous place for children, while, paradoxically, street children are commonly considered a danger to the community (see Swart 1988; Glauser 1990). Consequently, most of the discourse on street children is centred on their living an uncontrolled life. Alejandro Cussianovich (1992) claims that urban societies generally consider street and working children as children out of place and that, 'this does symbolic violence to such children'.

As shown above, home-based street children in Addis Ababa are not marginalized from the broader culture of the rest of the community. They are not dysfunctional families. They associated freely with non-street children in the neighbourhood they live in and were accepted as *yesefer lijotch* or neighbourhood kids. They walked to school and socialised with children with no connection to street life. They play football with neighbourhood kids on Sundays. There was no stigma attached to their street-related activities. In fact, neighbours praised such children for helping their mothers. Those I worked with and their families were part of the neighbourhood they lived in. Their parents belonged to a burial association and/or to a religious association. Children and parents alike were members of one or more rotating credit schemes. Those who could not afford to become members of any of these community-based voluntary associations were the most destitute. Street children connected to a social network or community are able to add to their potential pool of social ties and this strengthens their chances of creating their own support network in adulthood.

An added element in the socialisation process of street children had implications for the economic bonds between these children and their mothers. The economics of street life compelled street children to acquire adult-like behaviours and responsibilities in early childhood, both at home and in the street. The age restriction in the Ethiopian Labour Proclamation no. 64 of 1975 expressly prohibits the employment of children under the age of fourteen. In view of the abject poverty they lived in, street children and their parents pointed out to me the absurdity of the age restriction in reference to child labour or street-work. The alternative to their not working or begging in the street would be starvation or crime.

In general, mothers considered any money earned by their daughters to be household income, which they were entitled to dispose of for the good of the family. This caused constant rows and recriminations between mothers and daughters. Most of the boys I knew rebelled against handing over their entire day's earnings a few weeks or months after entering street life and usually hid or used part of their money to feed themselves, watch videos, play pinball or buy little luxuries in the street. Mulu's and Lemlem's family stories starkly illustrate that disparities in housing, health and educational outcome make poverty inter-generational. It is hard for the poor to break the vicious circle of deprivation. Poverty is often an insurmountable barrier to the realisation of parental aspirations for a better life for their children.

Finally, I have shown how and why street children are obliged to behave and take on the burden of being more adult from an early age. They are also capable of acting as agents of socialization at home and as entrepreneurs in the street. Homeless children face the same challenges in the street and more, but they do so with the absence of any caring adult in their lives or the comfort and solace of having a home to see them through the difficult years of adolescence and puberty. The more such children are forced to cut themselves off from the adult social world, the more difficult it is for them to enter into the wider circle of life. The following chapter describes the peripatetic and perilous journey from childhood into adulthood of youth gang members.

4

BORCO

The Give and Take of Gang Membership

The literature on youth gangs reveals the breadth and depth of the now globalized terrain of gang research (see Schneider and Tilley 2004). Although the term *gang* is used universally by researchers, police, social workers, media and the general public, there is still a lack of definitional consensus on the term. The central theoretical assumption within ethnographic and survey research is that youth gangs are social groups bounded by common affiliation and this separates them from other street youths. Membership of the group feeds their common need for supportive networks, identity, protection, power and solidarity. These bonds are bolstered by recognizable symbols such as a gang names, colours, drugs, choice of weapons and apparel. Additionally, gang members often share a common identity or territory usually demarcated by 'racial' and ethnic boundaries. The above description comes with a label that has a huge stigma. This is because delinquency and crime are said to be the main attributes defining youth gangs and that gang membership increases the likelihood of violent behaviour and drug abuse (see Short and Hughes 2006). All this has been written of in volume after volume, from every conceivable perspective, but mainly within the domains of experimental psychology, policing and criminology.

Ever since Frederic Thrasher (1927) studied over one thousand juvenile gangs in Chicago, increasing scholarly attention has been directed towards developing a theoretical framework and a methodology to study the etiological significance of gangs. His influence is perhaps most evident among what is now known as the Chicago School, who have paid considerable attention to the micro-social level of explanation of gang cultures. Patrick James's (1973) book *A Glasgow Gang Observed* and a number of studies and books in the UK have dealt with the social construction of 'Mods', 'Rockers', 'Yardies' and 'Teddy boys' including popular and media reactions to them in the 1960s and 70s. Recent books on the comparative study of European youth gangs report on the current situation of what they refer to as 'problematic' youth groups (see Klein et al. 2001). Violence is a chronic feature in Latin American and Caribbean studies of youth gangs (Rogers 1999). On the other hand, Lewis Aptekar's (1988) long-term study of the Gallada and Gamada in Colombia focuses on such children's economic and affective support networks. In Africa, Clive Glazer's (2000) study provides the historical development of youth gangs in the Johannesburg/Soweto area from 1935 to 1976. His book delves into personal network formation and reformation among the *Bo-Tsotsi* and sheds new light of how themes of masculinity and territoriality, exacerbated by the then apartheid-driven political climate, led to their formation and actions. Other Southern African studies include the Strollers in Cape Town plus the Ibanda and Malunde in Johannesburg. Both books discuss the friendship, support, security and sense of belonging membership to the group offered its members (see Sharf et al. 1986 and Swart 1988). This chapter provides ethnographic evidence of 'another angle' to the now familiar and often told stories about youth gangs.

My long-term data on youth gangs concerns three all-male gangs and one mixed-sex gang of teenage children. I got to know them all well during the six years I was doing my field research. I also met a group of jobless young men known as *bozene*.[1] They were a part of the numerous groups of people who had an impact on the boys' lives. My entry into the world of the mixed-sex gang was made possible through my association with members of one of the all-male gangs who subsequently joined the mixed-sex gang formed by one of the *bozene*. I have provided the details of the *bozene*'s group and life circumstances in chapter 5.

The age range of all three male gangs was ten to sixteen when I began my research. Depending on the circumstance, group membership varied from four to twelve boys. Due to the great number of children I was working with, and in order to represent the children as whole people, with their own biographies, attitudes and actions, I needed to restrict my scope. I have therefore chosen to concentrate on one all-male youth gang in this chapter and one mixed-sex gang in the next. Focussing on specific personalities from the two gangs enables me to include the voices of members of the other two all-male gangs and their entourage into the discourse at times as second- and third-person narratives. In addition to providing a context for the narratives by the people around them, this helped me avoid talking about the children as an abstraction.

Much is made in the literature about youth gangs having a name for their group. Since none of the gangs I worked with had a name for their group, I have named the all-male gang in this chapter 'Zelalem's gang' in order to facilitate their identification. Zelalem was not the first member of the gang I made contact with. Even though I paid equal attention to his comrades, he was the only one who remained part of the boys-only group until it disintegrated. He then joined the mixed-sex group I discuss in chapter 5, before making vain attempts to extricate

---

[1] *Bozene* means unemployed youths.

himself from street life as a young adult. The emphasis in this chapter is on the individual child and the specific behaviour in which each was engaged, individually and as a collective, while filtering the reality of their lives through their own words and actions.

The *Borcos* and their Kind

Studies after studies indicate that gang self-group identification is connected to the ethnic enclave from which the children's families come or to the communities where they operated. This contains elements of street level loyalty and neighbourhood solidarity. This was not the case with the children I studied. In contrast to home-based street children, the city-born homeless boys and girls I worked with did not self-identify with a neighbourhood or a community. Different migration experience and city life had altered the physical and cultural location of migrant children's families for them to identify too much with any ethnic enclave. Besides, all the children lacked the supportive networks of a family around them. They nevertheless adhered to a range of behaviours imbued with the same sense of *yilunta* that was acceptable to the wider community. This is because they were socialized by their families before entering the murky world of the street and the violence that accompanied it. Furthermore, as Clive Glaser (2000: 190) so succinctly put it: 'Underpinning all of this is a stress on gender based socialization, the historical construction of masculinity and the transition from adolescence to manhood.'

I did not have at my disposal the surprisingly substantial source material and official documentation, which Glazer (2000: 12) had access to on youth gangs in South Africa prior to embarking on my field work in Addis Ababa. There is still a paucity of written material about youth gangs in Ethiopia. I had read very little about youth gangs prior to entering the field and my involvement with them was accidental. The initial targets of my enquiry at the time were home-based street children and their entourage. Right at the outset of my field work, I had noticed groups of boys sleeping on the pavement oblivious to the traffic. Pedestrians either walked on as if they were not there or dropped a few coins. The *borcos,* as they were known by the street-working fraternity, were different in behaviour and appearance from other street children. Even when awake and about, they looked and acted indifferent to their surroundings. Unless they were playing, street children were usually alert to begging, working and selling opportunities. They were constantly on the move, and approached people and cars all the time. The *borcos* seemed to exist outside this space.

My initial impression was that such street groups were overwhelmingly male. However, as I show in chapter 5, I was eventually to discover the existence of girls in the gang. The male-only gang members I met were predominantly homeless boys who had chosen to abandon their families. They all knew the whereabouts of their native families but valued their independence from parents and adults alike. I kept trying to make contact with them when they were up and about. Since I did not offer them money for their time, they invariably ignored me. I persevered and made sure to greet one or two on my way up and down the street while locating my other informants. Fortuitously, I met one boy outside a pharmacy looking very worried. I walked over and asked him what the matter was. He told me that his friend was very ill and was given a prescription from the hospital but that the money he and his comrades had put together was not sufficient. I bought the prescription and told him to keep the money he had on him. I found him and his friends later in the afternoon. They called me over and thanked me. They had purchased sodas and other treats for their injured comrade. The boy had been badly beaten the night before but even though this was obvious, they insisted that he had been knocked down by a runaway car. The hospital where they took him gave him first aid and a prescription. They tolerated my presence from then on. The first boy I met left and joined another gang and eased my entry into that group. My friendship with Zelalem's gang was gradual and more rewarding in terms of data gathering.

Zelalem and the Gang

Mulu was the first person I heard calling youth gang members *borcos*. Isaac had told her that he had seen me with one of them. She warned me not to go anywhere near them. She told me that they were drug addicts, thieves, vagabonds and dangerous criminals and that they would eventually beat or rob me. I told her that *borco* sounded like an adulteration of the Italian word *porco* meaning pig or dirty. This pleased her to no end. She exclaimed that it was exactly what they were: filthy, vermin-ridden pigs. She also asked me not to bring them anywhere near her 'because people may think that they are her children'. Ephrem Tessema (1996: v), an Ethiopian anthropologist, has translated *borco* as follows: 'One who lives in the streets and is unable to return to a normal way of life. A person who falls victim to addiction and other deviant behaviour.'

Mulu was not the only person to warn me off frequenting the *borcos*. From the friendly traffic police officer, to shopkeepers and other street children, the same admonition was repeated: I would rue the day I met them. The fact is that I was never attacked, robbed or insulted by any members of the youth gangs I worked with. Lied to, let down, repeatedly fooled, yes, but never assaulted. I shall begin by giving a brief overview of the physical environment in which Zelalem's group operated. This is because territory rather than group alliance was the key factor that held them together and which distinguished them from the other two youth gangs I followed.

Territory

Youth gangs live widely dispersed throughout Addis Ababa, with little or no contact with one another. Apart from Zelalem's gang, territory seemed to be immaterial to group cohesion or existence for the other youth gangs. The places where
the two other groups milled or hung out had no clear boundary. They frequently
changed their sleeping places. This was due to constant harassment by the police
and night watchmen guarding shops. Since they gambled with/or robbed rival
gang members, they also had to occasionally escape the gangs they were at war
with. This incessant shift in circumstances meant that they slept on pavements, in
roadside ditches, on shop verandas and at traffic roundabouts. Locating the latest
emplacement of the two all-boy gangs was always a major crusade for me. The
longest time that one gang stayed in any one place was five months. They were
able to build plastic and cardboard makeshift shelters behind an empty dilapidated apartment building. Their shacks were propitiously hidden, away from the
main road and police vigilance, by shrubs and trees and were only accessible via
the excrement-strewn alley. As soon as the owners of the building started carrying out repairs, the police forcibly removed them by burning down their shelters
and blankets (*durito*),[2] and encouraged security guards to harass them day and
night. Such constant physical relocation and the fact they were not attached to
a neighborhood or a community like home-based street children accounted for
their geographical dispersion around the city.

Conversely territory, rather than social network or life circumstances, was the
pivotal factor that brought and held Zelalem's group together. Zelalem and his
friends slept, lounged and gambled next to a church wall, behind a cluster of
trees, which provided shade from the sun and shelter from the rain. The wall was
propitiously positioned opposite an intersection with busy traffic lights where
they begged from passing cars. They received alms from parishioners outside the
church on particular saints' days. Due to their fixed territory, I was able to find at
least one boy from Zelalem's gang any time of the day or night for the next four
years. Zelalem and his friends were cleaner, since they could wash themselves at
the water tap provided by the church for the use of the poor. The other two gangs
were invariably unkempt, unwashed, barefoot and dressed in filthy tattered rags.
They used riverbanks or indescribably dirty public toilets to wash themselves and
considered most public spaces to be open-air latrines. Zelalem and his friends
were also barefoot but used the shrubs further down the road and the church wall
to urinate and defecate.

Zelalem and the gang were able to leave their *duritos* behind the trees growing
alongside the church wall. Older beggars or unlicensed street vendors operating

---

[2] *Durito* is the ubiquitous patched-up blanket homeless children and adults consider their most
precious possession to help them ward off the invariably cold nights in Addis Ababa.

nearby kept an eye on their belongings. This was important since the other two gangs were obliged to wear or carry everything they owned or leave someone behind to watch over their personal effects. This gave them a more menacing and sinister look than they wanted. Zelalem's gang did not need to go far to earn their living, find entertainment or food. The area was alive with shoppers, pedestrians, minibuses, cars, church-goers and revelers until late into the night. The other two gangs operated late afternoon on main roads and dark alleys where the shebeens, bars, bordellos and restaurants were concentrated. There were several affordable tea-shops, bars, restaurants, and video parlors and a bakery in the vicinity of the church. All the children in Zelalem's group were considered credit-worthy in most of these places. This was not the case with the other two gangs who had to pay in cash for everything.

Another crucial point was the existence of one of Mother Theresa's hospices for the dying two miles up the road. As mentioned in chapters 1 and 3, public health centres and government hospitals require patients to present *kebele* identity cards or a letter of reference from the *kebele* before admitting them. In order to acquire an identity card a person has to be domiciled or at least registered in a *kebele*. Since this excluded most destitute persons, the hospice was a last-resort for homeless adults and children. Practically all the children I knew had been patients of the hospice at one time or another. The sick usually waited for the nuns to open their gates before daybreak and hoped to be included among the lucky few desperately ill children and adults admitted each day. The nuns usually admitted those who looked at death's door.

Zelalem's gang shared the church wall with an assortment of jobless young men aged nineteen and over. As already noted such people are called *bozene* (un-employed youths) in Amharic but gang members referred to them as the *gul-betegnotch,* the tough ones or the bullies. The *bozene* looked cleaner and were better dressed than the *borcos*. They had a better social image because they had a home to go to. Although they lived with their families, they had no job prospects or an alternative to loitering in the street. The police seldom harassed them. Those hanging around the church wall offloaded trucks and generally did odd jobs for the numerous bars and restaurants found in the vicinity. They also helped the nuns at Mother Theresa's hospice carry the sick and the dead in exchange for food. These were occasional job offers. Most days, they just sat around waiting for some-thing to happen. They subsidized their meager earnings by extorting 'protection' money from Zelalem and other street children, forcing them to gamble and lose money or arbitrarily robbing them of any cash they had on their persons. Chapter 5 deals more directly on the relationship between the *bozene* and the gang.

Finally, a number of studies have examined how the role of territory, 'race', ethnicity or class plays a pivotal part in the formation and behaviour of youth gangs. As depicted above, territory, rather than group loyalty, was important in shaping the formation of Zelalem's gang and immaterial to the existence or cohesion of the other two gangs. Even so, the group's entry into street life and joining the gang was also inextricably linked to their pre-street childhood experiences and it had little to do with 'race', ethnicity or class. I shall begin by connecting how Zelalem's group came into being with their life histories and territoriality.

Group Formation

There is a paucity of information about how youth gangs begin. In this section, I shall attempt to establish how the Zelalem group came together. All the youth gangs I knew were highly mobile and volatile entities. Their size and composition were in a constant state of flux with new children joining and old members disappearing. Old-timers disappeared and reappeared after quarrelling with their comrades; new recruits replaced some. Individual gang members regularly interacted independent of gang affiliation. I was not able to establish how the other two all-male groups were established, but as I demonstrate in this and the next chapter, I was able to record and then witness the formation of Zelalem's group and the mixed-sex gang.

Five boys from the Zelalem group formed the nucleus of the gang. At least one or two of them were part of the group at one time or another throughout the six years I was in constant touch with them. It took one year before they stopped lying to me and three years before I felt that I had completely won their trust. Eventually, I was able to meet some of the boys' families, visit their homes and talk to their neighbors and siblings. All the children had abandoned their families and not the other way around. This insight into their pre-street family life helped me understand the causes that led each child to abandon his family. It also enabled me to find out how gangs come into being, the nature of intra- and inter-group relations as well as the group's demographic composition. Due to the long period of time I knew them, I was able to witness the painful process of the boys' attempts to disengage themselves from street life and their vain search for non–street-based supportive social alternatives as post-adolescent boys.

There are numerous reasons and ways in which gangs are formed. Since each child is a singular personality, the following pre- and post-street life histories of five members of Zelalem's gang will provide an insight into how the group came together.

Life Stories

Wolamo

Wolamo was born in Wolayta Province. He was short and squat. He was blind in one eye and had the face of a wizened old man. He spoke softly and kept his head lowered when talking to adults. He was unkempt and walked barefoot. The tattered rags he wore were always dirty. He looked as if he had never had a bath or a change of clothes. He was the only one of the group who was loved by the entire gang, and adult beggars, as well as practically all the shoeshine boys eking out a living near the traffic light and the church wall.

Wolamo's family owned a patch of land in a remote village on which they lived. It was too small to support them. His father had to find work periodically in other parts of Ethiopia to make ends meet. He was often away and his mother and two older sisters and brother ran the home most of the year. In 1990, just before the overthrow of the Derg's government, his father disappeared without telling his family where he was going. Wolamo was eight years old. His 18-year-old brother followed suit soon after. After his brother's and father's departures, his mother and sisters were obliged to work on other people's farms. He claims that his two adult sisters beat him constantly and made him skip school in order to help them gather fuel wood and chop logs, which they sold at the local market. Whenever he complained, his mother told him that as the youngest child he was duty-bound to obey blindly his older sisters and they had the right to chastise him. He remembers with some bitterness that his mother did not punish one of his sisters when she threw a stone and blinded his left eye when he was six years old. His father and older brother were away at the time. They were told that it was an accident on their return. Wolamo said that he was too scared of being beaten, or worse, having his other eye taken out by his mother or sisters if he informed his father or brother how he really lost his eye. He often wondered whether he was born out of wedlock and his father had brought him to live with his wife and her daughters and then abandoned the whole family.

Wolamo ran away from home after throwing a stone at the sister who had blinded him in one eye after yet another beating for disobeying her. He was ten years old. He remembers leaving her lying motionless on the ground, with blood gushing out of her head. He made his way to Addis Ababa by boarding an over-crowded cross-country bus. Adult passengers saw him lying under a bench crying and shaking and took pity of him. He told them his father had died and that his stepmother was abusing him. A homeless boy approached Wolamo as soon as he got off the bus and took him to his friends. Wolamo gave them a false name, but they nicknamed him Wolamo after his birthplace. Although the word is at times considered derogatory because of its association with the history of slavery in Ethiopia,[3] he not did mind his friends or anyone else using it to refer to him. He wanted complete anonymity because he did not know whether he had killed his sister. He lived in fear of being caught by the police and hanged for murder. For a long time after he had arrived in Addis Ababa, he kept hoping that he would run

---

[3] Slavery (the actual buying and selling of human beings of Ethiopians by Ethiopians) was abolished by edict in Ethiopian in 1924, although the practice did not end until 1949.

into either his father or his brother. He was often in tears because he was beginning to forget what his father looked like. In time, he began to admit that the chances of him meeting either one or the other on the street were very slim.

The first boy who approached Wolamo when he got off the bus became his mentor, protector and guide. Wolamo followed him to another part of the city when the boy was pushed out of his group for refusing to share his money with the others. The two walked to the airport and joined a new group of boys. Wolamo fell very ill a few weeks after they moved to the new place. His comrades brought him to Mother Theresa's hospice. He was released from the clinic before he was strong enough to walk back to where his friends were. He reached the church wall and fell asleep behind the trees. The next morning people coming to pray gave him food and money. Most of the street children operating around the traffic light and the church at that time were *Gurague* shoeshine boys and newspaper sellers. The rest begged at the traffic lights or from church-goers or carried parcels for taxi and bus passengers, but they went home at night. Those who took refuge near the church wall were older homeless male beggars. He was the first homeless boy to sleep in the rough behind the trees next to the church wall until Tadele joined him.

Wolamo was thirteen years old in May 1995 when I first met him. He had been living near the church wall for about two years. He and I estimated that he must have come to the church wall in April 1993, a few days before Ethiopian Easter. He vividly remembered begging food from rich households and celebrating Easter with old beggars as well as eating meat and butter-saturated leftover food. Wolamo came from a poor rural-based family. On the other hand, Tadele, who joined him approximately three months later, was city born and came from a relatively well-off family.

Tadele

Tadele was born and brought up in Addis Ababa. He was tall, skinny, of dark complexion and handsome. He was argumentative, aggressive, bad tempered and rude to everybody, even to blind and handicapped beggars. He was addicted to cigarettes and *tchat*. No one liked him. He was the only one of the group who did not look like a typical *borco* unless he was wearing his tattered *durito*.

Tadele's father was sixty-eight years old and his mother sixteen when they got married. She gave birth to him soon after her seventeenth birthday. The father had four married daughters from previous marriages. Tadele was his only son and he doted on him. He died when Tadele was seven years old. The mother re-married within a year and had other children. Tadele hated his stepfather. He made life impossible for everyone by his disruptive behavior. I met his mother briefly during one of her visits to the church where she occasionally came to enquire about his well-being. She told me that, after Tadele's father's death, his wealthy family made life impossible for her because they feared that she would claim her rights to his estate. She married her second husband to get away from them and because he agreed to let her keep Tadele with her. She sent Tadele to live with her mother when he tried to throw his newborn half brother out of his cot.

Tadele started running away from home when he was ten years old. His mother and grandmother sought him out and forcibly brought him back home several times. His paternal uncles were frequently asked to talk some sense into him or to physically chastise him. After each beating, Tadele stole money or destroyed property before disappearing again. By the time I met him, his family had finally given up and asked a distant female relative who had a video rental shop not far from the church to keep an eye on him. She alerted them whenever he was in trouble. Tadele knew about the arrangement but refused to have anything to do with her. Tadele's mother, grandmother and other members of his family often came to enquire about his well-being. He invariably accepted whatever gifts they brought and hurled insults at them for everyone to hear. He went back to see his mother or grandmother from time to time. I was there when he came back from three such visits. The first time he boasted that he had destroyed enough property to bankrupt his mother. The second time he stole money from his grandmother. He bought new clothes and spent the rest partying with his friends. The third time he stole jewellery and the housemaid's salary and remained drunk and high for a week.

Tadele had been detained at various police stations and jailed several times for fighting or stealing before I met him in 1995. He told me that his grandmother was present when he appeared in court for the third time. She pleaded with the judge to send him to prison or to a mental institution because she was too old and feeble to control him. They sentenced him to a year in the only remand home for boys in Addis Ababa and released him seven months later. He considered his time in prison as the second betrayal from his family. The first was because everyone consoled and sympathised with his half-sisters while completely ignoring his pain when his father died. He said that he has been in pain and angry since his father died, when he first felt the urge to destroy family property and inflict pain on all his relatives.

The following is a reconstruction of bits of narratives about how he joined the group:

> I landed near the church by accident. I helped carry one of the homeless boys I was hanging around with to Mother Theresa's. I met Wolamo outside the hospice's gate. He was ill but the nuns refused to re-admit him. We started talking. I followed him to the church and nursed him. I was happy to stay with him. The older boys I used to be with beat me if I did not give them money or join in their fights with other gangs. They sometimes forced me to go to my mother's house and steal things. Wolamo and I were the only children sleeping here until Melit joined us and then we let the others become part of our group.

Tadele at fifteen was the oldest boy in the gang when I first made contact with the group. As opposed to the excitable and explosive Tadele, Melit was the epitome of 'masculine cool' and commanded respect from his comrades and the *bozene*.

Melit

Melit means 'baldy' in Amharic. It was his street nickname, which was inspired by his fondness for shaving his thick curly hair. He looked dirty and unkempt. He frowned all the time and this made him look older and more aggressive than he was. He spoke with a very soft voice and avoided making eye contact. He turned his head away from whomever he was talking to. He said little and stood apart from the group. He even slept a little way away from the others. His comrades feared and respected him.

Melit was born and brought up in Addis Ababa, even though he told the others that he was a rural-urban migrant like Wolamo. It took two years before he trusted me enough to tell me his real name and his life story and another year before he asked me to accompany him to his family home. His Oromo mother left him with his *Dorze* father when he was three years old.[4] He did not know her whereabouts. His father was a weaver and owned three wattle-and-daub walled one-room houses. They lived in one and they rented the rest. The place had a large enough compound for three weavers to built a sheltered space in which they could work in comfort. It had a shared kitchen and a pit latrine. Melit's father doted on him but brought another woman to look after him within days of his mother's departure. The women gave birth to two sons and his father married her. Melit's father died when Melit was seven years old. Soon after, his stepmother brought a daughter and son she had from another union to the house. This is how he expressed it:

> My life became hell after that. The woman enrolled all her children in the school and gave them the choicest foods. She bought them all, including the two she had from my father, new clothes, shoes and all their school equipment when school resumed. She told me that she did not have enough money for all of us. I did not have all the exercise books or pencils I needed. I stole from her children and she beat me. I complained but she called me a selfish child. She said that I ought to have some *yilunta*. Her children had never had anything. My father had spoilt me and it was now time for others to have the things I had always taken for granted. My stepsister and I are about the same age. We quarreled all the time. My stepmother beat me every time the girl complained, even if she reported that I had given her a dirty look. I had no one I

---

[4] Ethiopia is a composite of more than seventy ethnic groups. The Oromo group represents approximately 40 per cent of the population. There are concentrated primarily in the southern half of the nation. The 1998 ethnic population census puts the *Dorze* population as being 28,990. They live mostly in the North Omo Region but have a significant community in Addis Ababa. They are famous for their weaving skills.

could tell what was happening to me. She gave my bed to her daughter and bought a bed for the others. She made me sleep on the cold cement floor with a dirty blanket. I had no one to protect me against her oppression. The *dorze* weaver tenants looked on in silence but did nothing because they feared that she might ask them to move out and rent the rooms to other people.

I suffered even more when school was closed during the rainy season. I used to go out in the morning and stay out all day to get away from them. That is when I started begging for money and food. I was always hungry. They all pretended not to notice. I was too angry and ashamed to ask them to feed me. The whole family, including my half-brothers, started calling me a beggar and a vagabond. Finally, I couldn't take it anymore. I stole twenty *birr* and ran away. I thought it was a lot of money; I was ten or eleven years old at the time. I am not sure anymore. It is as if I have always lived like this, an unwanted dog. I prayed everyday that the police or my stepmother would not find me. I have since found out that she never even tried to look for me. I met other children the same day. They helped me spend the money I had on me and then taught me how to live like them. I was very happy at first. We were four children. We slept near a big mosque for a while.

Melit and one of the boys decided to move to another location because of the constant harassment they received from a gang of older street boys. They moved to the city centre and joined another group which Melit did not fit into. He walked to another part of town and joined a group of older street boys. Melit was the only one of the gang who worked during the day. He earned a lot of money by watching cars, carrying out garbage for people living in apartments and begging from traffic lights. The others found out that he was saving up money because he wanted to become a street vendor. They asked him to contribute a certain amount of money each day towards their nightly drinking sessions. If he did not have enough to hand over they beat him. Eventually, Melit refused to give them any money. They found out that he was keeping his money safe with a shopkeeper and forced him to fetch the money. They then went on a drinking spree and gave him a severe beating:

> It was very late at night and I was afraid that they might kill me. I ran and ran and ended up near the church wall. I just lay on the ground and cried myself to sleep. The next morning, Wolamo walked over to where I was. He told me that I could share his *durito* until I acquired my own. He paid for my breakfast and I stayed. Wolamo fell ill soon after this. Tadele and I carried him to Mother Theresa's. He was released two weeks later at the same time as Zelalem. They were both very weak. Zelalem decided to stay with us after we nursed him back to health. Zelalem and I came to the church within weeks of each other.

According to my calculations Melit joined the group on 7 January 1994, Ethiopian Christmas Day. He was fourteen and had been homeless and living on the streets for four years when I met him in 1995. Zelalem joined the group sometime in February 1994.

Zelalem

Zelalem had been homeless and living with other groups for sixteen months before settling with the others near the church wall. He was good-looking, tall, skinny and light-skinned. He had a permanent infection in one eye. This made him look sickly. He had periods when he went to great lengths to keep himself clean and well groomed. These never lasted more than a few days. Most of the time, he was unkempt, barefoot and dirty and looked like a typical *borco*.

Like Tadelle, Zelalem came from a fairly well-to-do family. They both used their real names in the street. They told me that they did not mind people knowing their names because they felt that they were victims of parental abuse and not guilty of any crimes.[5] Zelalem's father was a minor civil servant. His family owned the large villa they lived in. It had four rooms, wattle and daub walls, a cement floor, a corrugated iron roof, a telephone, a big garden, electricity and running water. His mother was an Amhara and his father an Oromo. They met in Harrar where his father was working as a schoolteacher. His mother was visiting her married sister. Soon after they were married, the Derg offered Zelalem's father lucrative government jobs around the Country. Zelalem and his two older brothers were born outside Addis Ababa. Zelalem's father was posted to Addis Ababa in 1988. That is where his two younger sisters were born. This last posting had a negative impact on the entire family:

> We had too much money when my father worked as a high-ranking government of-
> ficial in the rural areas. Father had been a Derg official in charge of land allocation.
> People used to give him gifts of money and food in order to influence him. My mother
> could open the safe and take all the money she needed. He built our house in Addis
> Ababa with the bribe money he accumulated during his service around the country.
> We lived off my father's salary in Addis Ababa. She had to ask him for money all the
> time. She hated doing that. They fought constantly over money and everything else.

Apart from the family's financially more-restrained circumstances, Zelalem's mother was not able to build up the type of support network she had with other women in rural areas. Even though she was born in the city, she claimed not to have relatives or know anyone in Addis Ababa. She told me that they bought their villa with money saved from previous postings, moved in, closed the main gate and her children became her friends and neighbours. Besides choosing to be socially isolated and having marital difficulties, she had to cope with her spirit possession. Zelalem explains it better:

> Because of her *wokabi*,[6] Mother is not able to hire a domestic servant. She had many
> women friends in the rural areas; they knew what to do. The spirit accepted them.

---

[5] I have changed their names to respect their privacy.

[6] *Wokabi*, also known as *Zar*, is spirit possession but can also refer to the person possessed by the spirit.

Since we came to live in Addis Ababa, 'HE' does not want to see anyone in the family, let alone outsiders when 'HE' wants to be with her. When the spirit possesses her, she goes into a trance. 'HE' throws her from wall to wall, from bed to floor. 'HE' makes her bleed from the nose and mouth. She appeases him by performing a special ritual every Wednesdays. I am the only one she is allowed to admit into her room. I know exactly what to do; I started participating when I was five years old. I brew coffee. I get some fresh *tchat* and help her calm 'HIM' down. This can take the whole day and night or just a few hours. If she gets upset or quarrels with father, 'HE' attacks her very, very badly. Even my father fears 'HIM'. Mother cannot help it. 'HE' has taken over and has power over her. She cannot be cured by drinking holy water (*tebel*) or prayers. If she tried, 'HE' might even kill her. 'HE' is very powerful. It will stop when 'HE' wishes to leave her. There are no contradictions about being a Christian and believing in spirit mediums. My family is Christian. We have all been baptised and fast regularly. We even have several bibles at home. Both my mother and father fast during lent and we have all been baptised.

According to the entire family, Zelalem assumed the role of an assistant house-maid as well as being his mother's confidant after they settled in Addis Ababa in 1988. He was then barely seven years old:

I was the only one who helped mother with household chores. I have done ever since I could walk properly. I even helped her when she gave birth to my two little sisters. I did not mind at the time. I love her very much. I am her favourite. The others resented her praising me all the time. She let my father beat my older brothers but he did not dare touch me in front of her. They were all jealous of me.

I left because my siblings and my father treated me like an outsider, a woman and a slave. My brother Samson is an alcoholic. He and my father used to boss me around and beat me if I did not obey them promptly. My father used to call me a girl and say that I would never grow to be a real man. He often said that he was not sure that I was really his son. At the same time, he ordered me to make him tea, serve him his meals or fetch him this and that. He hates me and I do not love him.

Zelalem's father and older brother readily admitted to having physically and ver-bally chastised him in the past. His father justified this by saying that Zelalem was a complicated child who needed to be constantly praised and coaxed into doing anything. He claimed that his wife had spoilt Zelalem and turned him into a whingeing female. Zelalem gave me a multitude of reasons for running away from home. The two recurring themes were his mother going to a Middle Eastern country in 1991, coupled with his hatred of his father and his brother Samson:

My mother acts as a spirit medium from time to time. She cannot help or talk to just anybody. Many go back without an answer to their problems. 'HE' tells her whom to assist. My mother's clients are Christians and Muslims alike. Some give her money and others gifts, although she never asks for anything. She can read coffee cups, interpret dreams and bring luck to unfortunate women who cannot have children or need help with marital problems. My aunt came to visit from Harrar and introduced her to a rich Arab woman. My mother solved her problem and the women took her to the Middle East.

Zelalem's older brother fell very ill soon after their mother left for the Middle East. All the housemaids they hired left, complaining that it was too much work for them to cope with such a big and unruly family. His two sisters were three and five years old at the time and therefore too young to be of any use. Zelalem was the only one who was willing to nurse his brother Samson and take care of domestic work. Father and brother told me repeatedly that Zelalem ran away because he missed his mother too much and not because of their constant abuse. Zelalem says he had run away from their tyranny:

I ran away from home when I was eleven years old, a year after Mother abandoned me. Father ordered me to pay his rotating saving scheme (*iqub*) in another part of town. I told him that I was tired from doing the housework alone and that he should ask one of my older brothers. He slapped me and even refused to give me taxicab money. I felt very bitter. I just walked aimlessly for hours. I entered a church and cried until dark. A very old beggar approached me. I told him that my mother had died and that my step-brothers and stepfather were making my life impossible. He offered to raise me. He took my money for safekeeping and told me to sell my shoes and wear tattered clothes so that we could earn more money begging. I was not very happy with him but I was too proud to go back home and beg my father for forgiveness. I hated him then; I hate him even more now. One day with God's help, I shall show him that I am a man and that he has no right to treat me like a female. No, I cannot ask my mother's *wokabi* to curse him. It is her thing. I fear 'HIM' very much. He is very powerful and unpredict-able. 'HE' may want to have me in his power. I do not want this to happen.

I left the old beggar after three weeks because I resented doing for him what I did for my family and handing over the money I earned from begging. I forced him to give me back the money he was keeping for me by threatening to go to the police. I think it was just over fifty *birr*. I joined a group of street children I used to meet while I was begging with the old man. I felt happy and free with them. We spent the money partying and eating good food. They taught me everything I know about hustling and begging. I fell ill and the children carried me to Mother Theresa's hospice. Wolamo and I were re-leased at the same time before we were well enough to take care of ourselves. Melit and Tadele nursed us back to health. Wolamo is the only other human being apart from my mother that I love and trust. I decided to stay. Godje is a relative newcomer.

Zelalem was fourteen years old when we first met and had been living in the streets for four years. Although he pretended to be a rural-urban migrant, he looked and acted streetwise. Godge was the personification of a rural-urban run-away child. He looked out of place in the street. His attitude towards adults and language set him apart from the others.

Godje

Although I had already spotted the gang, it took me two months of walking past him or standing next to him trying to chitchat before Godje began to acknowledge my presence. Unlike the others, he was able to sit still and silent for hours. I found this fascinating. In desperation, I sat next to him, waited a long time and exclaimed that he was talking too much. This made him laugh and from then on we began to have a few words. It was through Godje that I was able to befriend the others, although Zelalem always claimed to have 'found' me first and that he therefore had a special relationship with me. This meant that I had to constantly prove to the others that they were all 'my friends', especially when he was around.

Godje was born in Godjam, hence the nickname Godje. He did not want anyone to know his real name. He joined the group in January 1995 and had been with the group for five months when I first met him. He was twelve years old. He looked younger than his age. He told me that he knew his age because he was born on Christmas Day and his mother told him how old he was every year. He had a very 'pretty' girlish face, beautiful teeth and an impish smile. His clothes were always dirty and tattered. He kept his hair short and washed his face frequently. He looked out of place among the others because of his small size and obsequious demeanour. He looked more like a home-living street child than a *borco*. He was self-effacing and did not say much. He had run away from home aged ten because of the constant beatings he received from his father. This is how he explained it:

> We had two cows, one bull, a few goats and sheep. We were four children. My mother was barely fourteen when she gave birth to me. I had two younger sisters and a baby brother who was only four when I ran away. As the oldest boy, it was my duty to care for the animals. Girls do not herd; they help around the house and in the fields. I used to get up before dawn to take the animals to a shepherd before going to school. I went back later in the afternoon to lead them back to their stable. This was very difficult for me. I had to run up and down to keep them together. All along the way, the sheep strayed into people's fields. I think the shepherd did not allow them to wander around and feed because he was afraid of losing them. They were always hungry. Whenever the farmers complained to my father, he beat me with a stick or pinched my thighs and arms. He also beat my mother and all of us whenever he was drunk.
>
> I ran away from home because I lost two cows on a Christmas Day. I took the herd to the field and joined other boys in a game of Christmas hockey (*yegena tchewata*). It was my birthday and I felt happy. I forgot all about the animals until late afternoon but by then the cows had disappeared. I had lost one cow before. She was new and headed for her original home. It took three days to get her back. My father beat me so hard that I could not walk for a long time. He did not even stop when my mother begged him to beat her instead and threw herself on my body. He beat us both until he was too tired to lift his stick. These two cows had been with us a long time. I had no way of knowing which way they had gone. My friends and I looked for them until it got dark. One of my friends went to look in my family's compound and could not spot them. I decided

to run away there and then. I made my way to the bus station. I threw myself at the feet of the drivers and begged them to take me to Addis Ababa. I told them that my father had died, that my stepmother was oppressing me, and that I wanted to join my older brother in Addis Ababa. I was crying so hard that they felt sorry for me.

Godje met two boys soon after he got off the bus and joined their gang. After a few weeks, the two boys fell out with the others and decided to move on. Godje followed them. They joined a large group of older boys in another part of the city. His friends stole two *duritos* and disappeared. Even though he had nothing to do with it, the others beat him up. It was late at night. Godje walked up the road and fell asleep outside the church gate. Godge again: 'The next morning Tadele spotted me. They all saw that I was hurt and that I had been crying. They told me that I could stay with them if I wanted to. At first, I slept with Tadele because I did not have my own *durito*. He was soon fed up with me, so I borrowed money from the others and bought my own. I am now twelve years old. I think I came to Addis Ababa two years ago.'

Summing Up

As can be deduced from above, the children come from varied ethnic backgrounds and poverty was not always the cause that led the children to abandon their families. Even though I have been able to reconstruct how Zelalem's group came into being, there is no fixed pattern to how street children form a gang or enter a group. I heard all sorts of combinations from the other two all-male groups; none could tell me for certain who started the gang or how they came together. Some of the boys' stories contradicted what another boy had told me. As indicated above, the causes that spurred each boy to enter street life or join the group were as diverse as their family and ethnic background. All of them had previous experiences of surviving in the street and gang life before joining the group. Tadele and Zelalem had some contact with their families since they lived in Addis Ababa. They both considered the emotional relationship they had with their parents unsatisfactory. They also had complete control over the amount of contact or type of relationship they had with their parents, siblings or close relatives. Although his stepfamily lived in Addis Ababa, Melit lived in the abject emotional and material abandonment that followed the death of his father. He had run away from the constant abuse of his stepmother and stepsister. Wolamo and Godje were runaways from rural areas. Both had been physically and mentally abused by family members. Both knew where to find their families but had decided never to see them again.

Like most of the homeless boys I have talked to, Zelalem and his friends had all been badly abused by their respective families. This abuse is an extension of the culturally sanctioned practice of verbally and physically disciplining children that I have described in chapters 2 and 3. My data show that it is not only parents who abuse their parental authority. It is not uncommon for children to be mistreated by stepmothers, uncles and especially by half-siblings as well as stepsisters and stepbrothers. I have recorded seventeen cases of runaway boys and girls under the age of thirteen. They had all tried to escape the tyranny of one or more members of their extended families. They all joined a gang for a short period of time before being either reunited with their families or joining other groups of homeless children.

Gang Life

The literature on street children and youth gangs is full of stories about the enduring, supportive and affective relationships existing among them (see Ennew 1994; Aptekar 1988; Swart 1988; Sharf et al. 1986; Lucchini 1993). These traits were lacking among the gangs I studied. I found that all four gangs I knew had set up a highly unstable society. The instability stemmed from the over-riding concern held by each child with his own personal freedom of action and his need for immediate organisation. By immediate organisation, I mean that the children wanted to be part of a group and its loose, organisational structure, while being apart from it. They all liked the idea of being able to move in and out of the group at will and they frequently did so. They treasured their freedom to choose how to spend their money and their ability to socialise with any member of the group or with outsiders. Their need to act autonomously and to adhere to group life constituted two primary values that modified the ethic of reciprocity.

In spite of the absence of strict regulatory codes governing their conduct, the children themselves used Amharic words in current usage to describe their activities. They talked of group life in terms of *abro menor* (living together). They referred to working, begging and making a living as *meshekel* (hustling/trading). They described affective and friendly bonds that held them together as *guadenet* (friendship) and their economic transactions as *metebaber*, which loosely translated means co-operating. Health matters or nursing each other was *mastamem* and bereavement was *lekso*. Minor crimes and misdemeanours were *matchberber* (deceiving) and *mesrek* (stealing). Most forms of violence or fighting among themselves were explained away as quarrelling or *metalat*. In real life, these activities did not involve networking on the part of the individual child. It meant entering into a complex and imperfect system of reciprocity that did not always provide the individual child with the supportive companionship system he sought.

All the gangs I knew were highly mobile, volatile entities with constant changes in the composition of their groupings. This made it difficult for me to explain the interactions between them in terms of social network or exchange theory. The type of emotional and economic exchange that existed among the four gangs I followed is best analyzed in terms of reciprocity. In the social sciences, reciprocity as a concept refers to the establishment and maintenance of relationship between persons or social groups. Reciprocity is said to unite people through a relationship of exchange and divide them as separate members of the exchange relationship (see Mauss 1955; Polanyi 1968; Sahlins 1974). Marshall Sahlins (1974) elaborated the significance of reciprocity by creating three types of links between material flow and social relations, each correlated with social distance. Generalized reciprocity is the flow of free gifts or the sharing of resources without strict measurement of obligation to repay between close kinsmen or within a restricted or intimate social group. It is characterized by the existence of a diffuse obligation of return, which is moral rather than economic in nature. Balanced reciprocity is a form of exchange between structural equals, who trade or exchange goods or services with the strict expectation of return. It is less personal and moral and more economic in type. Negative reciprocity is characteristic of interaction between enemies or distant groups. It involves maximizing one's profit at the expense of others and may take the form of haggling, thieving or even raiding in war. Sahlins suggests that all three types of reciprocity form a continuum, which correlates kinship ties and social distance. He also affirms that as exchange creates groups, so it creates boundaries between individuals and groups. This double function of uniting and setting apart made reciprocity an apt analytical tool for interpreting the social, affective and economic relationship of the members of youth gangs I studied.

The above-listed recurring themes in their lives and narratives may not have covered the totality of their experiences in the street, but they were the issues I found readily identifiable as crucial to their way of life. The same issues are also an indication of the manner in which they developed personal relationships with other gang members and non-related adults in the street. I shall therefore use them as indicators to illustrate the link between economic exchange, group life, affective relationships and emotional distance among the groups of homeless boys I knew.

Living Together – *Abro Menor*

Many researchers have shown the importance of membership in the group for the individual street child's survival strategies and to allow each child to have a role to play in group activities (see Aptekar 1988; Swart 1988; Sharf et al. 1986; Lucchini 1993; Ennew 1994). All the gang members I knew expressed a pronounced desire for autonomy coupled with a need to feel part of the gang. This need for freedom and organization was exceptionally reflected in the ill-defined rules governing entry to and exit from the group. It was also made evident by the total lack of leadership and/or explicit roles for the individual child to join in group activities within the all-male gangs. In chapter 5, I describe how and why leadership and explicit roles for girls and boys were major issues in the mixed-sex gang. The following demonstrates how the rules governing entry into and exit from the group as well as leadership and other roles throw light on group dynamics.

Entry – Exit

Although the ease of entry varied from gang to gang, formal initiation rites destined for aspiring gang members were not present among the groups I studied (see Rogers 2003). I never saw or heard of any member of Zelalem's all-male group actively recruiting newcomers. They all admitted that as soon as their numbers increased the atmosphere around them deteriorated. More children meant more visibility, more fighting among group members and more trouble with the police and the *gulbetegnotch,* their bullies. As I shall demonstrate in chapter 5, recruiting other children, especially girls by girls, was more important to the mixed-sex gang. All those who joined Zelalem's group did so voluntarily. Entry into the group was problematic only when one of the established members took a dislike to a newcomer. Re-integration into the group was unconditional as long as there were no scores to be settled or debts to be paid. The price of assimilation was the extent of exploitation a child was willing to suffer initially at the hands of one or two members of the gang. Although there were no hard and fast rules for recruiting a newcomer, the one who talks to a newcomer first usually feels a sense of 'ownership' over him long after the event. There was an unwritten agreement between Zelalem and his friends that, when a newcomer joined them, the one who met him first had the right to exploit him. This explains why Zelalem kept insisting that he 'found' me first even when the others insisted that I was Godje's 'friend' first.

All the homeless children I knew have told me that they felt free and happy when they first joined a gang. A new kid did not have time to get scared. His finder became his special friend, adviser, patron and exploiter. If the child had any money or valuables that could be sold, his finder helped him spend the money. The new boy followed his mentor everywhere he went, ran errands, played and begged with him – that is, until he tired of his subservient role and refused to team up with his finder. More often than not, one of the *gulbetegnotch* would then assert his right to take over the role of mentoring and pressurized the child to either gamble or supply him with cash or cigarettes. This exploitative relationship therefore lasted only as long as the newcomer accepted the situation. All the street children I saw joining any of the three all-male gangs found ways of avoiding giving or sharing all their earnings within two or three weeks of joining a group. Many voted with their feet as soon as the situation became unbearable. Some disappeared and reappeared several times before giving up the idea of becoming part of the gang.

Twenty-three children joined Zelalem's group while I was carrying out my research. A few had already lived with other gangs of boys or were running away either from their families or from other street children. Only two remained with the group for more than a year, the rest were pushed out or left after a few days or weeks. Bed-wetting, excessive farting, talking too much, bragging, lying, being a know-it-all, cowardice, stealing from gang members and whingeing were some of the grounds for evicting a newcomer. However, I have heard the original five occasionally accuse each other of having one or more such undesirable habits. Since there were no set rules about staying with the group, those who left or were rejected were children who did not manage to fit in somehow.

Among Zelalem's group, Godje was the smallest and most vulnerable child. The *gulbetegnotch* forced him to run errands, gamble or hand over money on demand. He was often beaten or harassed by Tadele, his finder. Godje frequently left the group and slept across the street or behind the church with adult homeless beggars for a few days. This is how he explained his need to re-integrate himself in the group: 'What I really want is to live with them and have them leave me alone at the same time.'[7]

Simply stated, Godje wanted to be part of the group while at the same time being apart from the group. He wanted to be an insider and an outsider. The other reasons he gave for staying with the group were also similar to the countless explanations I was given by other such children. He felt lost, unloved, lonely and depressed when he was by himself. He was scared of sleeping alone. Even though older street boys and the *gulbetegnotch* abused Godje constantly, they also abused other children. Their abusive behavior did not hurt him as much as his own father's. Besides, he knew that he could leave the group any time he chose to.

Leadership and other Roles

In the literature, gangs display clear leadership, well-developed lines of authority and other organizational features including recognizable codes of conduct. Zelalem's group, much as the other two gangs of predominantly homeless boys I befriended, lived together in a loose-knit social group. Actually, all three gangs had no leader per se. There were no structural criteria delineating individual gang members' social roles within any of the groups I studied. They all assured me that they did not have a leader. If anyone declared himself as leader of the gang or wanted to be their chief, the others would plot his violent downfall. No, they did not have a name for their gang. No, they did not function like a football team or a household. No, they were not controlled marginally or otherwise by anyone in the group. They just had nicknames for each other, imposed or self-selected.

---

[7] This is how he expressed it in Amharic: '*Kenesu gar eyenork; arfew betewugn new emefelegew.*'

They did not necessarily have their meals together or go to watch videos as a group. They begged at the traffic light alone or in twos or threes. The only times they were all together was at night, early morning or during the hottest times of the afternoons when they lounged behind the trees to sleep, gamble and smoke cigarettes. However, there were times when one or two members of the group were able to force or pressurise the others to contribute to leisure activities or into doing other things that they did not want to do. This included roaming around town at night, gambling with other gangs of boys in other parts of the city, seeing the same film more than once or joining in inter-gang warfare.

Studies in South America and South Africa imply that gang members create a world with its own rules, style and status structure, including involvement in particular kinds of delinquent behaviour (see Aptekar 1988; Swart 1990; Glazer 2000). Even though Zelalem's gang did not adhere to any script regarding how they lived together, there were certain things they all agreed to. Stealing money, *duritos,* food or patrons from other members of the gang was not accepted. Informing the police, family members or any outsiders about the whereabouts of a missing comrade or his social and economic activities was considered an act of betrayal. Refusing to help an injured or sick comrade, not lending money for food and running away when complete strangers or other gangs attacked them were not tolerated. Infringement of the above proscriptions resulted in ostracism, exclusion or, more often than not, a severe beating. From time to time the above-mentioned principles were ignored, bent or changed at the whim of a bigger boy or a couple of boys within the group. These occasional betrayals, as they called them, more than the beatings, hurt the victims. I have seen Tadele kick and punch Wolamo for not wanting to gamble with him, for not waking him up on time to join the others for breakfast and other trivial reasons. Zelalem once severely beat Wolamo, his favourite person, for not warning him that the *gulbetegnotch* were waiting to pounce on him and steal his money. The list is endless.

The above notwithstanding, all three gangs had a special child who was the object of the entire group's affection. Wolamo was the beloved of his group. A sickly boy nicknamed Papas (the pope) and a very skinny boy called Tyson were the most liked children in the other two groups. Leadership qualities did not come into this. Wolamo was liked for being compassionate, self-effacing and kind. Papas was loved for being gentle, pious and patient. He did not drink, smoke or gamble and attended church regularly. His comrades empathised with Tyson because he was meek and harmless. He had innumerable scars all over his skinny body because of years of physical abuse by his stepmother. Melit was feared and admired in equal measure for being sombre, silent, self-sufficient, fearless and reflective. Even the *gulbetegnotch* were wary of him. They considered him fearsome in anger and steadfast when the group was at war with other gangs. Even though he was never the leader of the pack, he was the epitome of an Ethiopian alpha male. In short, he commanded respect for upholding the dominant values regarding manliness in the 'wider Ethiopian culture'. None was treated differently or given prominent positions within the group. No one physically abused Papas, perhaps because of his illness. Tyson was his gang's skivvy and was verbally reprimanded or slapped around by older boys and the *gulbetegnotch* for not obeying orders with alacrity. The same action would have resulted in any other boy being kicked or severely beaten. They judged and valued each other's qualities or defects with the same conventions and social expectations used by mainstream society. I did not have to ask the children what they meant by this and that. It was very easy for me to grasp the rationale governing their code of behaviour, since it was imbued with the same communal sense of *yilunta* I was raised with.

Street Work – *Meshekel*

Many factors separated gangs of homeless boys from the adult-organized social world but not from adults. Zelalem's group survived by begging from adults and by interacting on a daily basis with waiters, shopkeepers, the police, adult beggars and numerous jobless youths and unemployed adults. However, their lifestyle, their homeless status and their identity as *borcos* militated against any of them gaining a foothold into the already desperate job market or a place in the public health and formal education sectors. As far as work was concerned, they either did not have a *kebele* identity card or the pay was so low that they could not have fed themselves as well as they did from street life, let alone afford to rent a house or pay for leisure activities.

Street children living with their families had some kind of permanence, or at least continuity, in their lives. Their mothers were located within various social network systems, which enabled the children to access a modicum of education and health care. They, or their mothers, were able to derive some material or social support from neighbors and connections with community-based voluntary associations. Zelalem and his kind were not even able to rely on each other to secure their daily bread in times of hardship. Their need to live 'as part' of and yet 'apart' from the group superseded their need to work as a team. Apart from times of illness or bereavement, the same imperfect reciprocity that existed in their work relationship permeated every other aspect of their lives.

There was some kind of division of labor within families of street children, street-working children and the jobless youths who preyed on them. Street vending, portaging, working and begging activities were taken up by anyone when the opportunity arose. Since there were few opportunities for either group to earn a decent living, this often caused skirmishes among the street children, jobless youths and older men. The worst fracas occurred when cars broke down and several of them wanted to help push-start it or when they all offered themselves to help carry parcels. Zelalem's group operated outside this fray, unless they had hopes of picking the pockets of onlookers.

I seldom saw the older gangs beg or work during daylight. Whenever I met them in the late or early morning, they were either asleep or looked as if they had just woken up with a severe hangover. They operated at night or very early in the morning. They roamed around supermarkets, traffic lights, bars, nightclubs and restaurants and begged from drivers, shop owners and clients alike. At times they woke up to find money left there by pedestrians on their way to church or work. On particular Saints' Days, they mingled with the lepers, the handicapped and other beggars in order to receive alms in the form of food, clothing and money from worshippers. Their physical appearance and age precluded them from evoking the same kind of sympathy that younger street children, women with babies and the handicapped elicited from drivers. Pedestrians, especially women, were intimidated by the way they looked. Most shop owners did not want them in their car parks or outside their shops. They hired guards to keep them away from their customers. This is how one of the older boys explained their predicament:

> We cannot keep ourselves clean. We sleep on pavements, on shop verandas, in ditches, anywhere convenient. We have no homes. The *bozene* may be young and jobless but they have families and homes to go to at night if they want to. We are *duriyes* (vagabonds) and people know it. We cannot fool them. Many of the *bozene* you see hanging around here were born and raised in this neighborhood. They have home addresses and identity cards from their *kebele*. When they are caught doing something by the police, one of their friends alerts their family. We have no one to rescue us. If we try to compete or take over some of their jobs, they will call the police and have us evicted from here for good.

When I began my enquiries in 1995, none of the children I met had any kind of identity document, because none were registered in any *Kebele*. On September 1999, three gang members proudly showed me identity cards with their pictures on them stating that they were registered with an NGO. They told me that they could finally go about their business without fear of being harassed by the police. Although this did not help them get out of street life or shield them from police violence when they were caught misbehaving, they were the lucky few. In reality, such children had no established network system they could count on for leisure, shelter, nurturing, feeding or protection from physical danger for any length of time.

Zelalem's group experienced many of the problems faced by the older gangs. However, their ideal geographical position enabled them to survive more or less by begging from drivers at the traffic lights opposite the church. The group faced hardship whenever the traffic lights were not working. Since power cuts were and are still common in Addis Ababa, these occurrences could last a few hours or days. The first thing they did when they ran out of money was to run up credit from the few tea-houses and very cheap restaurants where they were considered credit-worthy. The problem was that, when one of them defaulted, the owners held them collectively responsible. This caused rifts and recriminations within the group since it went against their desire to act autonomously. Debt-ridden children facing their comrades' resentment either disappeared altogether or left the group until they could pay back their debts. Restaurant owners made sure that they were paid in full and informed each other about defaulting gang members.

Every now and again the police intensified their vigilance and violence in order to rid the streets of homeless adults, street children and handicapped beggars. These exercises often lasted several days or weeks and were the only times when Zelalem and his friends were unable to feed themselves. The group had a range of options during such times. Their first coping strategy was to risk police violence or detention by continuing to beg at the traffic lights. Their second coping strategy was to compete with other destitute people for begging opportunities outside the church and from rich households in the vicinity of the traffic lights. During such lean times they also bought or begged leftover food from adult beggars on credit, or worse still, rummaged in municipal garbage bins. Their last-resort coping strategy was to either migrate to other parts of the city or beg away from the streets and as far away from the police as possible. It meant begging from door to door. Watchmen or maid-servants either gave them leftover food or told them to go away. They had to work for several hours in order to obtain enough leftover food to make it worth their while.

Zelalem and Wolamo were very good at begging for food. They often went begging together. Melit and Godje preferred to beg on their own. Tadele was the only one who refused to beg from house to house. His comrades said it was because he was aware of the class position of his rich family; he was too proud to beg. This is in spite of the fact that he was supposed to have no *yilunta* whatsoever about begging from comrades and other beggars including lepers when he needed money for cigarettes and other things. Tadele said that he was not as lucky as the others at eliciting pity from people because he was too tall and looked older than the average street children.

Although they all earned their living by begging from drivers at the traffic lights, Zelalem, Wolamo and Godje earned extra money from their patrons. These were Ethiopians and foreigners who gave them more than a few coins in preference to other children. The boys referred to such people as their customers or *dembegnotch*. Several newcomers were severely beaten and evicted for trying to 'steal' a gang member's customer. This type of patronage never gravitated to another level since these were brief and chance encounters at the traffic light. The three boys occasionally hit the jackpot and had regular clients who gave them money or unwanted garments. Tadele was the only one who did not have a special customer. The others explained that he was too arrogant and had not learnt to act humble in front of adults. His mother had not physically chastised him enough or inculcated him with a sense of *yilunta*.

Zelalem's group did not attempt to combine their begging activities with working as street vendors or porters or watching cars. They explained that they earned
more money from begging at the traffic lights in a few hours than did most street
children in a day. Besides, the *gulbetegnotch* would rob them at night of anything
they were selling. Other street children and salespersons from around the church
told me that the boys loved gambling and were addicted to liquor, hashish and
cigarettes. They regularly roamed around all night and got drunk. They therefore
had hangovers or were too tired be able to function normally during the day. This
was not far from the truth.

Friendship and Cooperating – *Guadenet* and *Metebaber*

Zelalem and his friends displayed the same need for individual freedom and being part of group life in their emotional and financial dealings with each other
as they did in everything else. Friendship bonds (*guadenet*), especially during leisure activities, meant establishing temporary emotional bonds with one or several
comrades. Such affective relationships brought them closer to achieving Sahlins's
(1974) generalized reciprocity, where free gifts or resources, as well as emotional
support, are shared without strict measurement or obligation to repay. Conversely,
economic exchanges, which they euphemistically called cooperating (*metebaber*),
involved a complex system of reciprocity, with the individual child entering into
intricate debit/credit relationships with one or more members of the group. These
in-group economic exchanges reflected some form of balanced reciprocity, i.e.
more of an economic than a personal or moral type of material exchange between
structural equals. However, like most things in their life as a group, the rules and
regulations governing their affective relations and material transactions were at
times discarded, evaded or arbitrarily changed. Unrequited love and unrequited
reciprocity are words that best express these emotional and economic exchanges.
I shall therefore use unrequited love to describe their affective relationships and
unrequited reciprocity to describe their economic exchanges.

Unrequited Love

Gang affiliation did not foster emotional bonds among all the three gangs I knew.
The moral standards by which Zelalem and other homeless children judged each
other's behaviour and described their emotional bonds were similar to those used
by most Ethiopians. This was because like the home-based street children, their
natal families had imbued them with local cultural and universal human values,
including a sense of *yilunta,* before they entered the street world aged ten and
older. However, the *borcos* had an extreme need for autonomy, which precluded

the formation of enduring affective emotional attachment among themselves and therefore a long-lasting sense of responsibility for one another. Since none of them felt that they belonged anywhere nor felt secure in the warmth of the group, their sense of *yilunta* or shame shifted with circumstances. In fact, the *only* constant in their lives was the importance of displaying masculine traits such as not loosing face or being called a woman.

All the homeless boys I knew spent most of their time forming temporary or inconsequential alliances with one another. In addition to appreciating the beloved of the groups like Wolamo, Tyson and Papas, each child strove to establish a long- or short-term attachment to one or two members of their gang. However temporary, the friendship bonds that united an individual child to another were vital, both to the quality of their emotional well-being and relationship to the group as a whole. Emotional attachment to another member of the group meant having someone special with whom to share leisure activities or unburden one's grief. It also meant that there might be someone who would stand up for you during a quarrel with another member of the gang, or failing that, someone who would console or nurse you after a beating or verbal abuse by other comrades.

The most distressing thing I have heard them recount is betrayal by that special friend in whom they had invested all their emotions and trust. Zelalem was forever trying to be Melit's or Wolamo's special friend. He also desperately sought to endear himself to one and all with kindness and generosity. He was unfortunate in his quest since everyone he got close to eventually rejected him. He was emotionally very needy but so were all the others. His problem was that that he could not hide this vulnerable and 'unmanly' trait. Wolamo explained this better:

> Zelalem wants to force us to love him. He is very kind and helpful and we all love him but he spoils it by trying very hard to please one or the other. He wants to be praised for every little thing he does. He is not ashamed to cry openly like a woman and for hours if he is upset with one of us. We all get embarrassed by the way he bootlicks the *gulbetegnotch*. As soon as one of them raises his hand to hit him, Zelalem begs for mercy like a girl. I sometimes feel like beating him again after they have finished with him. He is always threatening to leave town, to leave us and so on whenever he feels rejected. He never goes very far. We sometimes beg him to stay just to shut him up.

Ironically, Zelalem's need to be loved, appreciated and praised all the time were the very same accusations leveled against him by his father and siblings. Melit explains:

> Zelalem can be elated, happy and your best friend one day and depressed or angry the next. If Wolamo or I refuse his invitation to party with him when he has a lot of money, he gets very upset or tearful like a girl. He nags and nags like a woman and emotionally pressurises one of us to go with him. He chooses where we go, how long we stay in one place and what we must do and eat. The problem starts when he runs out of money because he expects whoever he has chosen to spend his money with to

be grateful and hang around with him forever. I just pick a quarrel with him before he finishes his money and let him cry and sulk for a while.

Tadele's erratic behaviour and lack of socially desirable traits such as compassion, sense of honour and shame (i.e. *yilunta*) or fairness, more than his bad temper and violence against smaller children, condemned him in the eyes of his comrades. The traits Tadele was said to lack are the very same personal characteristics that are considered culturally unbecoming in a decent person in the 'wider Ethiopian culture'. Godje explains:

> No one loves Tadele, not even Wolamo the saint. Tadele tries very hard to be Melit's special friend but Melit avoids him all the time, even when he knows that Tadele has money for partying. Tadele has no sense of shame. He does not care what people think of him (*yilunta yelewoom*). He does not fear God's retribution. He even begs from the beggar girl with the newborn baby living on the other side of the church wall. He thinks he owns me because I am the only child he has ever 'found'. As soon as I sense that our quarrels are irritating the others I give in for peace sake.

Wolamo put it as follows: 'Tadele is capable of starting a quarrel about anything. He accuses someone of having lied to him or anything. He beats up and threatens the smaller boys unless they buy him cigarettes or lend him money that he never pays back. Even the *gulbetegnotch* get fed up eventually and let him have his way. He abuses me because I do not like fighting and Godje because he is the smallest.' Wolamo basked in the knowledge that they all liked him. He was praised for displaying culturally recognised attractive qualities such as generosity, compassion as well as being self-effacing and helpful. They all liked spending time in his company and often chose to spend their money with him when they felt like partying unless they were trying to endear themselves to a particular comrade. This did not stop Tadele or Zelalem from insulting or beating him or the *gulbetegnotch* from abusing him. Wolamo felt deeply hurt by this abuse. He liked being with Melit most. Melit returned his affection. They often joshed and hugged each other, walked with their small fingers entwined or performed *Dorze* and *Gurague* traditional dances in unison. They deloused each other's heads and mock wrestled. These were occasional displays of affection. Neither Wolamo nor Melit stood up for one another against the others or the *gulbetegnotch,* nor did they team up for leisure activities.

Melit was said to be self-assured and dependable. He minded his own business. He did not try to endear himself to anyone else but Wolamo. He was the only one who occasionally stood up to Tadele and the *gulbetegnotch*. He was feared, admired, hated and respected for having masculine traits. Although he never showed any weakness in front of his comrades, he often cried when he was alone with me. Two years after I met him, he sobbed for hours while he was telling me about his tragic relationship with his stepfamily.

The whole group had ambivalent feelings towards Godje. On the positive side, Godje minded his own business; he was polite, friendly and humble. On the negative side he was considered too much of a loner, too secretive, selfish and wrongfully unfeeling. Godje was easily hurt by his comrades' behaviour towards him. He just made sure that none of them saw him cry or knew the depth of his feelings. He liked to project the image of a tough, self-assured man. He often named Melit as his male role model. The others often called him a *hodam* – a glutton or one who only thinks about his stomach. Zelalem put it this way:

> We all contribute a few cents if one of the comrades is short of money to buy his lunch, especially once we are in the tea-shop. Godje pretends not to notice and/or claims that he has no money. Worse still, we all know that he prefers to go to restaurants and eat alone and that he spends most of his money on food. He is very selfish and can only think of his safety and stomach. He has to be pressurised or intimidated in order to join in when we want to party or have to fight other gangs. I do not know why he stays with us and why we let him stay with us. I suppose it is because he minds his own business most of the time. Besides, the *gulbetegnotch* focus on him and Wolamo because they earn the most money. This makes them go easy on the rest of us.

Godje explained that he did not care for drinking, playing pinball machines, watching violent videos or gambling. He liked food, especially meat.

> I used to think that my father was rich. I now realise how poor we were. I was always hungry at home. There was not much food. We hardly ever ate meat, unless it was during festive times. My mother knew that I liked meat and would put pieces of meat in my mouth (*goursha*) at such times, since the adults ate the choicest pieces. She kept chickens. From time to time, she would boil an egg and secretly gave it to me before I left with the cattle in the morning. I hate lending the others money. Apart from Wolamo, no one else pays me back. I spend most of my money eating because I know that either the *gulbetegnotch* or one of them will expect me to either gamble or contribute to buying cigarettes or booze. I regularly hide most of my money, leave some cash in my pocket, and let the *gulbetegnotch* rob me in order to be left alone. I have to make sure that Tadele the coward or Zelelem the wimp do not tell on me.

Godje told me that he really liked being with Wolamo, but he could not compete with the others for his affection. If Zelalem were not such an emotionally erratic fellow, he might have liked him more. He loathed Tadele and was wary of Melit. He hated spending his money partying with the others and resented being forced to do so. His comrades remarked that he remained an insider/outsider by design as well as by default. Zelalem told me that, although Melit minded his own business, they all felt that he was part of the gang. Godje did not project Melit's sense of belonging to the group to the others. This was why no one tried to be his special friend or to protect him from Tadele or the *gulbetegnotch*. They were all amazed and in awe at his capacity to endure pain in silence. No matter how hard he was beaten, he never cried or pleaded. He just took all the beating, walked across the street and sulked in silence.

Godje hated all the *gulbetegnotch* for being bullies and for extorting money from him and the others. He also told me that he never cried in front of the others, just as he never cried when his father beat him. He knew this infuriated them. It was the only revenge he could muster against their tyranny. He was always in tears whenever he told me how one or another of his comrades had been cruel to him or when he described his father's violence against him and his mother.

Unrequited Reciprocity

Jill Swart (1990) states that the Malunde practised a complex system of reciprocity that involved an intense network of debit/credit relationships. They also kept a mental record of who owed what or who lent what. The result was that those who did not reciprocate ended up being excluded from the network. A somewhat similar form of purely economic exchange existed in the organisational set-up of all the three groups I studied. They assisted one another or exchanged foods and other goods with the strict expectation of return. They generally abided by this principle but occasionally made crucial exemptions when it suited them, thus distorting Sahlins's classic 'balanced reciprocity' model.

Conversely, other research showed that the Strollers of Cape Town continually reinforced each other in their survival activities, in their joys and fears. In the majority of cases, they shared their earnings equally among themselves (see Sharf et al. 1986). In other words, the Strollers practised Sahlin's 'generalised reciprocity'. In real life, the manner in which Zelalem and the rest of the gang regulated their material transactions was flawed and unstable because of the boys' individual need to act autonomously while belonging to the group.

The type of reciprocity that existed among all three groups encapsulated a loose obligation of a moral nature sometimes with and sometimes without expectation of restitution or a strict economic inter-change of money and other goods. The borderline between obligations of a moral or of an economic nature was blurred since it shifted according to circumstances and the whim of the individual child who would forget all sense of *yilunta* in order to achieve his goal. This lack of strict measurement of economic or moral obligation created an unstable set of circumstances they all had to deal with. They considered lending or borrowing from each other to be an economic transaction. They often abided by this principle but made exceptions when it suited them. The key to their behaviour can best be perceived in the way they talked of food in either purely economic or purely cultural terms. Paying for someone's lunch or tea was considered a loan and the transaction narrated in economic terms. The partaking and sharing of begged food or partying were explained in cultural terms as a kind of moral obligation.

Monetary Exchanges

Each child tried hard to keep the money he earned and dispose of it as he saw fit unless he was robbed by the *gulbetegnotch* or pressurized to spend it by the other boys. Generally speaking, the whole group lent each other money with the expectation of being paid back in cash and in full. However, it was not uncommon for one of them to deviate from a supposedly non-altruistic exchange by making an exception when dealing with a special friend, the group's 'beloved' or someone in particular he wanted to win over. Conversely, the dispenser of an altruistic obligation of a moral nature might change his mind and demand immediate restitution for past good deeds. Melit said: 'Sharing or pooling our money together would create fights, with those who contribute the most complaining or wanting to have a vote about how things are distributed. It is easy to keep account when we borrow money from each other, or pay for lunch or tea or cake. Sometimes we pretend to forget the loan when we want to be nice to someone. However, if a boy I have lent money to upsets me, I demand that he reimburse me the money on the spot even if I know that he does not have it.' Wolamo explained: 'The only time we share our money willingly is when we invite a special friend or friends or even the entire group to have a good time with us. We do not care how much we spend when the mood takes us. We can even sell our *duritos* or borrow from everybody to have a better party.'

Food Exchange

The rules governing obligation to reciprocate bought or begged food were different. If a boy paid for a comrade's meal or shared bread or food he has paid cash for, he expected the recipient to reimburse him the exact price of the meal or food item. Individual children readily made up a shortfall if a comrade lacked the necessary money to order a meal of equal value to what the others were eating. Such gestures were expected to be reciprocated in kind by the recipient if or when the occasion arises. It was not the amount of money contributed but the rapidity and willingness of the donor to contribute which made him look generous. On the other hand, the exchange of begged food was more of a moral than an economic nature. They all agreed that begged food ought to be shared with hungry comrades. They treated the sharing of begged food and food gifts the same way as most Ethiopians. It is common behavior in Ethiopia to invite whoever drops in while food is being eaten or served even if there is not enough to go around. The children spoke of such food obligations in cultural terms, emphasizing what is commonly accepted behavior in society at large. Zelalem put it as follows:

> If I am ill, the others will feed me without expecting me to pay them back when I am better. If I sit down to eat begged food and one of my friends comes, I have to ask him to join me. It would be unseemly if I ate alone while my friends are hungry. It is a big *yinlunta*. Even Tadele, the hyena, would agree to that. We behave the way we would behave at home when we are eating begged food. This rule does not apply when we are in a tea-house or restaurant. Where money is involved, we keep a strict account and consider it a loan and not an invitation.

They all affirmed that they never fought over begged food obligations. First of all, it would be shaming (*newur new, yilunta new*) to ask for food back. Secondly, how can anyone measure how much food a friend has eaten? However, even the rules governing begged food were not as straightforward as they seemed. During one of the periods when they were unable to earn enough money from the traffic lights due to police harassment, Zelalem was able to secure several plastic bagfuls of begged leftover food. He gave everyone enough to eat and sold the rest to adult beggars. Tadele insisted that he share the money as well. Zelalem refused and they exchanged blows. The others did not come to Zelalem's defense and this, more than the blows, upset him very much.

Imediatismo

Being depressed or elated caused more than one of them to behave erratically and dispense kindness and generosity. Their need to gratify their whims immediately, or *imediatismo* as Ricardo Lucchini (1993) calls it, personified their attitude towards leisure activities, and further demonstrates what I call unrequited reciprocity. Judith Ennew explains the apparent lack of long-term planning and their inability to defer gratification or *imediatismo* among such children as 'swift adaptive strategies'. This is because, as she (1994: 417) put it, 'They have a sense of reality and recognize that such plans are not congruent with their present resources.' Jill Swart (1990) and Richardo Lucchini (1993) say that *imediatismo* among homeless children is due to the fact that they cannot protect their money from thieves or are at risk of danger if they have money on themselves. The above statements hold true for all three groups. Zelalem and Godje spoke for all their friends when they summed up additional reasons that stopped them from having long- or short-term plans. Zelalem speaks: 'The real problem is that we do not earn enough money to cover all our expenses every day of the week. There are days when some of us make twenty or forty cents only. We are then obliged to borrow money from our friends or let them pay for our meals. There are other

days when we have a lot of money. We pay back our debts; we may buy a better *durito,* clothes or other necessities. If we feel sad or lonely, we may decide to
spend it on food and drinks entertaining our friends.' Godje's explanation:

> I have never tried to enter a rotating saving scheme (*iqub*) because I never know how
> much I will be able to earn in a week. If I fall ill, I may not be able to earn enough
> money. If I am obliged to contribute to some activities or if the *gulbetegnotch* rob me,
> I will be obliged to either borrow from others or default. There is no point in having
> long-term plans when you live like us. In any case, if I had a substantial amount of
> money, the others would encourage me to spend it on food and drinks. If I refuse, they
> might beat me or make me feel guilty.

Leisure – *Meznanat*

Most home-based street children, including the *gulbetegnotch,* took every opportunity to play football or handball with other children. Apart from gambling,
the members of the two older gangs I worked with did not join in any kinds of
fun and games in the street. Their principal leisure activities were playing cards,
chewing *tchat* or drinking alcoholic beverages very late at night in the numerous
shebeens found in the back streets of Addis Ababa. The only time I have seen
them act like children is when they mock wrestle with each other while walking
side by side.

Zelalem's group's idea of a good time was throwing a big party and getting
drunk, smoking hashish or chewing *tchat.* They also liked watching videos and
playing on pinball machines. They spent hours lounging about under the trees
by the church wall. They did not go to football matches or play football or other
games like the other street children. I once offered to buy them a football, but
they told me not to bother because they would sell it before I had reached the
end of the street. Ultimately, unrequited love and unrequited reciprocity as well
as *imediatismo* were the result of the unstable society they had created.

Health – Nursing – *Mastamem*

Ill health and bereavement were two afflictions when membership of the group
mattered. Illness more than any other adversity spurred members of the group
to replace the family of the sufferer, so to speak. If close kinsmen and intimate
social groups are defined as people who provide or are thought to provide support in time of need, Sahlins's 'generalized reciprocity' comes closest to the type
of exchange that existed in time of illness and bereavement between members of
all the three all-male gangs I worked with. This is because it involves the exchange
of free gifts or the sharing of material and emotional resources without any strict

expectation of return other than the existence of a diffuse obligation of a moral rather than economic nature.

Gang members are exposed to multiple health risks stemming from, among other factors, a lack of hygiene, violence, substance abuse and sexual behavior. Ill health, like bereavement, is a social event in Ethiopia. People go to great lengths to visit a sick relative or friend. Although gang members rely primarily on each other in times of illness, it is not uncommon for other street children or adult beggars to offer help or even contribute to medical expenses. None of the homeless boys I knew looked malnourished since they all managed to eat two or more times a day. Yet, since they did not have regular body-washing habits and lived in indescribably unhygienic conditions, they were prone to all sorts of infections. There was never a time throughout the years I have known them when one or the other was not suffering from something. The major ailments I have recorded in my diaries are: mouth and leg ulcers, abdominal or chest pains, coughs, eye, ear, mouth, skin or throat infections, toothache, headache, nausea, diarrhea and vomiting. The private clinic where I took some of them diagnosed bronchitis, pneumonia, asthma, diarrhea, amoebic dysentery, abdominal pains caused by anxiety and various forms of intestinal parasites. Five under-15-year-old boys had sexually transmitted diseases. They all admitted that most street boys have or wish to have sexual relations with women from age twelve onwards. Most pharmacists sold them antibiotics and tranquillizers over the counter whatever their ailments. One pharmacist told me that since they are infected with all sorts of things, the antibiotic will sort these out as well and the tranquillizers will keep the children quiet until they get better. None of the children knew the difference between the antibiotics, vitamins and tranquillizers. They only knew that aspirin cures headaches.

Economic constraints and their status as homeless children made it difficult for the *borcos* to gain access to health-care facilities. They had a limited number of options when they fell ill. Since they did not have a home address and therefore *kebele* identity cards, it was practically impossible for them to be admitted to government-run hospitals unless they were severely injured. They therefore usually waited until they got worse before taking any action. The first option was to tell a pharmacist what ailed them and take whatever he suggested. Those who had money readily chipped in to buy the prohibitively expensive drugs. They also resorted to all sorts of traditional herbal medicine and/or took holy water (*tebel*) from the church. If all this failed, they took it in turns to nurse the sick comrade. The patient's special friend usually took it upon himself to be there as often as possible. No expense was spared to buy the types of foods or drinks they thought would help the patient recover. The last-resort option was Mother Theresa's hospice for the dying. Gang members helped each other drag or carry a sick comrade to the hospice in the hope that he would be 'chosen', as they put it. If they failed, they carried or dragged the comrade back to their shelter and tried again the next day.

Bereavement – *Lesko*

In chapter 3 I have elaborated on the importance attached to belonging to a burial association (*idir*) by rich and poor alike and how the poor strove to keep up their membership of such organisations. The truly destitute were those who had to operate outside the social network system provided by voluntary associations such as rotating saving schemes (*iqub*), burial associations (*idir*) and religious associations (*mehaber*). As in most countries, weddings and funerals are significant events in Ethiopia. While wedding parties are by invitation only, funerals are a must for relatives, friends and acquaintances. Since Ethiopian Orthodox Christianity and Islam require that the dead be buried within twenty-four hours, it is not uncommon for factories or whole offices to come to a complete standstill while everyone attends a funeral. The presence of a priest to officiate and purify the dead person's soul before burial is considered an essential part of the ceremony. The body is washed and prepared by family members or friends beforehand.

The homeless children and adults living near and around the church where Zelalem's group operated went to great lengths to observe funeral rites even for people they barely knew. It was not uncommon for beggars, street children and unlicensed street vendors to contribute towards funeral expenses and the obligatory fees for priests to officiate at the funeral of homeless, destitute children and adults. There were several young girls with babies sleeping and begging on the other side of the wall where a high rate of infant mortality was the norm. Zelalem and all the homeless boys I knew invariably contributed small amounts of money and paid their respects to the dead baby and the bereaved mother. Even when they barely knew the mother, many of them joined the funeral procession.

As mentioned above, Tadele was very unpopular. His comrades often commented that he was shameless, selfish, cruel and very quarrelsome. Tadele's grandmother died in April 1997. He refused to go home for the funeral. He cried for a whole week, shouting to all who could hear him that he was finally truly alone. His comrades took it in turns to be with him and supplied him with food, alcoholic beverages, *tchat* and cigarettes. Other street children and even older beggars brought gifts and came to condole with him, thus re-creating in the street the dominant values held in time of bereavement by the rest of society.

Crime

Clive Glazer (2000: 61) states that 'open defiance of the law was "natural" to the *Tsotsi* subculture'. Crime was more than simply a material issue: it became a central sub-cultural theme during the 1940s and 1950s. In South America and the Caribbean delinquency and crime are said to be part of the economic objective of youth-gang cultures (see D. Rogers 1999). As I have demonstrated above, the *borcos* earned most of their living by begging and doing small jobs when an opportunity presented itself. Crime was an opportunistic rather than a ritualized or planned activity among all the youth gangs I knew.

Membership in the gang conferred the individual child with an identity as a *borco* and this either incited or buffered real or potential violence by complete strangers or other gangs. The same public image militated against such children being considered anything but a danger to society, especially by the police. In contrast to the vast majority of street children living with their families, gang members were indeed capable of criminal behavior. Many homeless boys have told me that they had been in police custody several times, most of it for petty theft or fighting with other children. Zelalem and his friends were regularly picked up for vagrancy. They were either beaten up on the spot or kept for a few hours or days in police cells with adult prisoners and released after being told to desist from begging or sleeping in the street.

There is one remand home in Addis Ababa housing approximately one hundred boys. Neither the courts nor the police stations were able to cope with the influx of street-related crimes committed by children and young adults. The cells at police stations were always full. The police usually dealt with petty crimes by 'disciplining' street children on the spot or in the over-flowing police stations. I have seen them order 8–10-year-old street boys to march up and down for hours or jog in place until they fell helplessly to the ground. Unfortunately, another of their solutions included administering severe beatings in order to teach the children a lesson, as they put it.

Before I met them, Zelalem, Tadele and Melit had had longer sentences imposed on them for stealing and were sent to the only remand home for boys found in Addis Ababa, or to an adult prison. Zelalem's worst nightmare was his family finding out that he was imprisoned for five months for stealing a jerry-can full of kerosene from outside a shop. As mentioned before, Tadele's grandmother encouraged the judge to pass a longer sentence on him when he was jailed for stealing shoes left outside a church by worshippers. Melit was jailed for six months for snatching a woman's handbag. All the children I spoke to found their experiences behind bars harrowing and were very bitter at having been sent to prison in the first place. Melit explains why: 'Jail is the worst thing that can happen to you. They only feed you once a day. None of us has relatives and friends to bring us food parcels. The prison guards do not allow people without *kebele* identity cards to visit prisoners. Our friends cannot visit us because they do not have any kind of official identity card. We were left completely alone. I used to cry at night from hunger and bitterness. I was so unhappy. I even thought of killing myself but could not find a quick way to do it.' The following comments from two law enforcement officers reflects how most of them view the *borcos:* 'They must have stolen money or done something dreadful before running away from their families and entering street life. They are hardened criminals; they steal and fight because they really enjoy it. No one picks a fight with them because they are capable of murder. We regularly find screwdrivers, hammers, knives, razor blades, and even used syringes on them.' He was not far off, since even Godje carried razor blades and a rusty three-inch nail on him. The two older male gangs I knew proudly showed me their scalpels, screwdrivers and flick knives, and went into graphic descriptions of the use to which these weapons could be put.

From one traffic policeman:

> I know that some are very poor and abused children but as soon as they enter the street world they get 'damaged'. You do not know how hard it is for us. We have to beat them up to stop them from stealing everything they can remove from cars. The *borcos* you like so much spoil plants and bushes along the street and in the roundabouts. They rob people at night. They fight each other with knives. Sometimes, when we see them beating each other, we just ignore it. We are fed up. There are too many street children, too many beggars and too many poor people in this town.

The public image of *borcos* as dangerous thieves is hardly warranted. By the time I heard and noted the following narratives, none of them had a reason to lie to me. Zelalem explained it as follows:

> Professional thieves do not look or live like us. They are very clean and well dressed. They use razor blades and other instruments to cut through people's bags and pockets in taxis and buses. They even go to church to steal from worshippers. We only steal when the opportunity arises. It is very difficult to steal from people or from cars at the traffic lights and get away with it. Most of us do not even dream of stealing. If we got caught, people would kick us to death. If something drops from someone's pocket, bag or parcel and no one sees it, it is ours. If a person goes in the church and leaves a packet behind to pick it up later, he is a fool. If they rush to watch a car accident or skirmishes and do not pay attention to their bags, it is their problem.

> MELIT: The bigger the crowd after a traffic accident, the better the chances we have to pick people's pockets. If we find someone drunk at night, especially at the end of the month, we go through his pockets and take everything he has. If he is unconscious, we take his shoes, clothes or anything that can be sold and leave him there naked. Most of us are too scared to steal things. Some of the other gangs have no *yilunta*. They rob the drunks and then kick them almost to death out of sheer pleasure. We are very careful. We do not want to end up in jail or, worse still, receive a beating from the public. If someone shouts 'thief', every pedestrian, even women, spit and kick the man or boy without asking whether he is innocent or not. It is just as bad if a policeman is present, because they beat you before asking if you are implicated.

> GODJE: Tadele steals from us. We have beaten and thrown out newcomers because they try to steal from us. We mainly rob drunks or ladies who have too many parcels

to carry. We confuse them and try to take something from the bags. When I was with the other boys, I saw one of them grab a foreign woman's gold necklace and run away with it. They were fearless. They also stole hubcaps, wing mirrors and the covers of petrol tanks and sold them to garage owners. There are too many people around here and people know us. We have to be careful.

I have shown above that there was a low level of crime among the *borcos* compared to what is said to exist elsewhere in the world. Violence is another major issue that is constant in the literature on gangs. Violence was indeed a permanent aspect of the *borcos'* way of life, but as I shall depict below and in chapter 5, intra-gang violence was more frequent and harmful to group cohesion and the well-being of the individual child.

Violence – *Metalat*

All the surveys and studies I have consulted highlight the role that violence plays in gang culture. This includes violence committed by gang members on the public and inter-gang violence (see Rogers 1999, 2003). Clive Glazer (2000: 4) explains that masculine identity for the *Bo Tsotsi* hinged around fighting skills, independence, street wisdom, feats of daring, law breaking, clothing style, proficiency in the *tsotsitaal* argot and success with women. Intra-gang fights among the *borcos* were mostly revenge attacks over being insulted by other gang members, and over sleeping or begging territory. Quarrels also occurred due a child refusing to show respect, keeping secrets, sharing food, drugs or money. Not paying gambling and other debts or not participating in inter-gang fights resulted in fisticuffs or outright beatings. The presence of a third party as participant, mediator or protector amplified or deflected the seriousness of the insult or fight. An insult proffered in the presence of others was more serious than when just two boys of unequal strength were present. Most of the time those involved in the violence were left by their friends to find the best to way to assuage their resentment; or as they put it, '*elehatchewoon yauutut*'. I was incapable of remaining impassive when they fought in my presence. I would, with only a small degree of success, try to remonstrate or attempt to get the boys to resolve their conflicts amicably. Most of the time, the loser would grab me by the waist from behind and continue to insult his assailant or run a short distance and throw stones and threats while I did my best to restrain the other from retaliating.

Zelalem and his friends often suffered from injuries due to violent attacks by the *gulbetegnotch,* the police, other gang members and each other. Jill Swart (1988) gives vivid descriptions of the kind of unconditional and altruistic support provided by group members towards injured comrades among the *Malunde.* Among the gangs I knew, the group acted as a team only when confronting other gangs. The type of support which existed among the *borcos* prevailed only for injuries sustained at the hands of the police or outsiders and did not apply to injuries from violence within the inner circle or from the *gulbetegnotch*. Inter-gang violence generated varied forms of reciprocal support but each case was judged on its own merit. If the sufferer was said to have triggered the wrath of other gang members or the *gulbetegnotch,* he was left to fend for himself or he could count on being nursed or consoled by his special friend. If two gang members have a punch-up, the others usually let them fight it out, or as they put it, 'let them exhaust their anger'. Conflict and violence were nevertheless everyday occurrences. They fought for trivial reasons.

> ZELALEM: It is not easy to remember what triggers a fight among us. We would all be lying down and if someone has his leg in the way, Tadele's instinct is to kick it. I am prone to shout, 'Get your filthy leg out of the way.' Someone would say something and another one would tell him to shut up. Anything or anyone can make us angry when we are sad or hungry. Tadele hits anyone near him when he is angry or has a craving for *tchat*, a cigarette or something to drink. Wolamo is the only one who never gets on anyone's nerves. Tadele and Melit, even I, still manage to find reasons to beat him up from time to time. Trivial insults, the wrong look, lack of respect or a threatening pause are often considered grievous affronts needing retaliation. We just go on living together as before after a quarrel. If someone sulks or tries to make any one of us take sides, the others gang up on him or make fun of him. They have made me cry so many times because I side with the small ones.

> MELIT: The worst fights happen at night. The *gulbetegnotch* often cajole or pressurise some of us to roam around at night in search of other gangs with whom they can gamble. Tadele and many newcomers willingly go along. The problem starts when they are unable or unwilling to pay their gambling debts. Enemy gangs occasionally raid our group at night and steal our *duritos.* The scene is then repeated the other way around, until one of the gangs calls it quits. Any boy who does not show alacrity in joining inter-gang fights is robbed, beaten up and hounded out of the group for being a coward and a traitor. Re-entry into the group is made intolerable by the contempt and mockery poured over the coward. On the positive side, those who are attacked by outsiders, especially our enemies, are more or less assured of our sympathy and support. However, you can only get help from your own friends if they are physically present when trouble starts. If not, it is your fight. Even your best friend will not go back there to defend your rights. It is too dangerous. However, if they come around and attack anyone of us, we must defend our friends.

In addition to the above, the *gulbetegnotch* regularly took advantage of Zelalem's group's lack of permanent cohesion or loyalty to each other. Zelalem explains: 'Tadele regularly reports to them everything we do, say or earn and they leave him alone, even though he knows that they are robbing us. He kowtows to them in the hope of appeasing them and partaking of the spoils. He is without shame or consciousness. He has no *yilunta* whatsoever.'

GODJE: Two nights ago the *gulbetegnotch* wanted more 'protection' money from us. They shook Zelalem up and found nothing on him. They said that they would let him go if he told them if anyone else had money. He showed them the place where I had buried my money. They took it in turns to punch and kick me. Zelalem and Tadele watched them beat me up, they were both laughing. I got very angry and told them that Zelalem was keeping his money with the teahouse owner. They made him go and fetch the money he had saved up. They all got drunk. Zelalem hit me all over the body with a stick the next morning because he had no money to pay for his breakfast.

As they grew older, sex-related conflicts added to the already high incidence of violence in their lives. Even little Godje contracted a sexually transmitted disease. Towards mid 1997 several homeless young girls started visiting the group at night. Godje explains:

> Many girls join us at night. They are like us; they are in trouble with their families. Genet, who we call *Datchi* [run them over] is the worst of the lot and a great sinner. Her nickname stems from the way she comes into the group and within hours everything breaks loose as if she had run us over with a big truck. At first we all liked her and felt sorry for her. She lost her mother last year and her three brothers began bringing girls home and treating her like their housemaid. They beat her when she refused to cook and run errands for them. I now hate her because she causes trouble. They have started quarrelling over her. The *gulbetegnotch* invite her to smoke cigarette or hashish, chew *tchat* or drink with them. Some of them refuse to pay her after they 'have done it to her'. In retaliation she makes them fight each other. I cannot explain how she does it but she and her girlfriends manage to involve all of us in their quarrels with the *gulbetegnotch*.

> Tadele received a severe beating the other night because the newest and prettiest girl told them that she did it with him for free. They slapped Zelalem because the same girl made him stand up for her when they beat her up for insulting them. The girls know how to provoke all of us. As soon as the punching and kicking begin, they disappear. They wait a few days and reappear one by one or with new girlfriends and the whole thing starts all over again.

This notion of face saving and proving to be 'manly', inculcated to boys through having a sense of *yilunta,* explains most of the violence in inter-personal relationships. Aggression was often the only means of saving face during such confrontation in which opponents sought to establish or maintain 'face' at the other's expense by remaining steady in the face of adversity. Most of the intra-group fights I heard about or witnessed were instant one-on-one, often brutal and quickly solved quarrels. The predatory type of violence, that is premeditated and ritualized, existed among the mixed-sex gang, and it was usually meted out on girls by other gang girls. As I shall relate in the next chapter, some girls from the mixed-sex gang either disappeared completely, joined other gangs or took-up full time begging or prostitution.

Summing Up

Clive Glazer (2000: 2) states that the concept of youth coheres around the no-tion of transition between childhood and responsible adulthood; for males it is a phase of mobility, rebellion, experimentation, floating identity and asser-tive independence. Relatively speaking, street children living at home are usually made to feel useful or even productive by their families; this includes friends and neighbours because their street related activities subsidize their school expenses and help support their families. They have therefore a better sense of self-worth and self-esteem than homeless street children. Some are able to use their parents' networks or at least the stability of a positive social identity to get a foothold in the job market and the adult organized social world in their own right. Very few homeless children find a satisfactory alternative to gang life as they grow older. Their lack of a home to go back to or any kind of socio-economic network in the community make it extremely difficult for them to be re-absorbed into family life and mainstream society.

The runaway children who are welcomed back by their natal families are few and far between. The successful ones I knew had been on the street for less than a month. They were all aged fourteen or younger and mostly girls. These children had at least one member of their family they could trust to care for their welfare or someone who they knew was prepared to protect and defend them from what-ever they had run away from. Throughout the years when I worked in the street, I witnessed the efforts NGOs' employees made to reunite runaway children with their families. Two children from the rural area who were part of one of the gangs I was following were taken back to their home villages. Both were back on the streets within months. They told me that they found it difficult to readjust to rural life and that they faced the same situation they had run away from, namely hunger, family discord, beatings and being constantly asked to do menial or hard work around the house.

Homeless children's lack of family ties, home addresses and, therefore, *kebele* identity cards reinforce the already negative and criminal image they project. The very same factors exacerbate their ability to disengage themselves from street life or criminal activities with the onset of adulthood. The gang members I knew were prone to mood swings and depression. They had more opportunity to en-gage in criminal and problem behaviour. The boys were more than likely to have initiated sexual activity at a much earlier age, some as young as twelve. In addi-tion, street-based homeless girls inevitably enter or had been forced to enter into premature, exploitative and at times violent sexual relationships with adolescent street boys, unemployed young men or other adult males prior to or after becom-ing homeless. Girls and boys alike have the means and opportunities for alcohol abuse, addiction to cigarettes, *tchat* and hashish. They also have more trouble with the police because of minor criminal activities like begging, petty thieving, gambling and vagrancy.

Finally, the homeless youth gangs in Addis Ababa do not exist outside the adult social world. They are inextricably linked to the outside world after entering street life. This is because of their reliance on the generosity of various groups of adults for their survival and their inevitable associations with the police, other street children, older beggars, the *bozene,* their patrons and food sellers. The low-level crime they engaged in was not their main source of income. The social resources and social support systems available to home-based street children differed considerably from those of street-based children. Therein lay the most important factors that integrated or separated the two categories of children from the adult organised social world but not necessarily from the adult social world. In contrast to street children living with their families, homeless children lacked the reciprocity expected of close relatives and friends that goes along with the nature of social support and social network available within the family unit. The vast majority of home-based street children attended school part-time; none of the homeless children I knew attended any kind of educational institution. Street children living at home could count on some form of continuity in their lives. They had someone to provide them with emotional support and with a place of sleep, and on whom they could rely for help and affection. The following chapter describes Zelalem's gang's varied attempts to 'mature-out' or extricate themselves from gang life and adjust to adulthood as their group disintegrated with the added burden of sex and girls in their lives.

5

SEX, GIRLS AND GANG LIFE

Zelalem's gang were all under fifteen when I first met them. The other two all-male gangs were in the thirteen to seventeen age groups. The mixed-sex gang that I followed next consisted of boys from nine to twenty-four and girls under sixteen. The painful, not to say confused, transition from childish naivety to adulthood all children go through has already been the subject of anthropological enquiry (see Le Vine and New 2008). As David Bainbridge (2009) has shown, even in 'normal' settings, teenage years contain the most intense physical, emotional and mental experiences of our lives and can leave us feeling joyful or suicidal, or send us reeling between the two. This is complicated by the value-laden and sensitive subject of children's sexuality, which produces anxiety in adults by children knowing things that are thought to be too adult for them. We want to educate them, but at the right time in the right way (see Moore 2006). Just as I was getting my head around the fact that the boys I was working with were all becoming sexually active, after I began following the exploits of the mixed-sex gang, I was soon confronted with child-on-child sexual abuse and ritualized violence.

The boys in Zelalem's gang faced the upheaval of adolescence and transition to adulthood in far-from-ideal conditions. The fear and dislike the *borcos* generated as young men tempered people's erstwhile generosity towards the helpless street children they used to represent. As Lewis Aptekar (1988) aptly put it, age becomes their worst enemy. Police officers and ordinary citizens ceased to look upon them and their personal appearance with tolerance. Age and sexual maturity increased the boys' needs to be re-absorbed into mainstream society. The painful process of disengaging themselves from the street, establishing alternative relationships outside the gang structure and entering the complex world of heterosexual relationships began at the stage of their lives when they were least likely to succeed. Furthermore, because of the fragmented and troubled ties they had with their families, they lacked any kind of social resources that they could count on for any length of time. Due to the unstable society that they had created for themselves, they could not even count on each other for emotional, material or social support. Even though they were engaged in relatively minor socially harmful, violent or vicious criminal conducts, the hellish life they had led as pre-pubertal boys barely altered as they reached adulthood.

As I have already stated, my involvement with the mixed-sex gang in this chapter was accidental and due to my connections with Zelalem's group. A review of the literature on girls in gangs suggests the presence of girls even in youth gangs that are completely controlled by males and orientated towards male activities. Their role in these gangs varies from being subordinate to male members' authority to being romantically involved with one or more boys. Girl gang members tend to be little more than sexually exploited appendages to the gang. Female gang members, like males, seek respect, but the content differs. For males, it has to do with masculine power and control. For girls, the pursuit of respectability involves not being taken for granted and includes being feminine. Gang membership is said to be viewed by both sexes as a collective means of coping or surviving in low-income slums of the city, and centers on economic activities, including drug dealing, prostitution and violent robbery. There is constant reference to the violence committed on girls and by girls. There is also abundant evidence that girls often join gangs for the same reasons as males, such as a sense of belonging, whereby the gang becomes a sort of close 'family' (see Rogers 1999, 2003; Chesney-Lind 2004). The girls living among the tough, emotionally damaged, sexually charged post-pubertal boys in the mixed-sex gang I studied did indeed exist as annexes to the male gangs but they criss-crossed the line between victims and victimizers. They had to volunteer to be sexually available to the boys, including prostituting themselves to contribute to the gang's livelihood or face the ire of the group. Even though they had all joined the group voluntarily, they were either constantly depressed or angry. Much like the territory which kept Zelalem's gang together, they were the raison d'être for the existence and economic survival of the gang.

Girl gang membership, just like boy gang membership, is best examined in the context of the severe disadvantages and abuse such children had experienced at home. The girls in the mixed-sex gang had all run away from home because of physical or sexual abuse by familiar adults. Unlike the description found in some of the literature on girls in the gang, they had not joined the gang for excitement or because they were rebelling, or for economic reasons (see Campbell 1984; Decker and Weerman 2005). I shall therefore concentrate on individual children and their actions. This is in order to examine patterns of intra-group relations as well as the collective behaviour, which influenced other contextual factors, such as level of violence, livelihood, the corporate behaviour of the group, leadership and other roles. This chapter takes up again the case of Zelalem and his comrades in order to demonstrate how the imperfect society that they had created meant that each boy had to find and fight his own way out of street life as a post-adolescent boy. I shall begin by describing the various causes for the breakdown of Zelalem's gang.

No Home To Go To

Zelalem's group started disintegrating towards the end of 1997. Territory and age were pivotal to the break-up of the group. The first push factor came in January 1998, when the church authorities surrounded the front of the church with barbed wire and began building offices for their officials. Soon after building work began in earnest the police and church guards made sure that no one slept or defecated anywhere near the church wall or round the traffic lights. The traffic police worked in pairs preventing any child or adult beggar from approaching cars by physically attacking them, with their truncheons if necessary. This made it impossible for the gang to use the trees as a substitute home. The gang relocated to the back gate of the church and began sharing sleeping space with adult beggars. Apart from the tensions and aggravations which followed this increase in population, they were not able to claim a special corner for themselves where they could lounge, socialize and sleep together behind the church. They began acting autonomously and this constricted the already tenuous relationship they had with one another. Zelalem's gang's life took a turn for the worse when they were obliged to fight over patrons and customers among parishioners with adult beggars and handicapped children. They began migrating to other parts of the city and competing with other street children and adult beggars, this time as young adults rather than children.

Not Homeless but Jobless: The *Bozene*

At around the same time, the gang's arch foes and bullies, the *gulbetegnotch,* who had used the same church wall and the trees as their territory, crossed over to the other side of the street and began congregating in front of the bakery and shops opposite. Since these establishments opened directly onto the pavement and main road, there were no secluded places, trees or verandas to hide behind, shelter from the heat of the sun or the deluge of the rain. Furthermore, this was a less ideal spot for jobless, penniless young men to loiter unnoticed because shop owners made it clear that they did not want them around. After a few weeks, several stopped coming altogether. The few who had nowhere else to go shifted their position according to the whim of shop owners and the weather.

Four jobless youths established some kind of truce with me and became my informants. I was astonished by the courtesy and kindness I received from these *bozene/gulbetegnotch* since they had made my life difficult in the past. They told me that when they saw me befriending Zelalem's group they all thought that I was a *pent'ay,*[1] out to convert the kids or some kind of NGO employee. After they

---

[1] *Pent'ay* is a slang and derogatory term used by many Ethiopians to refer to followers of a foreign-

realised that I was neither a religious zealot nor an NGO employee, they made bets on how long I would last. In time they resented the fact that I always took Zelalem's gang's side and ignored their plight completely. As one of them put it:

> We are completely invisible to you and to everyone else. We are the forgotten humans. Everyone is concerned with helping street children. NGOs and other do-gooders come and go without improving their lives or decreasing their numbers. Everything is relative. We do have a home to go to. We do not starve because we can always rely on our families to feed us. What is not so apparent is that there is hardly any money left over to clothe, feed or pay for any kind of training. The police leave us alone because we are not the problem, the *borcos* are the problem. We sometimes act as police informants and they appreciate that.

> There is no hope for the *borcos*. They are truly damaged. We would do anything; go to any length to find a job. We cannot compete with the already saturated market in the informal sector. Besides, most of these street traders have two, three jobs and supplement their income by peddling in the streets. Many have employed relatives who provide them with the capital or the goods for them to retail merchandise. We know that some shop owners offload some of their stock, including contraband goods, by handing it to a jobless relative to sell in the streets for a cut in the profit. You do not know how inventive they are, and the type of contraband goods they have access to. We do not have the capital, the network or the know-how to compete with them.

This informant solved his existential problem by lying about his age and family background and joining the army to fight the Ethiopian-Eritrean war in July 1999. Another 26-year-old jobless young man put it even more succinctly:

> We did try to befriend you at first, all of us hoping that you will employ us as informants or assistants. We were surprised that you did not fear us. We were all angry at your indifference to our plight. We used to encourage Tadele to steal from you until we found that you carry very little money and keep it with your driving licence in a special belt around your waist. Why do you think that we fight over any kind of jobs? Even menial jobs, like offloading trucks, carrying garbage to the skip or moving dead bodies for the nuns at Mother Theresa's hospice for the dying? We never accepted leftovers from the church or fight for the dead people's garments that are distributed from time to time. It would have been a shameful thing to do because of our family's reputation. We are too conscious of what the others think or say about us including our own comrades. We have *yilunta* and have to keep the outward appearance of being respectable. There are too many like us in this city, educated, from good family and jobless. And yet, we are invisible: no one sees us, no one hears us and no one wants to help us.

> The truth is that even though some in our group were not that good at school, the brilliant ones did not make it either. Our parents sacrificed everything for our education in the hope that we could have a better future. Even university graduates find it hard

---

based and financed Pentecostal/Evangelical church. *Pent'ay,* Ethiopian Protestant converts, are renowned for being zealots and at times resented for their presumed incessant drive to convert people by any means necessary.

to find jobs these days. Our families and relatives have tried everything to secure a job for us. We still strive to find a solution to our plight.

This informant moved in with a mature, well-off childless widow who owned a small shop. Since she has many relatives in the USA, he lived in hope that she will enable him to migrate to the States in search of a better life. Another 25-year-old *gulbetegnoch* explained it as follows:

> We hang around here to get out of the house. We are too ashamed to stay at home doing nothing, earning nothing. We have no way of knowing how to get out of this existence. We are men after all. Before they began building this wall, I could get out of the house in the morning then go back home and say that I had eaten and not lie about it. I could even give a few *birr* to my mother and pretend that I earned it doing some kind of respectable job, like assisting a motorist instead of telling her that I stole it from a *borco*. I think my family knows where I spend my days. We do not speak about it. We are all too conscious and ashamed to admit that there is no hope for me. I have betrayed my parent's faith of securing a good job and helping them. I have not developed into a man with a proper job and wife. I am still a dependent child with the mind and delusions of being a real man.
>
> I have school friends who have jobs, girlfriends and even wives. I pretend to have plans to go abroad and am waiting for a visa and other lies when they ask me how I am doing. I am twenty-five years old. I have never even had a proper girlfriend, just occasional sex behind the bushes, outdoors in front of others like an animal and with girls who have run away from home. Trust me, I am not the only one, there are many like me around here. I often wish for some kind of calamity, like a big earthquake or major war to happen and obliterate the whole city or even the country. I hate my life and the government.

This informant's way out was to acquire a passport and, with financial help from relatives, make his way to Kenya in the hope of eventually landing in any Western country.

As I grew to know the *gulbetegnotch* better, I noticed that they had a volatile relationship with one another almost comparable to the one I witnessed among the *borcos*. The following sums up the reasons behind the existing enmity between some of them, as told by Alemu, one of the *gulbetegnotch* who eventually formed his own mixed-sex gang, which I talk of in this chapter.

> We were not such good friends. We quarreled all the time, over who had the right to rob one of the *borcos*, gambling debts, how to share any money we took from the kids, even about boasting who has the better family's standing in society. Your *borco* friends were the only constant source of ready cash for us. This forced us to either gamble with them or steal from them. There was no way any of us would have had the courage to demean ourselves and beg from cars. There is too much *yilunta* involved. First of all, there is the name and reputation of our families to consider. This is our neighbourhood (*sefer*); everyone knows us. We do not look or act like *borcos*. We come from good

families and are aware of who we are. We have to constantly strive to appear respectable to everyone around, including the *borcos* and adult beggars. Second, it would have been pointless any way. We used to watch each other's move and if one got a chance to do something to earn money; another would immediately copy what he did or compete for the same job. This created periods of tension and resentment among us. Depending on who took the side of whom, some would be forced to come in the afternoon and others in the morning until the air was clear. I preferred the peaceful times. None of us enjoyed hanging around here with no future or hope for a better life. We all wished we were university students or better still in a secure job.

Alemu's solution to leaving the church wall was to lure several under-16-year-old homeless girls and boys and members of Zelalem's gang into forming a new gang, with him as their leader. This was sometime in October 1997, shortly after the big rains had stopped. They went to live in an uninhabited no man's land near the airport, an hours' walk from the church. They built makeshift shelters, acquired two stray dogs as pets and guards and encouraged as many children as possible to join their group.

I stopped going to the church because it became harder for me to have a private moment with Zelalem's group. I was mobbed by the begging fraternity congregating at the back gate of the church as soon as I stopped to talk to them. I had to ask the *gulbetegnotch* to cross over the street and call one of them or tell me where they had gone and generally act as go-betweens for me and the boys. With time even this became hard to accomplish since the gang found it increasingly difficult to live with adult beggars. They resented being constantly told that they were wasting their youth; that they should improve their behavior, find gainful employment or go back to their families. They went back and forth trying to find other gangs or locations where they could fit in. Since I could not follow their increasingly peripatetic existence, I stopped going to the church altogether and gave the boys a phone number where they could leave a message when they wanted to see me. Soon after Zelalem and his friends lives took a turn for the worse and the only place I could find them was in Alemu's camp.

Sex and Gang Life

Alemu's establishing his own gang in another part of the city provided an alternative escape route for Zelalem and his friends. All of them were to join this gang at one time or another. The sanitary conditions in the camp he set up near the main airport were appalling. It was situated about a mile off the main road. There was a small river a short walk away where they fetched water and attempted to wash themselves. They defecated and urinated all around the camp. The girls had no access to privacy or sanitary towels. Alemu's gang lived mainly off what the girls earned from prostitution. They followed the same routine: at dusk the girls made their way to an informal parking space on a cliff overlooking a quarry and waited for male motorists to ask for their services. The most lucrative times were the end of the month on pay day or after midnight when minicab drivers and other men came alone or in pairs. Sundays were their busiest night when men came for casual sex before going home. One girl explained it as follows: 'They drive out of town and have picnics with their virginal girlfriends and fiancées and then they come to us for sex.'

There was minimal violence from male customers parked in cars because the girls either had one of the boys watching from afar for their safety or if they were operating alone, pretended to have their brothers around. In any case, the girls worked in groups of twos or threes. The more entrepreneurial and more experienced girls sought customers alone on the main road or outside bars and shebeens. Younger male members of the gang supplemented the girls' earnings by begging for leftover food from rich households in the vicinity or carrying parcels for people alighting from taxis and buses.

The three other, all-male, gangs I knew did not have structured organizations with hierarchies. As I have detailed in chapter 4, they did not live according to strict rules but had a diffuse mutual understanding about living together, which they either adhered to or broke according to their whim. The only similarity with the mixed-sex gang was that those who found their membership intolerable voted with their feet. Alemu's gang has a structure, with him as the leader of the pack. He chose or discarded his lieutenants as well as his male and female discipline enforcers. Both girls and boys handed over everything they begged and earned – that is, food, money or clothes – to Alemu. He took what he considered to be his share and provided what he deemed appropriate to individual members. The rest was used for food or partying all night. The girls did all the cooking and washing, including washing the boys' cloths. Boys were invariably in charge of buying booze, cigarettes, *tchat* or marijuana and carried the money while the girls shopped for food.

Alemu distributed 'wives' to those he favoured. Although he would at times consult with the boys on their preferences, he rarely allowed a girl to choose a 'husband'. He expected gratitude and complete obedience from one and all. Those who did not obey his orders, and hand over their earnings, were beaten into submission by Alemu or his henchmen. The membership size of the gang changed constantly because many children, especially the girls, left the group, sometimes within days. As a 15-year-old girl put it:

> Some girls stay because they are in love with one of the boys, others because they have seen it all and find peace here. I accepted the beating and handed over my money at first because I had nowhere else to go. I now prefer to live here with other children who have suffered like me. We are all very bitter because we have been sexually abused by close male relatives or friends of the family. Some of my friends have been raped by their stepfathers, stepbrothers or their mothers' boyfriends.

I can only remember the constant beatings from all the adults in my family. All my childhood was 'do this, do that', a slap for being too slow, a *kurkum* for getting it wrong or a curse for not looking happy about being abused. No one believed or protected me. We are free here. No one insults us or judges us. We are not lonely or alone here. We often buy all kinds of things that we like in order to have a good time. We make a big fire and smoke and drink all night. For many of us, this is the first time in our lives that we have had any kind of fun. The girls who leave us are usually very unhappy about sharing their money or do not like the 'husbands' Alemu assigns for them. A few rebel against any form of beating or insults for disobeying Alemu's orders. They had enough insults, curses and beatings at home; that is why they ran away in the first place.

I do not mind giving Alemu my money. I was one of his favourite 'wives'. We have remained close. He discusses things with me and I help him discipline some of the girls. I know how to handle the boys. You don't know what 'that little thing can do'. Most of the girls get along with the boys. I give them good advice. Those we punish deserve it.

The type and severity of discipline girls received varied. Girls who did not accept the 'husbands' assigned to them were pressurized by other girls into acquiescing. If Alemu appreciated the girl, he would let the matter rest. Otherwise, the girl was lulled to think that all was well, until the partying started and, once drunk, boys were told to have their own way with her. One girl explained that this gave the chance for boys who did not have 'wives' to have sex. Girls who constantly stood up to Alemu or their 'husbands', or who withheld money earned from prostitution, received group beatings, mostly at the hand of other girls. A girl described one such beating as follows: 'The girls grabbed me and held me down. One sat on me and the others pinched my thighs and private parts while the first one slapped and scratched my face. What humiliated me most was the boys standing around encouraging them and laughing, even those I considered my best friends. I feel so ashamed; I did not have panties on.' The above more or less sums up what I was told by female gang members throughout the year I frequented them. I often enquired whether it would not be better for the girls to form their own gang. The answers were they were all afraid to be alone in the dark in this no man's land, especially of the hyenas. Besides, the boys would eventually find them and punish them for deserting. Tadele, Melit and Zelalem were part of Alemu's gang at one time or another. Wolamo and Godje had short, tumultuous relationships with Alemu and the girls. Each case provides examples of life as a gang member in a mixed-sex group, living outside the confines of the street and its public setting, and being neither a child nor a man.

Wolamo

Wolamo had three brief spells as a member of Alemu's gang. He was very popular with the girls. He was put in charge of accompanying girls and buying supplies for their parties. This was a trusted position for a non-lieutenant, since it was common for boys and girls to abscond with the money. Alemu assigned him a 'wife'. The girl claimed to be twelve years old and looked it. Wolamo accompanied her and other girls to where men were waiting to have sex with them. He did not attempt to have sex with any of them. He said he found it difficult to even think about it. He was also afraid of contacting some venereal disease or, worse still, HIV/AIDS.

Before he left the first time, Wolamo told me that he did not feel at home with the gang and felt uncomfortable with the constant violence and swapping of wives. He thought that it was immoral for them to live off what the girls earned from prostitution. He considered the other boys, including Zelalem and the gang, as lacking a sense of *yilunta*. He was the only one who admitted that prostitution was taking place. The others, including Zelalem, either talked about the girl's working or that the girls merely sat around with their clients and helped them 'relieve' themselves but did not have penetrative sex.

Wolamo left after Alemu had beaten up an 11-year-old boy who was withholding money. He then joined other boys sleeping on verandas and working by day not far from the airport. Soon afterward he was lured by an Ethiopian *pent'ay* (Pentecostal) preacher into joining their sect. He went back to the camp two weeks later. He told us that he felt like an outsider among the *pent'ay* family where he was fostered. He was too old, barely literate and felt uncomfortable with the constant praying. The *pent'ay* Ethiopian preacher who had recruited him came to talk to him every evening and eventually persuaded him to join a group of other street children that he and his wife were trying to reform in another part of the city. Wolamo stayed with them for two months. He reappeared one evening, saying that one of the supervisors in charge of daily routines at the shelter beat him and the other children regularly. He also resented not being able to come and visit his friends. The preacher came back and persuaded Wolamo to join a home for street children, which the sect had established forty kilometres outside Addis Ababa. Wolamo's rationale for following the preacher was that he could not stay a street child forever, at least if he conformed he could build a better life for himself among the *pent'ay*. He was thirteen years old when I first set eyes on him. He was eighteen years old the last time I saw him on 19 December 2000.

Tadele

Tadele, then aged seventeen, joined Alemu's gang soon after it was established. He lasted three weeks the first time and three days the second time. He was severely beaten by Alemu for insubordination and inciting others, especially the girls, to disobey his orders by withholding some of the money they earned. He went back to the church wall. Sometime in October 1998 he was caught again stealing shoes left outside the church by worshipers and held in a cell at a nearby police station. The rest of the gang took food parcels and begged other visitors to pass them on to him while he was in the local police station awaiting trial. He was sentenced to one year and transferred to a prison for adults in December 1998. Since visitors to prisons are required to show their *kebele* identity cards, his comrades were not able to visit him. They soon gave up and forgot about him.

Tadele was released in November 1999. I saw him frequently throughout December 1999. He tried to enlist in the army and join the soldiers fighting the Eritrean-Ethiopian border war but was rejected twice. He resumed begging and sharing sleeping space with adult beggars behind the church. He was invariably depressed when I met him. He often pretended to be mad and walked up and down the street without any clothes on. The adult beggars with whom he now associated told me that he often slept outside various churches on different saint's days and pretended to be mentally retarded or very ill. He told me that he had tried to work on a building site but left after two days. He said that he was too ashamed to ask his mother for help.

Tadele then became convinced that his half-sisters had put a curse on him or worse still that they had consulted a shaman (*wokabi*) and had fed him some juju, which had made him behave as he does. He took holy water (*tebel*), saw a male and then a female *wokabi*, and talked to anybody who would listen to him. After that he began clamoring that he should have inherited his grandmother's estate and that he was robbed of the inheritance his father left him. His mother disappeared from the area without telling him where she had moved. The family friend with the shop near the church, did not know, or pretended not to know where his mother had gone. After that, his maternal and paternal family cut themselves off from him completely.

The *gulbetegnotch* despised him the most for not respecting his class position in society and behaving accordingly. Every thing another man would have hidden or been too ashamed to divulge – cowardice, petty theft from family and friends, addiction to all sorts of drugs, snitching on his comrades, having sex with any women including beggars – was a matter of exultation to Tadele's diseased mind. They could not understand why instead of being bloated with family pride and feeling lucky to have been born in a well-to-do family, he was doing everything possible to shame them. Their class position mattered to them, since there was nothing else they could hang on to. They watched and kept me informed as his life spiraled out of control.

The only person who tolerated Tadele's behaviour was a young mother with a 6-month-old baby. They frequently drank and smoked together. They also quarrelled constantly. Tadele baby-sat for her as well as begged from passing cars with the baby in his arms; eventually the baby died. She got pregnant again and everyone was convinced it was Tadele's. She gave the child up for adoption and disappeared. Tadele felt betrayed. He accused her of selling his child. He was fifteen when I first met him. The last time I saw him in July 2001, he was lying down drunk and incoherent. In May 2004, I was told that he had been severely beaten and taken to hospital and no one has seen him since. He was twenty-five years old.

Melit

Melit refused to join Alemu's gang at first. I accompanied him to his father's house three times because, as he said, he wanted his stepfamily to know that he had decent friends. They all refused to talk to me. On his third visit, he threatened to contact the *kebele* court and tell them what they had done to him. His stepmother allowed him to share a room in a house rented by a single mother and provided bedding material. I met Melit at Alemu's camp a few weeks later. He said that he felt unwanted and unloved by his stepfamily. The silence with which the other tenants surrounded him brought back memory of how lonely and lost he felt after his father died. He stayed at the camp for three weeks. He left because he did not like acting as Alemu's henchman and having to beat girls and boys on order. He did not fit in. It was difficult for him to be a crowd follower. He had helped burn down Zelalem's makeshift shelter in the camp and joined other boys to beat his old comrade and the girl. He was ashamed of what he had done and feared that he might end up killing Alemu. He went back to live with his stepmother once more. He found a job as a day labourer on a building site but lost his job because he could not keep up with the other workers. He felt too proud and depressed and did not want to give his stepfamily the satisfaction to seeing him fail in life again. He went back to the church wall.

Melit teamed up with a boy and a girl and went to live with them near another church wall. They pooled their resources and began selling cigarettes and other small items. The partnership lasted three months. The two boys quarrelled constantly about the proceeds of the sale and the girl. They had a big fight and the girl sided with the other boy. They held Melit down and she slashed his ears and arms with a razor blade. Melit went back to the church wall. I last saw Melit sometime at the end of March 1999. He told me that he found it very difficult to beg from cars because people did not feel sorry for him. He was also too ashamed to beg for food from door to door because he looked too grown up and healthy. He had had enough of being insulted by maidservants and watchmen and everyone telling him to work for his living. Some time in May 1999, he sent word to let me know that he had joined the army and was going to the front to fight in the war with Eritrea. He asked that I pray for him from time to time. He was eighteen years old.

Zelalem

Zelalem was the first one of the group to join Alemu's gang. The exact date was 22 September 1997. Although he resented Alemu's tyranny, he was very diligent at carrying out his orders and fitted in with the group. His gentle nature made him popular with the girls. He spent his days begging leftover food from rich households and his evenings regaling his friends with wild stories about his childhood experiences all over Ethiopia. Alemu awarded his contribution to group life by assigning him a 'wife' he had discarded. He gave them the necessary material and helped them build their own shelter. Zelalem nicknamed his girlfriend Misir, which means 'lentil' in Amharic. Even though the girl continued to prostitute herself, they were happy to be together.

Sometime in February 1998, Alemu's latest 'wife' disappeared with another girl. Since there were very few girls in the camp at the time, he demanded that Zelalem hand over his 'wife' to replace her. Zelalem and Misir refused, claiming to be in love with each other. Alemu and his henchmen, helped by Melit, dragged them out and beat them up in broad daylight. They then poured kerosene on the hut and burnt it to the ground. Zelalem was more upset by Melit's betrayal than of the beatings he and the girl received at the hand of Alemu's gang. They left the group and set up their own camp about a mile away from the others. Three days later, Alemu came back at night, burnt their hut and three boys gang raped the girl.

The next day, while they were scouting for a new place to hide, Zelalem and Misir met a farmer who had planted vegetables on the riverbanks. He was looking for someone to watch over his crop because he lived too far away. He let them build a shelter and promised that every time he visited and found his crop undamaged he would pay them five *birr*. The girl ceased to prostitute herself. They survived by Zelalem begging food from rich households. They supplemented this by collecting bottles, plastic bags and various types of containers from the airport garbage dump, washing them in a stream and selling them to open-air market retailers. After Zelalem and Misir left the group, Alemu ordered gang members not to speak to me. From then on I could only derive information and harrowing stories of gang life from boys and girls who had left the camp. In any case I had started to stagger my visits because I was suffering from constant back and stomach pain and was planning to leave Ethiopia. This was eventually diagnosed as three perforated ulcers.

Other runaway girls and boys joined Zelalem and Misir for a short period of time. A girl who had beaten up the 'husband' assigned to her, and who had subsequently been stripped naked for a whole day by female gang members, stayed with them for two weeks. Her story was unexpected and poignant. When she was nine years old, after her mother's death, she had gone to live with her much-older half-sister and her husband. The sister had treated her as a substitute servant and child minder. By the time she was fourteen the girl had had enough. Due to the constant fights she had with her sister, and the beating she received from her brother-in-law for refusing to help out, she decided to steal money and run away. The girl was permanently angry with Alemu and his gang. She talked incessantly of getting her revenge. She left when Misir and Zelalem refused to help her lure the girls to their camp and beat them up.

Zellem and Misir lived happily until Misir fell pregnant. They eventually found a way to abort the child. She was ill for quite some time after that, even though she did manage to have medical attention. Zelalem nursed her throughout. A few months later Misir found out that she was pregnant again. This was in spite of the fact that the clinic had given her extensive instructions on family planning. Zelalem left one morning without telling Misir and returned home. He called to tell me that he could not cope with the responsibility of taking care of Misir and a child. He came back a week later and disappeared again. He phoned me on 19 April 1998 (Ethiopian Easter Day) to tell me that he had gone back to see his mother for good and did not have the courage to leave her because she was very ill. His older brother was bed-ridden and she could not cope with him. He asked me to inform Misir and to encourage her to go back to her mother.

Misir had no intention of going back to her mother or contacting any relatives. She had been repeatedly raped and molested by her stepbrother and his friends. Her own mother had been thrown out of her family home after they discovered that she was pregnant when she was sixteen. The father was a married teacher. He refused to assume any responsibility and threatened to kill her if she persisted in claiming that he was the father. Her godmother housed her until she had Misir. She also helped her to acquire a *kebele* house. As soon as Misir could walk, her mother's godmother found her mother a job as a cleaner and general assistant in a boutique. Misir's mother earned very little and worked long hours but kept her daughter in school.

Misir was ten when her mother began her affair with a rich elderly man. He encouraged her mother to quit her job and work for him. He asked her to live with him and his two teenage sons and agreed to raise Misir as his child. Even though he never gave her mother the job he promised, the man was generous and kept his word. They lived happily until Misir was thirteen, when his sons began molesting her. At first it was only kisses and fondling of her breasts. This progressed to the older boy bringing his friends over and forcing her to kiss them as well. One day, while the mother was out, her stepbrother's best friend raped her. The boys told her that they would tell their father that she had asked for it. The next day her stepbrother raped her, in order to 'make it larger' so that she would not feel so much pain next time. From then on she had to endure their attention regularly. She was too scared and ashamed to tell her mother or anyone. She felt it was all her fault. She ran away on impulse after yet another of her stepbrother's friends told her to go wash herself after she had endured the latter's attention.

This is how she explained it: 'I went to wash myself and as if in a dream I went to my mother's room took some of her clothes and just walked out and kept walking until I fell down exhausted. I was accosted by some girls in the evening. They told me that I could join them. I followed them to Alemu's camp. I cannot go back to my mother. I am too ashamed, even if she does not know what happened to me, I know what I did.' After I told her that Zelalem had decided to stay with his mother for good, Misir went to live with her mother's godmother and gave up her baby for adoption. Zelalem contacted her and they were together again for a brief period of time. He went home for his brother's funeral and stayed on another six months. He left and got a job for a wholesaler in the *Mercato*. I last saw him in July 2001 still working and sleeping in the same store. He was twenty years old.

In May 2004, an expatriate friend told me that he had seen and talked to Misir. She had a baby boy and was begging around the place my friend was living. She told him that Zelalem was now working in another store near the airport as a porter and cleaner. He had tried to be her boyfriend again. She had refused because he had left her too many times. The baby in her arms was not his. Her mother's godmother had refused to help the second time she got pregnant. Her mother had told her that she considered her dead and did not want to see or talk to her ever again.

Godje

Godje visited Alemu's gang once. He survived for three days. He was disgusted with the whole set up, especially the fact that the boys lived off their girlfriends' prostitution. He despised Zelalem for kowtowing to Alemu and fitting in so well. He said that he would rather kill himself than turn into a pimp. He left without saying a word and returned to the back of church until the owner of the tea-shop offered him a job in June 1998. He was not allowed to handle money and did not receive a salary. His duties included taking out the garbage, serving customers, running errands, cleaning the place throughout the day, and fetching water for the restaurant from one mile up the road. He worked every day including Saturdays and Sundays, from 6 AM to 11 PM. In return, he could eat two meals a day and all the leftover food he could handle as well as sleep inside the shop. He lasted six months. The cook and the cashier stole foodstuffs and money. Godje reported it to the owner out of fear of being accused of stealing. The cook and the cashier had been with the owner for many years. They swore that the thieving had started after Godje had joined them. The owner preferred to believe them. They took it in turns to slap and kick Godje and told him never to set foot in the shop again. A *pent'ay* preacher subsequently recruited him. He stayed with them for one week. He left because he refused to take off the Ethiopian cross that his mother had given him. Besides, he did not understand why he should consider their version of Mary, Jesus and Joseph a better one.

From January 1999 to March 1999, Godje befriended a street-working boy who invited Godje to live with him and his mother. They took it in turns to sell cigarettes and assorted sweets. Godje had left his job at the tea-house addicted to cigarettes and coffee. The boy's mother did not approve of his heavy smoking. She ordered her son to call off their friendship and threw Godje out of her house. Godje went back to the church wall. When I met him May 1999, he looked unkempt and unhappy. He told me that he felt too depressed to do anything. He wanted to go back to Godjam to see his mother. I bought him clothes, presents for his family, gave him enough money for travel and wished him well.

Sometime in December 1999, I found out from Tadele that Godje was still in Addis Ababa. He was living in the middle of the town in a makeshift shelter with older beggars and working as a porter during the day. Other children corroborated this story and helped me find him. He was in partnership with two men selling marijuana, contraband cigarettes and *tchat*. It was four in the afternoon and he looked drugged. He was embarrassed to see me because he felt he had let me down. He said that he had lost his nerve at the last minute. He could not face going back home. Even though his family did not know what a life he had led, he knew. He was ashamed of having let his mother down and that he could not show his father that he had turned into a fine man. He preferred them to think that he was dead. He could no longer beg because he felt self-conscious and ill at ease working alongside younger street children. He was seventeen. He told me to forget about him. I lost touch with him because he left the place soon after our conversation. I finally traced him to another part of town sometime in July 2001. He looked older, thinner, dirtier and rougher. His impish smile had gone. He had given up hope. He did not know what would happen to him and he did not care. He just wished he had died a long time ago. I told him that I was leaving Ethiopia. He begged me to take him to Europe. I explained that it was not that easy. He refused to take any money and tore up the piece of paper with a telephone number of a relative of mine who would have given him money on a regular basis on my behalf. He was nineteen years old.

Slow Descent into Hell

In spite of the many theoretical definitions of what it means to be a man, the ideal male is not a universal or fixed concept. As I have detailed in chapter 2, there were multiple ways of being and becoming a man, or at least appearing to be one, for boys. The girls' essential role in the mixed-sex gang was to serve and service their male counterparts. Most joined looking for affection and acceptance and ended up as child prostitutes and henchmen in charge of disciplining other girls for insubordination. The choice of assimilation to the group meant prostitution and luring other girls to the group as well as sex with male gang members, most times while their minds were dulled with alcohol and marijuana. Many voted with their feet. Some stayed because they were in love with a special boy. Others had no alternative. They either conformed to what the boys expected or faced group beatings by both girls and boys or, worse still, gang rape. As one runaway girl put it: 'I thought they would be like family members but they were worse than the devils I ran away from.'

The background and life stories of girl gang members were as diverse and tragic as were those of the boys I studied. As I have already indicated, they had all been physically abused by their parents or step-relatives. Additionally, many girls had been either sexually molested or raped by a close relative, stepbrother or their mother's boyfriend before running away. The most unsettling aspect of intra-gang rape, group or otherwise, was that most boys and some of the girls correlated it with a severe form of beating. In other words, a justly deserved punishment and humiliation for insubordination. For most of the boys, rape only occurs when the girl is a virgin. A common remark was that 'she is upset because they played with her and refused to pay her'. Girls who described their experiences of rape often felt shame, distress, a feeling of helplessness or extreme anger. They did not want to go to the police because they felt that they would not be helped or understood. One girl remarked that she had never seen female police officers; all the police she knew were male and prone to make lurid suggestions if girls approached them for help.

Once in the street, the girls did not want to go back to their families. A constant justification was that even if their relatives did not know what had happened to them after they left home, they knew. They all felt ashamed. This self-knowledge more than anything created their sense of anomie. Many blamed themselves for having been abused by male members of their own families and by gang members. Since they were convinced that they had no one to turn to and nowhere to go, they dealt with their pain in silent desperation or constant anger.

For Zelalem and his friends, growing up as street children was affecting and communal. Once they crossed over to the dislocated world of a mixed-sex gang, inhabited by indifferent gang members with mutable morals, they were on their own. A first glance, the situation in Alemu's camp appeared to be one of jocular interdependence, much like the impression I had when I first met Zelalem's gang. The sordid aspects of child prostitution, gender-based intra-gang violence and substance abuse became apparent as soon as I began increasing my visits to the camp. It was painful to witness how each child had to accommodate their shifting roles and identities as gang members. Intra-gang violence and inter-gang feuds among Zelalem and his friends were instant, direct and short-lived, often between two boys or the *gulbetegnotch* harassing a specific child. More often than not violence in Alemu's camp was a pre-meditated vicious group act with boys and girls straddling the line between victim and perpetrators.

Several writers maintain that there is strong evidence to prove that group life provides an adequate child-on-child socialisation environment for youth gang members (see Swart 1986, 1988; Sharf et al. 1986; Aptekar 1988; Ennew 1994a). There are numerous texts describing the lives of homeless children (see Swart 1988; Sharf et al. 1986; Aptekar 1988; Connolly 1990; Ennew 1994a; Tyler et al. 1997; Lucchini 1993). Most give vivid accounts of such children's child-to-child relationships in the street. All the gangs I worked with in Addis Ababa were in many ways dissimilar to their counterparts in Asia, Africa and South America. Apart from Alemu's mixed-sex gang, none of the all-male youth gangs I knew had a formal structure, nor were they engaged in organized purposeful social or criminal enterprises. The gangs I studied did not have a special name for their group or for their activities in the street, just nicknames for each other. Even though they gave the impression of living happily together, they were more often than not at odds with one another. Besides, in Addis Ababa such children are not socialised by some kind of child-on-child interaction. They were all initially socialised by their own families before joining a gang aged ten or older.

As I have explained in chapter 2, *yilunta* as part of the socialising process may require a great deal of enculturation to bring about and sustain. Even if they possessed shifting morals, all the children I knew mustered their feelings and behaviour in accordance with those found in the 'wider Ethiopian culture' and had a clear understanding of the notion of *yilunta* and right from wrong. Zelalem and his friends often invoked religious or popular maxims to put across their ideas. The manner in which they conformed to cultural practices related to the giving, taking and sharing of food is another case in point. The spirit they re-created among themselves and in the street and the dominant values held in times of bereavement and ill health are also fitting examples. Furthermore, the moral standards by which they judged each other's behaviour and the personal characteristics that they considered culturally becoming in a decent person, especially a man, were comparable to those used by mainstream adult Ethiopians.

The boys and girls from the gangs I worked with had created an 'imperfect community', which did not provide them with all functions of the family. Much as home life was unsatisfactory, gang life did not replace it with a better alternative. It did not bring about continuity, permanence or the emotional and affective bond the children needed or wished to have. They had all run away from the abuse of their immediate families and in adolescence entered into another form of abusive and exploitative relationship with children like themselves. In the six years I was in the field, I never met a child who had not been beaten by family members or teachers and this includes those who had nothing to do with street life. The crucial point among gang members was that both boys and girls felt less

loyal to others in the group, less obliged to obey orders from anyone or reciprocate in terms other than their own. None of the children I talked to had any faith
in police officers being there to defend them or their rights to be heard. None had
ever come into contact with female police officers or social workers. Many had
seen the inside of a remand home or a prison cell.

Unlike dispute-related violence, the desire to punish a 'norm' violator, save
face or exercise coercive power as a form of deterrence results in the aggressor's
desire to coerce someone else to engage in a certain behavior and to restore eq-
uity (see Short and Hughes 2006). In the case of Alemu's gang, the presence of
more children meant that small conflicts and predatory violence escalated from
verbal abuse to extreme physical aggression, in which some bystanders willingly
or unwillingly took part in punishing the 'norm' violator. For boys, the potential
status reward, not to mention acceptance by the group, for punishing girls was
access to a sex partner or sex itself. This was enough for them to value violence-
based coercion. In short, violence was necessary for the maintenance of order
but also for creating group cohesion. The girls' (victims and victimizers alike)
acquiescence was sufficient proof that violence was needed to re-establish order.
Individuals within the gang experienced a great deal of pressure to back down
or join in violent acts when circumstances required that they put the welfare of
the group above their honour or emotional needs. I stopped counting the times
when in answer as to why a girl deserved to be punished, I was told that she had
asked for it – 'she had made so and so lose face or had insulted him, or worse still
had disobeyed orders'. This reasoning was acceptable to both boys and girls.

Youth gang membership is a fleeting, if not transitory, experience, cut short
by the onset of adulthood and the need for an alternative lifestyle. Due to the
long-term interaction I had with the youth gangs, I was able to record how the
children straddled the line between childhood, adolescence and adulthood. As
can be seen from the above, Wolamo and Melit were the only ones who managed to be re-absorbed into mainstream society. Wolamo was an interesting case
of religion coming to the rescue. An unexpected war with neighbouring Eritrea
provided Melit an exit into the army. Zelalem found the complexities of an adult
heterosexual relationship as difficult to handle as home and family life had been
when he was a child. His way out was to keep running away from home, from
family, from his girlfriend and his responsibilities. Tadele's fate shows how the
break-up of his family ties destroyed his ability to extricate himself from street
life. Godje's destiny was more representative of what befell the other homeless
boys I knew: jobless and without future prospects in sight. By July 2001, apart
from Melit and Wolamo, none of them had found homes, jobs or had managed to secure *kebele* identity cards. They had discarded their wild hairstyles and
anti-social demeanour and were still looking for a way out of gang life and for
acceptance by society. In other words, they had all joined the ranks of jobless
destitute men and women found all over Addis Ababa. This belies the widely

held assumption in Ethiopia that such children become hardened and dangerous criminals when they reach adulthood.

Finally, NGO directors often asked me, while still in the field, to either train their staff or provide advice on how to find a solution to the street-children problem in Ethiopia. All those who have read this book, including my very helpful editor, have also encouraged me to propose a solution. Anthropologists are more concerned with meaning than with remedies or measurements. *Meaning* here refers to the investigation of intensions, purposes, desires, actions and reactions and other such subjective qualities in the people they study. It is difficult to move directly from descriptive analysis to prescriptive policy advice. In any event, there is no simple solution or panacea to the problem. I hope to provide an explanation as well as an answer to the problem in the concluding chapter.

DISCUSSION AND CONCLUSION

This book is an account of how Ethiopian society acts upon its children when they are too young to take action against it. The childhood of members of youth gangs that I have depicted were in all ways precarious, each experience being amplified by a lack of safety and certainty. Conversely, home-based street children have a family with its own secrets and needs, which binds them together by a nexus of loyalties and love. These are not dysfunctional families. As a whole, home life offered the children the warmth, contact, unbreakable loyalty and an intense sense of belonging they needed. As I have shown in chapter 3, it is not that female heads of household are inadequate mothers, or that filial devotion is lacking, it is that being poor gets in the way of mothering. Street children and members of youth gangs are not a counter culture or a sub-culture but a distorted microcosm of Ethiopian society. Their morality does not differ from that of mainstream society. They are adept at using their knowledge of the socio-cultural environment to their own advantage. Youth gang members do not reject the norms and values of the 'wider Ethiopian culture'. The problem is that they are obliged to exist within the sub-cultural life of poverty, and child abuse. This puts them in positions where they cannot fully function within its boundaries. They are therefore forced to break old rules and make new ones as they go along.

Issues related to child poverty, youth gang culture, delinquency and streetism are multiple, complex and varied. It follows therefore that no universal remedy to these problems will be foolproof. Nevertheless, practically all the sources I have referred to in this book conclude with policy recommendations. Suggestions invariably include more policing, more State welfare, health and education provisions and more crime-prevention measures. At times, the feasibility, or even applicability, of these remedies strains to match the authority of the preceding analyses and reflects prevailing political or economic realities.

Like the proposed solutions, the global discourse on child poverty, streetism, delinquency and youth gangs is staggeringly similar (see Schneider and Tilley 2004; Klein et al. 2001). Missing from the picture is evaluation of earlier reports or projects, indicating the practical measures that have worked or failed, and why. Soon after coming into power in 1997, Tony Blair, then Labour prime minister, listed an array of policies to end child poverty in the UK by 2010. His government promised to tackle the fundamental causes of child poverty, which he listed as being structural unemployment, poor education provisions and poor housing as well as a crime and drugs culture. His passionate speech that 'poverty should not be a birthright. Being poor should not be a life sentence. We need to break the cycle of disadvantage', was well received (see Polly Toynbee, 'This is one legacy target that Labour can't afford to miss', *Guardian,* 14 March 2009). In spite of rhetoric and the legion of child protection and welfare schemes that were put in place, statistics show that by 2009, 3.6 million children in Britain are classified as living in poverty (see Amelia Gentleman, 'A portrait of 21st Century Poverty', *Guardian G2,* 18 March 2009). Mainstream media named a host of problems – deeply flawed upbringing, dysfunctional families, loss of deference towards adults and authority, single mothers on welfare or unchecked immigration policies – as the causes for the proliferation of street crime and youth gangs. In a leading article, Kenneth Minogue writes, 'Deprived of fathers, boys growing up in the inner city, turn to gangs for some kind of structure in their fractured lives.' He blames the softly-softly approach to youth crime, the welfare state and the break-up of the 'traditional British family' (see Kenneth Minogue, 'The Evil of Niceness', *Daily Mail,* 28 March 2009). What is striking is that the above-mentioned issues, except for State welfare provisions and political stability, are the very same causes invoked to account for youth gangs, child poverty and streetism in the developing world and within the development discourse. There are over seventy local and international child-supporting NGOs based in Addis Ababa (see www.ethiopia-emb. or.jp/news_e/list-e.pdf). They cannot and will not replace State welfare provisions, and so the number of street children and poor families keeps on increasing.

Another central issue within the debate on youth gangs is that more policing and more welfare will not solve the problem. A report issued in the UK by HH Inspectorate of Constabulary states that the police have identified almost three thousand organized criminal gangs and that 'the UK law enforcement community now knows more about organised criminality than ever before. ... The scale of the threat is better understood but there is no firm grasp of how the gangs operate and interact' (See *The Times,* 24 April 2009). This book is an attempt to fill such lacuna in – it deals precisely with how street children and their families operate and interact with one another and the wider community. It is also about how youth gangs come into being and function and about the children's relationship with one another, their families, their peers and society in Ethiopia. Additionally, the book addresses the seldom-analysed vital behavioural development, which occurs when such children emerge from the toddler stage and their transition from childish naivety to adolescence. In short, their presumed 'deeply flawed' upbringing, which I have tackled in this book by referring to the concept of *yilunta,* its sense of morality, its variation and never-ending transmission from the long-past to the future in the socialization of Ethiopian children.

I shall begin by discussing the use of corporal punishment and verbal abuse in disciplining children at home, in schools and in the street. As I have indicated in chapter 2, male-female power relations in Ethiopia are maintained by means other than representation, legal or otherwise. The basis of this other power is the symbolic capital derived from *yilunta*-based imposition of cultural values, which are presented as universal norms but whose content and context are historically determined by patriarchal ideology, socially constructed and therefore arbitrary. *Yilunta* also raises questions about conformity and individuality. Women are encumbered with instruments of knowledge about raising their children that they share in common with men. The meaning behind the notion of *yilunta* relies strongly on the idea that parents, especially mothers, inculcate moral values to children, but adherence to those values is largely a personal responsibility. In Ethiopia, parental authority over children in the home is a by-product of a patriarchal social arrangement. The price of not conforming to societal norms is public opprobrium. This is not false consciousness. In the socialization process, by reproducing an entire system of gender-based differences constitutive of the social order, women consciously reproduce the structures of domination which undermine their own choices in life. Under-pinning all this is the historical construction of masculinity, which stresses the inculcation of masculine dispositions in boys, female acquiescence to this plus unquestioned obedience to parental or adult authority by both sexes.

Pierre Bourdieu's (1977: 95) notion of *habitus* refers to the ways in which an individual's instinctive sense of what may be achieved is structured into a pattern of behaviour, which she or he construes as 'normal'. The extreme physical and verbal chastisement meted out to children in Ethiopia traps girls and boys in the cultural dictates of Ethiopian 'womanhood' and 'manhood'. It also leaves most of them without the means to defend themselves or to escape poverty. All the children and parents I have talked to told me that they had been physically chastised or verbally abused in their infancy. There is an Amharic expression mothers often used to express how well they were brought up, *tekontitche new yadegoot*.[1] Many children claimed that the beatings they received were mostly irrational, and the descriptions in this book attest to this. They hated the beatings they received for things they had not done or had said wilfully, and that their parents would not listen to or believe them. They especially resented being physically chastised in public, in order for their parents to show others that they were good disciplinarians. Mini once said to me that if her mother had beaten an adult half as much as she had beaten her, she would be jailed for life. As I have shown in chapters 4 and 5, running away from home was often their only way of coping with the emotional pain. Some children return home, but many end up in the street as members of youth gangs. They all resented being beaten by their teachers and the police for what were typically very minor infractions.

---

[1] *Tekontitche new yadekut* means 'I was pinched while I was being socialized'. Pinching children's thighs, cheeks or ears is one form of physical punishment often used by mothers to chastise their children.

The breeding ground for the informal economy and streetism in Ethiopia is a combination of economic under-development and population growth, all caused by an inefficient political system. Rural poverty due to population growth is an incentive to move to an urban environment. Upon arrival in the city, migrants soon discover that the system is not prepared to receive their large numbers or provide them a better life. Urban areas in Ethiopia are densely populated. They tend to house the majority of informal workers and the enormous unemployed work force. The informal sector is distinguished by low entry requirements for children and adults alike. No skill, no education, no capital acquisition or registration is necessary to beg or illegally trade in the street, just desperate want. In the saturated informal sector, the competition for begging and trading opportunities is tough and suffused with an under-current of violence. Street begging and trading stem less from economic strategies and more from survival tactics. Although it allows poor people a great deal of flexibility and mobility, it does not provide security.

Poverty is an almost insurmountable barrier to the realisation of the fundamental rights to education, health care, shelter and love, to which children are entitled. It also makes it harder for such children to break this vicious cycle of deprivation as adults. In chapter 3, I have tried to untangle the different levels and types of economic relations street children had at home and with the community. I have demonstrated how home-based street children re-created, maintained or embodied the structure of their mother's social networks and used some of these to generate their own opportunities for economic survival. This is in order to indicate the inter-generational process of structural and financial factors, which perpetuates poverty. Unlicensed street traders are endlessly concerned that their assets may be seized or destroyed by the police. However hard they try to increase their income-generating capacities, they have no means of delaying current needs for food, medicine, rent and school-related expenses. Everything requires money. Street children's families live, rationalize and work for the present. Unlike rural people, the urban population lives in an entirely money-based economy. They pursue various occupations and are dependent on their wages and earnings for the satisfaction of all their needs. Most of the families of street children that I have worked with spent over 90 per cent of their earnings on food.

The data I have provided in chapter 3 show that mothers and children react in the same way to available opportunities to earn an income. The emphasis in this book is on the child as the origin point of this activity. More often than not, the children themselves decide to engage themselves in street work and begging. Many end up teaching other children and their parents the tricks of the trade. The problem is not why such children behave so much more like adults than they need to, but why they have to. Urban poverty for street children's mothers means not only securing their family's material needs but also ensuring the moral formation of their children. The fact that their children are obliged to contribute to family income destabilizes the opposition or dualism between the public and private sphere, with children and mothers straddling both. The result is that at times children end up parenting their parents. In such circumstances, children end up taking the lead in domestic matters. All the same, even the most realistic and best parents rarely accepted that their children were mature enough to exercise the power to decide how family income is used or how the family should behave. Apart from eroding the traditional authority and identity of mothers, parent-child economic relations increase intra-household conflicts; hence, the never-ending reasons for mothers needing to chastise their children.

Globally, youth gangs display significant variation in their organization, structure and the level of crime and violence they engage in. All-male gangs do act as a group in various types of collective behaviour, ranging from simply hanging out together, low-level criminal activities and inter-gang warfare. Those I knew did not form a mutually exclusive bounded group. They went in and out of the collective and interacted or engaged in activities that were not group-related. Conversely, within the mixed-sex gang, individuals or pairs who did not act on behalf of the group or acted without its knowledge were more than likely to be punished. The genesis of intra-gang violence was adherence to masculine codes of honour, which shaped the individual boy's reaction to any form of affronts to his honour and manhood. This does not under-estimate the face-saving property of violence or the benefits of being rewarded with a sexual partner or sex itself for participating in group-organized violence. Most of the time boys engaged in violent behaviour in large part because they felt they had to and not necessarily because they wanted to. Violent confrontations were often motivated by a desire to appear manly and avoid loosing face or being shamed in front of others. Among Alemu's mixed-sex gang, rape and violence were contests for displaying status and masculine power as well as controlling the girls' sexuality and behaviour.

The word *gang* usually conjures up images in the popular mind of juvenile delinquency, street crime and violence, drugs and knives. Among the groups I worked with, crime was opportunistic rather than the sole reason for gang membership. This difference could be linked to familial circumstances and to the fact that the majority of youth gangs emerge in the context of urban poverty. As I have shown in chapter 4, the youth gang members I worked with did not forge their own identity so much as it was forced upon them. The police and members of the public invariably viewed them as a threat to social order. They depended less on the presence of adults in their lives and more on their relationships with other children or on their own resources for their survival in the street. They had most of the essential characteristics associated with streetism. They occupied a well-defined territory in street life. They did not live with adults. They worked, begged or hustled for themselves or shared the proceeds of their street activities with the community of children they live with. While a few may have accepted the occasional temporary job offer, most were engaged in full-time begging and hustling. They also share non-gang motivated, multiple relations with the street-trading and begging fraternity, the police, shop owners and benefactors as individuals.

The street was not only their work place; it was their home as well as their playground. They were the runaways from dysfunctional families, the abused, the abandoned, the destitute, the petty thieves, the drug abusers, the gamblers, the juvenile delinquents, the dropouts and vagrants. They were the most in danger of street violence since they lacked the patronage and protection of family members or other generous adults. Law enforcement officers and ordinary citizens did not look upon their way of life or personal appearances with tolerance. The police were harsher with them because they were unkempt and generally disruptive and because they begged from motorists and occupied verandas and street pavement. Many ended up in police custody for vagrancy because they did not have identity cards or home addresses. They could be arrested or beaten by the police because of minor criminal activities like begging from vehicles, gambling, being drunk or smoking hashish. All this made it more difficult for them to enter into the wider circle of life as adults.

Field research among vulnerable children highlights the complex position of an adult ethnographer in the field. As I have already mentioned, my choice of youth gangs as a research subject was accidental. I had not done the type of pre-field preparation that I did for studying street children. There was a gap between my practical experience of field work and my theoretical knowledge of how to do field work among youth gang members. I just wrote the script as I went along, learning through experience and expedience. Field work as a whole was therefore a personal odyssey. The most difficult aspect was exploring sensitive issues dealing with boy-girl sexual encounters, at both personal and cultural levels. It is imperative to realize the contextual situation that frames such discussion. Sexuality in children disturbs at the best of times. In the literature, gang membership is dealt with in a variety of frames alongside localized forms of activities and behaviour. Sex is generally tackled in terms of romantic teenage love, problematised within the discourse of child pornography, prostitution, paedophilia, human trafficking, violence and rape (see Campbell 1984; Chesney-Lind 2004; Dorais and Corriveau 2009). I had to deal with child-on-child rape and sexual exploitation as well as girl-on-girl violence for the benefit of boys in a world created by the children themselves. As I have shown in chapter 5, the roles of the girls in the mixed-sex gangs were that of sexual chattels to male gang members, as an incentive for other boys and girls to join or as a way for the group to increase their income-earning opportunities from child prostitution. All the children had run away from home due to constant abuse by familiar adults and had ended up abusing each other in the street.

The above notwithstanding, I hope that I have demonstrated that these children are not juvenile delinquents – they are not problem children – they are children with problems and in urgent need of assistance. I have described the fear, violence, loneliness and longings of confused adolescents confined in a parent-less prison. Youth gang members in Ethiopia are victims of an abusive or indiffer-ent adult world. Studies after studies show teenage years to be the most troubled years in a child's life, and yet little provisions or space are made for them as a special category of children in schools or within the development discourse.

The literature on youth gangs highlights the impact of immigration and eth-nicity, 'race', urban poverty, depravation, drug and crime culture, national influ-ences and local neighborhood circumstances on youth-gang development (see Covey 2005). In Ethiopia, gang membership is the result of child abuse and ne-glect and of attempts by such children to escape the confines of familial oppres-sion. My informants did not plan to join a gang when they left home; they just ended up being part of a gang. Membership in a gang did not provide them with the opportunity to make a sustainable livelihood. It did not integrate them into mainstream society as adults. Solutions such as getting children off the street, crime-prevention programmes and proclamations of ending child poverty are shorthand feel-good terms. They are routinely bandied about as being sustain-able forms of child-protection remedies. Too often, they disguise the magnitude of the problem in the developing world. More often than not, the State is either indifferent and unwilling or unable to end child or adult poverty. It is quicker to condemn children that seem 'out of place' in society and the anti-social acts they commit, than to accept that their failings are partly due to the lack of willingness by adults to accept responsibility for their fate or do something about it.

Poverty is not an isolated variable; it is inter-dependent with social, political and economic factors, which involve the State and its leaders. A recent study includes a discussion of the strategies of national development plans needed to address and to tackle childhood poverty more effectively (see Woldehanna et al. 2008). It is beyond the scope of this book to delve into the politics of Ethiopia. Two recent books provide well-informed treatises on the issues of bad gover-nance, conflict, poverty and the role of NGOs in the developing world (see Col-lier 2007; Moyo 2009). However, the degree to which the State is present, not just to impose social order but to put in place intervention programs, which are not suppressive, is important. Taking into account the local conditions in which they develop and operate, there are areas of government where the State *can* promote child welfare and accountability. The police and teachers are part of society and ought not be allowed function outside the law. Ethiopian teachers, especially those employed by the government, are under-paid and over-worked, but this should not be a licence for them to mete out corporal or verbal punish-ments on their students. In April 2010, I talked to several schoolchildren who told me that although the government has outlawed corporal punishment by teachers, verbal punishment and the power of teachers to have a student expelled is still a terrifying prospect for most of them. Police officers are there to protect people and apprehend culprits. This should not give them the right to beat up street children (or indeed suspected criminals) as a way of reinforcing their power and punishing them on the spot. Poor people are poor but they are not stupid or potential criminals.

I am a firm believer that change comes from within. As I have already indicated, the educated urban elites no longer deem it necessary to use excessive physical punishment to socialise their children. They are already setting an example. The State may outlaw corporal punishment by parents, but I doubt that they will be able to enforce or police it. Even though the Ethiopian constitution states that 'marriage shall be entered into only with the free and full consent of the intending spouses' and the legal age of marriage is eighteen for both sexes, 19 per cent of Ethiopian girls are married before their fifteenth birthday. Obstetric fistula and other health problems associated with child marriage are on the increase (see Central Statistical Agency 2005). The great majority of the street children's mothers I interviewed fall into this category. Since 1995, The Ethiopian Women Lawyers Association (EWLA) has been actively engaged in raising awareness about child marriage and women's legal rights in Ethiopia, ensuring that gender is central to the drawing up of laws, and have put in place practical measures to help economically poor women access legal services. The organisation has had great success in putting women's rights on the government agenda, with the ultimate goal of eliminating all forms of legally and traditionally sanctioned discrimination against women (see www.ewla.org).

I hope that NGOs helping such children will make an effort to create continuity in their lives when they attempt to assist them and their families. Children's needs and childhoods last longer than the lifetime of a specific project, which at times last only one or two years. A holistic and long-term approach to helping children and families living in difficult circumstances might be more costly and mean helping fewer children, but I believe it to be a more efficient way of getting some of these children out of poverty and providing an element of safety and certainty in their lives.

This book is an attempt to provide some vital information about street children and youth gangs for those concerned with the fate of destitute abused children. I hope that I have described and interpreted their lives and activities with empathy as well as an informed concern for their plight. Long-term ethnographic research afforded me the unique opportunity to examine from close proximity the dynamic processes of ongoing action and interactions among youth gangs and street children and the people around them. I hope that it will raise awareness, among many other things, of the tragic consequences of the effects of corporal punishment and verbal abuse of children by parents, teachers and police officers as part of disciplining children or crime prevention methods.

BIBLIOGRAPHY

Abu-Lughod, Lila. 2006. 'Writing against Culture', in Helen Lewin (ed.), *Feminist Anthropology: A Reader*. Blackwell.

Adamson, Christopher. 2004. 'Defensive Localism in White and Black: A Comparative History of European-American and African-American Youth Gangs', in Jacqueline Schneider and Nick Tilley (eds.), *Gangs*. Ashgate.

Alexander, Claire E. 1996. *The Art of 'Being Black': the Creation of Black British Youth Identities*. Clarendon Press.

Andargatchew, Tesfaye. 1976. 'Juvenile Delinquency: An Urban Phenomenon', in Marina Ottoway (ed.), *Urbanization in Ethiopia*. Addis Ababa University.

———. 1992. 'The Social Consequences of Urbanisation: The Addis Ababa Experience', *Ethiopian Journal of Development Research* 14 (1).

Anderson, Benedict. 1983. *Imagined Communities: Reflections on the Origin and Spread of Nationalism*. Verso.

Andranovich, Greg. D., and Gerry. Riposa. 1993. *Doing Urban Research*. Sage.

Andrews, Molly, et al. (eds.). 2000. *Lines of Narratives: Psychosocial Perspectives*. Routledge.

Andrews, Molly, Corinne Squire and Maria T. Tamboukou (eds). 2008. *Doing Narrative Research*. Sage.

Appadurai, Arjun. 2008. 'The Capacity to Aspire: Culture and the Terms of Recognition', in David Held and Henrietta Moore (eds.), *Cultural Politics in a Global Age*. Oneworld Books.

Aptekar, Lewis. 1988. *The Street Children of Cali*. Duke University Press.

———. 1994. 'Street Children in the Developing World. A Review of their Conditions', *Cross-Cultural Research* 28 (3): 195–224.

Aptekar, Lewis, and Paula Heinonen. 2003. 'Methodological Implication of Contextual Diversity Research on Street Children', in *Youth and Environments* Vol. 13 (1996).

Ardener, Shirley and Sandra Burman (eds.), *Money-Go-Rounds: The Importance of ROSCAs for Women*. Berg.

Bahru, Zewde. 1986. 'Early Safars of Addis Ababa, Patterns of Evolution', *Proceedings of the International Symposium on the Centenary of Addis Ababa, November 24–25*. Addis Ababa University.

———. 1991. *A History of Modern Ethiopia, 1855–1974*. Eastern Africa Studies. Addis Ababa University.

Bainbridge, David. 2009. *Teenagers: A Natural History*. Portobello.

Banks, Marcus. 1996. *Ethnicity: Anthropological Constructions*. Routledge.

Barker, Gary and Felicia Knaul. 1991. 'Exploited Entrepreneurs: Street and Working Children in Developing Countries', *Childhope-USA*. Working Paper no. 1.

Basin, Donna, Margaret Honey and Merle. M. Kaplan (eds.). 1994. *Representation of Mother-hood.* Yale University Press.

Bennett, Alan. 1997. *Writing Home.* Faber.

Berkman, Marcus. 2005. *Fatherhood: The Truth.* Teddybooks.

Bourdieu, Pierre. 1977. Outline of a Theory of Practice. Cambridge University Press.

Boyden, Jo. 1990. 'Childhood and the Policy Makers: A Comparative Perspective on The Globalisation of Childhood', in Alan James and Allison Prout (eds.), Constructing and Reconstructing Childhood. The Falmer Press.

Campbell, Anne. 1984. *The Girls in the Gang.* Blackwell.

Campos, Regina, et al. 1994. *Social Networks and Daily Activities of Street Youth in Belo Hori-zonte, Brazil.* University of Nebraska.

Carrithers, Michael. 1992. *Why Humans have Cultures: Explaining Anthropology and Social Diversity.* Oxford University Press.

———. (ed.) 2009. *Culture, Rhetoric and the Vicissitudes of Life.* Berghahn Books.

Central Statistical Agency of Ethiopia. 2005. *National Population Census.*

Central Statistical Authority of Ethiopia. 1999. *The 1994 Populations and Housing Census of Ethiopia.* Analytical Report V (II).

———. 2002. *National Population Census.*

Central Statistical Commission. 2002. *A Civil Society Forum for East and Southern Africa on Promoting and Protecting the Rights of Street Children.* Consortium for Street Children.

Chege, Michael. 1979. 'The Revolution Betrayed: Ethiopia, 1974–7', *Journal of Modern Afri-can Studies* London 17 (3): 359–380.

Chesney-Lind, Meda. 2004. 'Girls, Gangs and Violence: Anatomy of a Backlash', in Jacqueline Schneider and Nick Tilley (eds.), *Gangs.* Ashgate.

Children, Youth and Family Welfare Organisation (CYFWO). 1992. *Addressing the Situation of Children in Especially Difficult Circumstances in Addis Ababa.*

Clifford, James. 1986. 'Introduction: Partial Truths', in James Clifford and George E. Marcus (eds.), *Writing Culture: The Poetics and Politics of Ethnography.* University of California Press.

Clifford, James, and George E. Marcus (eds.). 1986. *Writing Culture: The Poetics and Politics of Ethnography.* University of California Press.

Cohen, Stanley. 1972. *Folk Devils and Moral Panics.* MacGibb and Kee.

Collier, Paul. 2007. *The Bottom Billion: Why the Poorest Countries are Failing and What Can Be Done About It.* Oxford University Press.

Connell, Robert. W. 2000. 'Arms and the Man', in Ingeborg Breines, Robert Connell and Ingrid Eide (eds), *Male Roles, Masculinities and Violence.* UNESCO, Paris.

———. 2001. 'Introduction and Overview', *Feminism and Psychology* 11 (1).

Connolly, Mark. 1990. Adrift in the City: A Comparative Study of Street Children in Bogota, Colombia and Guatemala City, in *Child and Youth Services*, vol. 14 (1).

Cosgrove, James. G. 1990. 'Towards a Working Definition of Street Children', *International Social Work* Vol. 33, 185–192. Sage.

Covey, Herbert. C. (ed.). 2005. *Street Gangs throughout the World,* Libra Publishers.

Cussianovich, Alejandro. 1992. 'Analisis historico del trabajo infantil en America Latina', in *Informe Talleres Latino Americanos, Desarollo Comunitario Urbano Y Ninas/Ninos Trabaja-dores de/en la calle.* Lima, Peru.

Dawit, Shifaw. 2002. *Diary of a Terror: Ethiopia 1974–1991.* Book Surge LLC.

Dawit, Wolde-Giorgis. 1989. *Red Tears: War, Famine and Revolution in Ethiopia.* Red Sea Press.

Decker, Scott. H. and Frank. M. Weerman (eds). 2005. *European Street Gangs and Troublesome Youth Groups.* AltaMira.

Devasahayam, Theresa, and Brenda Yeoh (eds). 2007. *Working and Mothering in Asia: Images, Ideologies and Identities.* Nuss Press.

Dorais, Michael, and Patrice Corriveau. 2009. *Gangs and Girls: Understanding Juvenile Prostitutions.* McGill.

Ennew, Judith. 1994a. 'Parentless Friends: A Cross-Cultural Examination of Networks Among Street Children and Street Youth', in Frank Nestman and Klaus Hurrelmann (eds.), *Social Networks and Social Support in Childhood and Adolescence.* De Gruiyter.

———. 1994b. *Street and Working Children. A Guide to Panning,* Development Manual 4. Save the Children UK.

———. 1996. 'Difficult Circumstances: Some reflections on Street Children in Africa', *African Insight* Vol. 26, no. 3.

Ennew, Judith, and Brian Milne. 1989. *The Next Generation: The Lives of Third World Children.* Zed Books.

Ephrem, Tessema. 1998. *Urban Adaptation and Survival Strategies: The Case of Internally Displaced Groups in the Arada Area of Addis Ababa.* MA Thesis in Anthropology, Addis Ababa University.

Eriksen, Thomas H. 1988. *Ethnicity and Nationalism: Anthropological Perspectives.* Pluto Press.

Ezekiel, Gebissa. 2004. *Leaf of Allah: Khat and Agricultural Transformation.* James Currey.

———. 2009. *Contested Terrain: Essays on Oromo Studies, Ethiopianist Discourses and Politically Engaged Scholarship.* Red Sea Press.

Fine, Gary A., and Kent L. Sandstrom. 1988. *Knowing Children: Participant Observation with Minors.* Sage.

Fine, Gary A., and Sherryl Kleinman. 1979. 'Rethinking Subculture: An Interactionist Analysis', *American Journal of Sociology* 85.

Fitsum, Resome. 1994. *An Assessment of the Conditions of Internally Displaced People in Addis Ababa with particular reference to the Churchill Road Area.* BA Senior Essay in Anthropology, Addis Ababa University.

Fortes, Meyer. 1970. 'Social and Psychological Aspects of Education in Taleland', in John Middleton (ed.), *From Child to Adult: Studies in the Anthropology of Education.* Natural History Press.

Foucault, Michel. 1981. *The History of Sexuality: An Introduction.* Pelican Books.

Geertz, Clifford. 1973. *The Interpretation of Cultures.* Basic Books.

Gellner, Ernest. 1983. *Nations and Nationalism.* Blackwell.

Glassner, Barry. 1976. 'Kid Society', *Urban Education* 11: 5–22.

Glauser, Benno. 1990. 'Street Children: Deconstructing a construct', in Alan James and Alisson Prout (eds.), *Constructing and Reconstructing Childhood: Contemporary Issues in the Sociological Study of Childhood.* The Falmer Press.

Glazer, Clive. 2000. *Bo-Tsotsi: The Youth Gangs of Soweto 1935–1976.* James Currey.

Goode, David. A. 1986. 'Kids, Culture and Innocents', *Human Studies* 9: 83–106.

Habtamu, Wondimu. (ed.). 1996. *Research Papers on the Situation of Children and Adolescents in Ethiopia.* Addis Ababa University.

Halsey, Greco D. (ed.). 1994. 'Social Network and Daily Activities of Street Youth in Belo Horizonte, Brazil'. *Child Development* 65: 319–330.

Hardman, Charlotte. 1973a. 'Can there be Anthropology of Children?', *Journal of the Anthropological Society of Oxford* 4 (1): 85–99.

———. 1973b. 'Children in the Playground', *Journal of the Anthropological Society of Oxford* 5 (30).

———. 1974. 'Fact and Fantasy in the Playground', *New Society,* 26 September 1974.

Hayward, Richard. 1990. 'Notes on the Aari Language', in Richard Hayward (ed.), *Omotic language Studies.* SOAS.

Hecht, Tobias. 1995. *At Home in the Street: Street Children of Recife, Brazil.* DPhil. Thesis, Department of Anthropology, University of Cambridge.

Heinige, David. 1982. *Oral Historiography.* Longman.

Heinonen, Paula. 1996. *Some Aspects of Child Rearing Practices in the Urban Setting of Addis Ababa (with special reference to street children).* Background Document, Radda Barnen, Addis Ababa.

———. 2002 *Early, Forced Marriage and Abduction and their links to Custom/Tradition, FGM, Poverty and HIV/AIDS.* Background Document, WOMANKIND Worldwide.

James, Alan. 1979. 'When is a child not a child? Confections, Concoctions and Conceptions', *Journal of the Anthropological Society of Oxford* 10 (2): 83–95.

———1993. *Childhood Identities.* Edinburgh University Press.

James, Alan, and Alisson Prout (eds). 1990. *Constructing and Reconstructing Childhood: Contemporary Issues in the Sociological Study of Childhood.* The Falmer Press.

James, Patrick. 1973. *A Glasgow Gang Observed.* Methuen.

James, Wendy, Donald. L. Donham and Eisei Kurimoto (eds). 2002. *Remapping Ethiopia: Socialism and After.* James Currey.

Jayaweera, Hiranthi. 1991. *Race, Ethnicity, Class and Gender: A Study of the Orientation and Identities of Afro-Caribbean Women in Oxford.* DPhil Thesis, University of Oxford.

Kabeer, Naila. 1994. *Reversed Realities: Gender Hierarchies in Development Thought.* Verso.

King, Anthony. 2000. 'Thinking with and against Bourdieu: A practical Critique of the Habitus', in *Sociological Theory* 18: 3.

Klein, Malcom, et al. (eds). 2001. *The Eurogang Paradox: Street Gangs and Youth Groups in US and Europe.* Kluwer.

Krumeich, Anja. 1994. 'Blessings of Motherhood: Health, Pregnancy and Child Care in Dominica', *Studies in medical anthropology and sociology.* Aksan.

Kurimoto, Eisei. 2002. 'Fear and Anger: Female versus Male Narratives among the Anywaa', in Wendy James, et al. (eds). *Remapping Ethiopia, Socialism and After.* James Currey.

Laidler, Karen J., and Geoffrey Hunt. 2004. 'Accomplishing Femininity among the Girls in The Gang', in Jacqueline Schneider and Nick Tilley (eds.), *Gangs.* Ashgate.

Lancy, David. F. 2008. *The Anthropology of Childhood.* Cambridge University Press.

Le Vine, Robert. A., and Douglas R. Price Williams. 1974. 'Children's Kinship Concepts: Cognitive Development and Early Development among the Hausa', *Ethnology* 13.

Le Vine, Robert A., and Rebecca S. New. 2008. *Anthropology and Child Development: A Cross-Cultural Reader.* Blackwell.

Lucchini, Riccardo. 1993. *Enfant de la rue: Identité, Sociabilité, Drogue.* Working Paper No. 224. University of Fribourg.

Lusk, Mark. 1992. 'Street Children of Rio de Janeiro', *International Social Work* 35: 293–305.

Mandell, Nancy. 1991.'The Least Adult Role in Studying Children', in Frances C. Waksler (ed.), *Studying the Social Worlds of Children.* The Falmer Press.

Marsden, Philip. 2007. *The Barefoot Emperor: An Ethiopian Tragedy.* Harper Collins.

Mauss, Marcel. 1955. *The Gift.* Cunnison, NY: Free Press.

Markakis, John, and Nega Ayale. 1978. *Class and Revolution in Ethiopia.* Spokesman Book.

Mayer, Philip. (ed.). 1970. *Socialisation: The Approach from Social Anthropology.* Tavistock.

Miller, Tina. 2011. *Making sense of Fatherhood: Gender, Caring and Work.* Cambridge University Press.

———. 2005. *Making Sense of Motherhood: A Narrative Approach.* Cambridge University Press.

Ministry of Labour and Social Affairs (MOLSA) and Radda Barnen Sweden. 1988. *Survey on Street Children in Addis Ababa.*

Ministry of Works and Urban Development: Addis Ababa City Administration, 1996 and 2006 Annual Reports

Mitchell, Juliet. 1966. 'Women: The Longest Revolution', *New Left Review* 40 (Nov–Dec): 11–13.

MOLSA, UNICEF and University College, Cork. 1993. *Study on Street Children in Four Selected Towns in Ethiopia.* Addis Ababa.

Moore, Henrietta. 2006. 'On Being Young', *Anthropological Quarterly* Vol. 29, no.2.

Moyo, Dambisa. 2009. *Dead Aid: Why aid is not working and how there is another way for Africa.* Alen Lane.

Naty, Alexander. 2002. 'Memory and the Humiliation of Men: The Revolution in Aari', in Wendy James et al. (eds.), *Remapping Ethiopia, Socialism and After.* James Currey.

Nestmann, Frank, and Klaus Hurrelmann (eds). 1994. *Social Networks and Social Support in Childhood and Adolescence.* De Gruyter.

Newman, Rebecca, et al. (eds). 1998. *Fatherhood.* Cambridge University Press.

Onyango, Phillista, and Peter Kariuki 1991. *Urban Poverty: Research and Policy Evaluation of Street Children and their Families in Kenya.* Ford Foundation.

Opie, Iona, and Peter Opie. 1959. *The Lore and Language of School Children.* Clarendon Press.

Oritz de Carrizosa, Susana, and John S. Poertner. 1992. 'Latin American Children: Problem, Programmes and Critique', *International Social Work* 35: 405–413.

Ottaway, Marina. (ed.). 1976. *Urbanisation in Ethiopia a text with integrated readings.* Addis Ababa University.

Pankhurst, Alula. 1992. *Resettlement and Famine in Ethiopia: The Villagers' Experience.* Manchester University Press.

Pankhurst, Richard. 1961. *An Introduction to the Economic History of Ethiopia.* Lalibela House.

———. 1968. *Economic History of Ethiopia.* Haile Selassie I University Press.

Perry, Donna L. 2009. 'Fathers, Sons and the State: Discipline and Punishment in a Wolof Hinterland', *Cultural Anthropology* Vol. 24, no. 1.

Polanyi, Karl. 1968. *Primitive, Archaic and Modern Economies.* New York: Georges Dalton.

Poynting, Scott, and Greg Noble. 2004. 'Middle Eastern Appearances "Ethnic Gangs", Moral Panic and Media Framing', in Jacqueline Schneider and Nick Tilley (eds.), *Gangs.* Ashgate.

Proceedings of the International Symposium on the Centenary of Addis Ababa, November 24–25, 1986. Addis Ababa University.

Rane, Asha. (ed.). 1994. *Street Children: A challenge to the Social Work Profession.* Bombay: Tata Institute of Social Sciences.

Richter, Linda. 1991. 'South African Street Children: Comparisons with Anglo-American Runaways', in Nico Bleichrods and Pieter Drenth (eds.), *Contemporary issues in cross-cultural psychology.* Amsterdam.

Rogers, Alisdair, and Stephen Vertovec. (eds.). 1995. *The Urban Context: Ethnicity, Social Networks and Situational Analysis.* Berg.

Rogers, Dennis. 1999. 'Youth Gangs and Violence in Latin America and the Caribbean: A Literature Survey', *Sustainable Development.* Working Paper no. 4.

———. 2003. 'Dying for It: Gangs, Violence and Social Change in Urban Nicaragua', *London School of Economics.* Working Paper no. 25.

Rosa, Anesi C. S., Rute de Sousa and George Ebrahim. 1992. 'The Street Children of Recife: A study of their background', *Journal of Tropical Paediatrics* 38: 34–40.

Sahlins, Marshall. 1974. *Stone Age Economics.* Travistock.

Sanjek, Roger. 1974. 'What is Network Analysis, and What is it Good For?', *Reviews in Anthropology* 1: 588–597.

Sciama, Lidia. 2003. *A Venetian Island: Environment, History and Change in Burano.* Berghahn Books.

Scharf, Wilfried., Marlene Powel and Edgar Thomas. 1986. 'Stroller: Street Children of Cape Town', in Sandra Burman (ed.), *Growing up in a Divided Society.* Northwestern University Press.

Schiefelin, Bambi. 1990. *The Give and Take of Everyday Life: Language and Socialisation of Kalulu Children.* Cambridge University Press.

Seifu, Ruga. 1976. 'Moulding Traditional Self-Help Associations to Meet Modern Demands: A Case Study', in Marina Ottoway (ed.), *Urbanisation in Ethiopia.* Addis Ababa University.

Selamawit, Mecca. 2006. 'Hagiographies of Ethiopian Female Saints: with special reference to Gadla Krestos Samra and Gadla Ferqerta Krestos', *Journal of African Cultural Studies* Vol. 18, no. 2, December 2006. Routledge.

Sen, Amartya. 1999. *Development as Freedom.* Oxford University Press.

———. 1983 'Development: Which Way Now?', in *The Economic Journal:* 93.

Shail, Andrew. 2004. 'You're Not One of Those Boring Masculinists, Are YOU? The Question of Male-Embodied Feminism', in Stacy Gillis, Gillian Howie and Rebecca Munford (eds.), *Third Wave Feminism: A Critical Exploration.* Palgrave.

Shari, Thurer L. 2004. *The Myth of Motherhood. How Culture Reinvents the Good Mother.* Houghton Mifflin.

Short, James, and Loraine Hughes. 2006. *Studying Youth Gangs.* Altamira Press.

Smith, Michael. P. 2001. *Transnational Urbanism: Locating Globalization.* Blackwell.

Schneider, Jacqueline, and Nick Tilley. 2004. *Gangs.* Ashgate.

Solomon, Gebre. 1993. 'The Condition of the Poor in Addis Ababa: A Social Problem not Yet Addressed', in Asfaw Desta and Dessalegn Rahamto (eds.), *Dialogue: Journal of Addis Ababa University Teachers Association* Vol. 2, no. 1.

Solomon, Gebre, and Kidanu Aklilu. 1993. *National and International Response to Internal Displacement in Ethiopia.* Addis Ababa University: Institute of Development Research.

Speier, Mathew. 1976. 'The Adult Ideological Viewpoint in Studies of Childhood', in Arlene Skolnick (ed.), *Rethinking Childhood.* Boston University Press.

Stone, J. L., and J. Church. 1968. *Childhood and Adolescence.* Random House.

Swart, Jill. 1988. 'Community and Self Perception of the Black South African Street Child', *Symposium on Theory and Practice, Street: Children in the Third World,* University of Amsterdam, 20–21 April 1989.

———. 1990. *Malunde. The Street Children of Hillbrow.* Witwatersrand University Press.

Tedla, Diressie. 1999. *Situation Analysis of Children in Especially Difficult Circumstances in Ethiopia.* Addis Ababa: Ministry of Labour and Social Affairs.

Tekeste, Negash. 2006. *Education in Ethiopia, from crises to the brink of collapse.* Uppsala.

Thrasher, Frederic M. 1927. *The Gang: A Study of 1,313 Gangs in Chicago.* University of Chicago Press.

Turton, David. (ed.). 2006. *Ethnic Federalism: The Ethiopian Experience in Comparative Perspective.* James Currey.

Tyler, Forrest. B. 1997. *Urban Settings, Youth Violence and Pro-social Communities.* Paper delivered at the Urban Childhood Conference, Trondheim, Norway, 9–11 June.

UNICEF. 1985. *Worksheet for the Regional Operating Plan for Abandoned and Street Children.* Bogota.

UNICEF. 1986. *Children in especially difficult circumstances. Annex. Exploitation Working and Street Children.* New York.

UNICEF. 1990. *Children and Development in the 1990s.* Proceedings of the World Summit for Children, September, New York.

UNICEF. 2003. http://www.unicef.org/infobycountry/ethiopia_early_marriage.html.

UNICEF/Transitional Government of Ethiopia (TGE). 1993. *Children and Women in Ethiopia: A situation report.* Addis Ababa.

United Nations Population Division. 2008. www.un.org/esa/population/unpop.htm.

Wainaina, James. 1981. 'The "Parking Boys" of Nairobi', *African Journal of Sociology* 1 (7–5).

Wang, Xia, and Rainer Hofe. 2007. *Research methods in Urban and Regional Planning.* Springer.

White, William. 1993. *Street Corner Society: The Social Structure of an Italian Slum.* University of Chicago Press

Whiting, Beatrice. B., and Carroline P. Edwards (eds). 1988. *Children of Different World: The Formation of Social Behaviour.* Harvard University Press.

Whiting, Beatrice. B., and John W. M. Whiting 1975. *Children in Six Cultures.* Harvard University Press.

Woldehanna, Tassew, Nicola Jones and Bekele Tefera (eds). 2008. Invisibility of Children's Paid and Unpaid Work: Implications for Ethiopia's National Poverty Reduction Policy. *Childhood May 15:177–20.* Sage.

Yunus, Muhammad 1998. *Banker to the Poor.* London: Aurum Press Ltd.

Zenebe, Mammo. 1996. 'Street Children: Nature and Magnitude of the Problems and Method of Intervention', in Wondimu Habtamu (ed.), *Research Papers on the Situation of Children and Adolescents in Ethiopia.* Addis Ababa University.

INDEX

54, 59–60, 155; qualitative, 2, 14, 67;
quantitative, 6; questions, 7, 49, 152;
research, 1–3, 6–16, 18, 28–9, 88–9,
107, 109, 118–9, 155, 157; sociality
theory, 8, 11–13
migrant, 17, 20, 23, 25, 27–8, 39, 43, 52,
153; children, 44, 91, 99, 103; families,
11, 19, 46, 58, 64, 90; men, 33
mother, 1, 2, 5, 8, 13–4, 28, 38–9, 40–5,
47, 62–7, 75, 78–88, 96–9, 111, 123,
128, 137, 150; daughter relationship,
33, 38–9, 42–3, 50–1, 57, 61, 76, 140,
144; son relationship, 33, 38–9, 42–5,
48–51, 55, 58, 77, 101–5, 113, 117–8,
134, 142–3, 145; stepmothers, 48–9,
60, 68, 96, 99, 100, 105–6, 110, 141
motherhood, 40–3, 43–5, 67–72, 78–88,
113, 150–7
moral, 3, 8, 30, 36, 107, 114, 118–9,
122, 146–7, 152; formation, 67, 153;
support, 59
morality, 30, 34, 87, 139, 150–1
Mulsim, 5, 18–9, 28, 102; chilren, 40;
mothers, 40

narrative, 7–9, 10, 14, 32, 37, 45, 64, 80,
90, 98, 107, 125; defined, 7–9, 11–3,
32
network, 15, 52, 58, 60–2, 64, 66, 78, 80,
106, 119, 129, 134; social, 6–7, 26,
47, 62–3, 67, 87, 93, 111, 130, 153;
support, 87–8, 90–1, 101, 123
NGO, 1, 3–6, 14, 27, 42, 61, 64, 78–9,
81, 84, 86, 112, 129, 133–4, 149, 151,
156–7
norms, 7–9, 33, 150, 152; cultural, 11, 67;
social, 7, 13, 35, 41

Oromo, 5, 19, 29, 48, 99, 101

parent, 1, 4, 8, 10, 13–5, 22, 25, 27, 30–4,
39, 40–5, 47, 49, 51, 62, 65, 67, 77,
87–8, 92, 101, 105–6, 129, 134–5,
146, 152–3, 157
parenting, 1, 2, 11, 14, 40–5, 67, 48,
83–4; father, 72–5; mother, 67–72,
153; the parents, 3, 83–4, 152; siblings,
3

pent'ay, 133, 134, 139, 144
police, 2–6, 14, 41, 42–3, 50–52, 62,
88, 92–3, 96, 98, 100, 103, 124–7,
140, 146, 151–7; violence, 47, 53–4,
84, 93–4, 108, 110–3, 120, 124,127,
130–1, 133, 148
poverty, 1, 4–5, 8, 14, 16, 22–6, 32,
42–4, 47, 67, 75, 79, 81, 88, 105,
151–7
power, 14, 19, 75, 102–3, 152, 157;
Bourdieu on, 31–2; defined, 30–2;
Foucault on, 30–1; masculine, 30–45,
132, 148, 154
pregnancy, 49–50, 58, 74, 79, 80–2, 140,
143–4
prison, 86, 98, 124, 140, 148, 158
prostitutes, 3, 26, 145; girl-child, 130–49
puberty, 2, 39, 42–3, 88
punishment, 67; corporal, 3, 14, 34, 40–4,
65, 66–7, 71, 75, 77–8, 98, 102, 105–
6, 111, 113, 133, 146, 151–7; verbal,
3, 14, 34, 40–4, 67, 77, 102, 107, 111,
115, 148, 151–7

quarrels, 15, 39, 59, 70–1, 74, 81, 83, 85,
99, 102, 106, 115–6, 123, 126–8, 135,
140–1

rape, 38–9, 51, 87, 137; gang, 14–5,
142–6, 154–5
reciprocity, 8, 106–130; food exchange,
119–20; money exchange, 119; Sahlins
on, 107
recruiting, 95, 139; gang members, 108–9,
145
rejection, 38, 150; group, 109, 115, 140
rent, 24–5, 54, 58–9, 60, 62, 66, 73, 77,
99, 100, 111, 141, 153
research, 1–2, 14, 88; researcher, 2, 8–10,
89, 107; ethnographic, 1, 8, 10, 15,
90, 108, 155, 157; field, 13, 90, 154;
findings, 6, 18, 28–9, 118
respect, 33, 123; family, 34–9, 134–6;
parents, 34–9, 70, 74; masculine, 70,
99, 111, 116, 120, 126–7, 132
revenge, 119, 143; group, 126
rob, 3, 53, 76, 84, 92–4, 102, 115, 117,
119, 121, 125, 127, 132, 135, 140

www.ingramcontent.com/pod-product-compliance
Lightning Source LLC
Chambersburg PA
CBHW060042030426
42334CB00019B/2445